The Art Galleries of Britain and Ireland

A GUIDE TO THEIR COLLECTIONS

The Art Galleries of Britain and Ireland

A GUIDE TO THEIR COLLECTIONS

JOAN ABSE

Rutherford · Madison · Teaneck
Fairleigh Dickinson University Press

Copyright © 1975 by Joan Abse

First American edition published 1976
by Associated University Presses, Inc.
Cranbury, New Jersey 08512

Library of Congress Catalogue Card Number: 75-24944

ISBN 0-8386-1850-2

Printed in Great Britain

Contents

8   CONTENTS

List of Illustrations

Introduction

The aim of this guide is to provide as comprehensive a survey as possible of the permanent collections of paintings, and to a certain extent, of sculpture, in British public galleries. The general principle which I have tried to observe is to mention all the paintings I thought could be of conceivable interest to sections of the public. Inevitably, because of the sheer number of works involved, this has meant a certain amount of selection, and in some cases mere mention of painters' names, but I have tried to keep my exclusions to a minimum with the thought in mind that sometimes what one man abhors another could possibly cherish. Certainly it can be the case that what is distasteful in one generation is in favour in the next. Thus the Victorian art so prevalent in some provincial galleries and shunned for most of this century has now once more come into its own. As far as the attributions of certain paintings are concerned I can only declare that I have for the most part taken in good faith the records of the various galleries. At times I have felt that a few attributions may perhaps be too ambitious but on the other hand it is just possible that some may err in being too cautious. Doubtless scholarly research will eventually clarify some of these matters but such problems are certainly beyond the scope of this book. My aim has been primarily to assist people in discovering the pleasure to be found in the art galleries of England, Scotland, Wales and Ireland. For it is a surprisingly rich heritage; I discovered how rich during the course of my own visits. Here I must acknowledge the assistance of the curators of many art galleries, too numerous to name, who kindly gave or sent me information and patiently answered my queries. My intention was to include all galleries with permanent collections; if any have inadvertently been omitted I hope I will be forgiven.

J.A.

Note

The times of opening of the galleries are stated at the head of each piece. All galleries are closed on Christmas Day and Good Friday. A number are open on Boxing Day and many are open on other Bank Holidays.

ABERDEEN
Aberdeen Art Gallery, Schoolhill
Tel.: 0224 23942
Open weekdays 10-5

Originally built in 1885, the Gallery was initially used for exhibitions of local artists and industrial exhibitions. In 1900 the Macdonald bequest of works of art and of a sum of money to buy such works (it was stipulated that they must have been produced within 25 years of the date of purchase) provided the Gallery with a substantial permanent collection, which was further increased by the gifts of another benefactor, Sir James Murray. The increasing size of the collection necessitated additions to the Gallery in 1905 but in 1925 it had to be radically extended again to the building's present size. The policy of the Gallery has been primarily to collect a representative group of Scottish works from the 17th century to the present day and of the English painting of the same period with which Scottish art was so intimately connected. Together with this the Gallery possesses a considerable group of European paintings from the mid-19th century onwards.

Of the Macdonald collection one of the most interesting portions is the group of artists' portraits, all of them oval in shape. Here are self-portraits by Alma-Tadema, John Brett, W. P. Frith, J. L. Gerôme, Frederick Goodall, Lord Leighton, Sir John Millais, J. S. Sargent, Sir Edward Poynter, G. F. Watts, and many others. Portraits by artists of fellow-painters include Philip H. Calderon by Sir George Reid, George du Maurier by Millais, Millais himself by Sir George Reid (the portrait which began the collection) and Briton Rivière by P. H. Calderon.

Aberdeen itself has produced a number of artists who have achieved considerable fame. Among these may be mentioned William Dyce, a painter much influenced by early Italian painting, in this a precursor of the Pre-Raphaelites; he became influential in art education as Director of the Government School of Design. His paintings at Aberdeen include *Titian's First Essay in Colour*, which was highly praised by Ruskin, *The Ferryman, Beatrice* and many other paintings, sketches and designs.

Another famous Victorian artist from Aberdeen was John Phillip, whose art benefited much from his visits to southern Spain, as can be seen in *The Gipsy Queen of Seville, La Bomba, La Lotería Nacional* and many others. Here too are many paintings and drawings by Sir George Reid and by James McBey, by whom there is also a large collection of etchings and drypoints and in whose memory the James McBey Print Room and Art Library was donated by his wife.

There is a prolific representation of other Scottish artists. Allan Ramsay is here with a portrait of Miss Janet Sharp and Sir Henry Raeburn is represented most notably by a portrait of the architect Robert Adam. There are several landscapes by Alexander and Patrick Nasmyth and later 19th-century Scottish artists include Sir William Quiller Orchardson with *Mariage de Convenance—After* and *The Broken Tryst;* Sir William McTaggart; James Cassie; and Sir David Wilkie with *The Duke of Wellington Writing Dispatches, The Turkish Letter Writer* and many other studies. Among 20th-century artists such figures as Sir Muirhead Bone, Sir David Cameron, S. J. Peploe, Anne Redpath, Duncan Grant, Russell Flint and Joan Eardley are featured in the Gallery.

Among the earliest English paintings are a *Portrait of a Lady* by Kneller, *Ruin in a Clearing* by Richard Wilson, two portraits by Hogarth, a conversation piece, *The Morse Family,* by Zoffany, and a watercolour, *The Raising of Lazarus,* by William Blake. A number of great 19th-century painters figure here too: Alma-Tadema, William Etty, John Linnell, J. F. Lewis and W. P. Frith. From Millais comes a watercolour, *Three Parables,* and *The Convalescent* and *Bright Eyes;* from G. F. Watts, *Orpheus and Eurydice;* from J. W. Waterhouse, *Penelope and her Suitors* and *The Danaides;* from Holman Hunt, *Past and Present;* from Rossetti, *Mariana.* There are a number of studies by Sickert and several oils including *Gaité Rochechouard,* and several works by Wilson Steer, among them *The Horseshoe Bend of the Severn* and *The Mirror.* The Camden Town Group are all here: there are works by Harold Gilman, Spencer Gore, Lucien Pissarro, Charles Ginner, Henry Lamb and Robert Bevan. Augustus John is well represented by, among others, *The Blue Pool, Gipsy in the Sandpit,* and a portrait of Lloyd George. There is a small, typically quiet work by his sister Gwen John, *Seated Girl Holding a Piece of Sewing. One of the Stations of the Dead* is an interesting example of the work of Wyndham Lewis, and other painters here include Sir Frank Brangwyn, David Bomberg, Laura Knight, Matthew Smith, L. S. Lowry, Stanley Spencer (*Reunion,* 1945, and *Crucifixion,* 1922-4), Paul Nash *(Wood on the Downs),* John Nash, Ben Nicholson, Victor Pasmore, Christopher Wood, Ivon Hitchens, Josef Herman, Alan Reynolds. Particularly powerful is Francis Bacon's *Pope—study after Velazquex,* 1951.

There is a sprinkling of French 19th- and 20th-century painting in the Gallery, the earliest being works by members of the Barbizon School or those closely linked with them: *Les Laveuses* by Daubigny; *Un Marais dans les Landes* by Théodore Rousseau; and paintings by Troyon, Lépine, Bastien-Lepage. There is a small work, *The Stream,* by Courbet; another by Monet, *La Falaise à Fécamp; Leaving Port* by Boudin; *Une Cour aux Sablons* and *Les Bords du Loing* by Sisley; *Sunshine on the Riviera* by Harpignies; and paintings by Decamps, Eugène Carrière, Fantin-Latour and Jean-Louis Forain. Most interesting is a sketch by Toulouse-Lautrec of Charles Conder for the painting *Aux Ambas-sadeurs—Gens Chics.* Both Bonnard and Vuillard are represented, the former by a landscape entitled *Vernonnet,* dated 1924, the latter by *La Partie de Cartes.* Also of interest are *Street Scene* by Maurice Vlaminck and *Nature Morte avec Vase* by Fernand Léger.

There are many excellent watercolours in the Gallery, among them works by Gainsborough, Turner, Girtin, Paul Sandby, J. R. Cozens, Bonington, Kokoschka, Signac, Graham Sutherland and others. Sculpture is also of a very high standard. Here are works by Degas, Rodin *(L'Homme Qui Marche),* Epstein (busts of Ramsay MacDonald and G. B. Shaw and *The Girl with the Gardenias),* Henry Moore *(Figure on the Steps,* 1956), Barbara Hepworth *(Oval Form—Trezion and Torso),* Ossip Zadkine, Benno Schotz and many others.

ACCRINGTON
Haworth Art Gallery, Haworth Park
Tel.: 0254 33782
Open weekdays 2-5; Sundays April-October 6-8

Oil-paintings in this gallery include *Castle near Lake,* attributed to Richard Wilson, *Venetian Scene,* attributed to Turner; *View of Lancaster,* attributed to Constable. Other artists represented include James Stark, William Collins, T. Sidney Cooper, J. F. Herring and J. B. Pyne. Among artists in watercolour here are Paul Sandby, Edward Dayes, Nicholas Pocock, Michael Angelo Rooker, David Cox and William Henry Hunt.

BARNARD CASTLE
The Bowes Museum
Tel.: 083 33 2139
Open weekdays 10-5.30 (October, March, April 10-5; Nov.-Feb. 10-4; Sundays 2-5; (Winter 2-4)

This is the only art museum of national importance to be found outside London and the larger provincial towns. It is situated in the small

country town of Barnard Castle, surrounded by the beautiful countryside
of Upper Teesdale and in its own park filled with lawns, trees and flower
beds. The building itself, in this northern county, presents somewhat of
a surprise to the visitor as it was designed by a French architect and has
all the massive appearance of certain French châteaux, being 300 feet
long and 130 feet high. The collection of over 1,000 paintings was
acquired by the founder of the Museum, John Bowes, ably assisted by
his French wife Josephine, during the decades between 1840 and 1880.
The Museum was built purely with the intention of housing the
collection, never with the idea of being a residence as well. Neither John
nor Josephine Bowes lived to see its completion and final opening in
1892. John Bowes bequeathed a large sum for the Museum's upkeep but
in 1956 the Trustees handed it over to the care of the Durham County
Council. The Museum now contains not only the collection of paintings
and objets d'art but also a large section devoted to the geology and
history of the region.

Among the works to be found in the Bowes Museum the collection of
Spanish paintings is the most remarkable, many of them having been
purchased in 1862 by John Bowes from the collection of the Conde de
Quinto, who had been Director of the National Museum of Painting in
Madrid. Outstanding is the moving *Tears of St Peter* by El Greco,
painted in the early 1590s and one of the five versions considered to be
from El Greco's own hand. Two earlier works by Juan de Borgona of
Fathers of the Church would seem by their rich colour and gold
backgrounds to indicate a Sienese influence. Another early work of great
beauty is *Christ, the Virgin and St John* by a painter known as the
Torralba Master from the Aragonese school of the first half of the 15th
century. Spanish devotion to the cult of the Virgin is illustrated in *The
Immaculate Conception* by the 17th-century painter of the Madrid
School, José Antolinez; this is one of the 25 versions of the subject
painted by him, while also here is his earliest known work, *The Agony
in the Garden*, painted in 1665. By Juan Carrena di Miranda, Court
Painter from 1671 to 1685, is a portrait of *Queen Mariana of Austria* (in
nun's habit as she was then the widow of Philip IV). A dramatic
Belshazzar's Feast is also by this artist. A panel, *St Eustochium,* was part
of an altarpiece painted by Juan Valdes Leal for a monastery in Seville;
by an artist of the circle of Juan Fernandez de Navarrete is an appealing
representation of *The Rest on the Flight into Egypt*. Other painters
represented include Antonio Pereda, Pedro Muñoz, Antonio Puga and
Pedro de Orrente, but above all not to be missed are *The Martyrdom of
St Andrew* by El Greco's pupil Luis Tristán, and two works by Goya.
The first of these is a penetrating portrait of the poet and lawyer,
Melendez Valdes; the second, painted on tin, is called *Interior of a Prison*
and is a moving evocation of the abysmal despair of the chained men.

A selection of Italian paintings is also to be found in the Museum. There is a small panel by the Sienese artist Sassetta, *A Miracle of the Holy Sacrament,* part of a predella for a polyptych painted for the chapel of the Arte della Lana in Siena in the early 1420s. An interesting portrait, dated 1528, is of Lelio Torelli of Fano by Domenico Caprioli, who came under the influence of Giorgione. From a little later in the 16th century comes Francesco Primaticcio's *Rape of Helen;* he was a Mannerist painter who worked for years on the decorations in Fontainebleau for Francis I. *The Holy Family with Saints* is by the Bolognese artist Prospero Fontana, among whose pupils were numbered the Carracci. *The Birth of St John the Baptist* is a late work by the Neapolitan artist Solimena, who was described in 1733 as 'by universal consent the greatest painter in the world'. By his pupil Corrado Giaquinto is the accomplished rococo work, *Venus Presenting Arms to Aeneas.* An excited composition, *The Triumph of Judith,* belongs to another Neapolitan, Luca Giordano. From 18th-century Venice come several fine works. Giovanni Battista Tiepolo's illustration of the story of Phaethon, *The Harnessing of the Horses of the Sun,* is a sketch for a ceiling in the Archinti Palace in Milan which he decorated in 1731 but which was destroyed in 1943. On long loan are a large pair of paintings by Canaletto executed in the 1730s, *Carnival Regatta on the Grand Canal* and *The Bucintoro Returning to the Molo after the Ceremony of Wedding the Adriatic.* Other Italian painters in the Bowes Museum include Mattia Preti, Trevisani, Viviani Codazzi, Giuseppe Salviati.

The collection of French painting, which cannot be shown in its entirety, is said to be the largest in England. The most notable works belong to the 18th century, although there are two portraits ascribed to a follower of Francis Clouet from the 16th century; and a *Holy Family* by Jacques Stella, painter to Louis XIV, together with a number of portraits of noblemen from the 17th century. Among the 18th-century works are a small scene by Fragonard, several architectural compositions by Hubert Robert, *Landscape with a Watermill,* dated 1743, by François Boucher, *Portrait of a Lady as Diana* by Nicholas de Largillière, numerous animal studies by Oudry, and a portrait of Louis XV by Louis Michel van Loo. From the 19th century there is a portrait of Napoleon by Girodet and *Charles X in his Coronation Robes* by Baron Gérard. The *View from Ornans* by Courbet is especially noteworthy and there are landscapes by Monticelli and Boudin and a flower-piece by Fantin-Latour.

There are a few works demanding particular attention from the German and Early Netherlandish schools of painting. From the former there is a panel of *The Raising of Lazarus* with *The Adoration of the Magi* on the other side by the Master of St Severin and *St Jerome and the Lion* by Hans Schäufflein, who was a pupil of Dürer. An out-

standing Gothic work is a triptych, dated 1470-80, of *The Crucifixion* by
the Delft painter known as the Master of the Virgo inter Virgines. *Christ
Appearing to St Peter on the Sea of Tiberias* and *An Allegory of Wisdom
and Peace* are two works by Maerten van Heemskerck, who worked
chiefly in Haarlem, A *Pietá with Two Marys* is by a member of the
school of Ambrosius Benson and there is a superb *View on the Rhine* by
the Dutch painter Herman Saftleven. *Ulysses and Nausicaa* by Lucas van
Uden and *Portrait of a Burgomaster* by Nicolaes Maes are two further
examples of Dutch works.

There are very few English works. Among them are a portrait of
Charles II attributed to Michael Wright, a portrait of Bishop John Butler
by Thomas Hudson, *Portrait of a Lady* by Reynolds and *Portrait of a
Gentleman* by Allan Ramsay. Of considerable interest is a view of
Barnard Castle by Thomas Girtin and there is also one of Elmsett
Church by Gainsborough.

BARNSLEY
Cannon Hall Art Gallery and Museum, Cawthorne
Tel.: 022 679 270

Open weekdays 10.30-5; Sunday 2.30-5

This gallery possesses a number of interesting English portraits: Michael
Wright's *6th Duke of Norfolk;* Sir Peter Lely's *Lady Houblon;* Jacob
Huysmans' *Sir Thomas Wendy;* Joseph Highmore's *Sir Willoughby Aston
and his Wife;* John Constable's *Mrs Tuder.* Other works include
Shipwreck off Rocky Coast by George Morland; *Mausoleum of Plautus
Lucanus* by David Roberts; *Dark West Wood* by Ivon Hitchens.

On permanent loan to the Gallery is the Harvey Collection of paintings (formerly known as the National Loan Collection) which consists of
a wide selection of 17th-century Dutch pictures. Among them are the
following: *Ponte Molle near Rome* by Jan Asselyn; three studies of cattle
and horses by Nicolaes Berchem; *River Scene with Ships Becalmed* by
Jan van de Cappelle; *River Scene with Town and Shipping* by Albert
Cuyp; *Child Holding an Apple* by van Everdingen; *View in Amsterdam*
by Jan van der Heyden; *Portrait of a Man,* possibly a self-portrait by
Cornelius Johnson, dated 1649; two genre paintings by Gabriel Metsu;
Portrait of a Lady by Caspar Netscher, signed and dated 1658; genre
scenes by Adriaen van Ostade and David Teniers the Younger; and
further land and seascapes by Jan Wynants, Aert van der Neer, Willem
van de Velde the Younger and Adam Pynacker.

Cooper Art Gallery, Church Street
Open weekdays 11.30-5

This gallery, formerly the old Grammar School, was given by Samuel Cooper, together with a collection of pictures, to provide a public art gallery for Barnsley. It was opened in 1914 and in 1934 an additional wing was built by Thomas Fox and a further group of pictures was donated by him. Sir Michael Sadler also made gifts of several groups of drawings which form the most important part of the collection.

The Gallery has an interesting group of paintings by minor 19th-century French artists of the academic school, particularly Eugène Isabey. Among works by him are *Hurricane before St Malo, The Wreck* and *The Duel.* Other artists of this school include J. L. Gerôme, Meissonier and Decamps, and there are studies by members of the Barbizon School and their associates including Théodore Rousseau, Corot, Diaz, Millet and Jongkind. Also here is a small work, *Notre Dame,* by the gifted but unfortunate Charles Meryon, who was much admired by Baudelaire.

Among the artists represented in the comprehensive selection of English watercolours and drawings are Alexander Cozens, J. R. Cozens, J. S. Cotman, Gainsborough, Constable, Girtin, Turner, De Wint, Ruskin, Millais, Burne-Jones, William Roberts, Stanley Spencer, Paul Nash, Wyndham Lewis, C. R. W. Nevinson, Duncan Grant, Augustus John and Wilson Steer.

BATH
The Holburne of Menstrie Museum, Great Pulteney Street
Tel.: 0225 3669
Open weekdays April-October 11-1, 2-5; Sunday 2.30-5; Nov.-March (except Sun. and Wed.) 11-1, 2-5

The collection of paintings and objets d'art which constitutes this museum is housed in a fine neo-classical structure originally built as a Pavilion in the Sydney Gardens in 1795-6. The Museum owes its origin to a bequest made in 1882 of the collection belonging to Sir Thomas William Holburne, one of whose ancestors had purchased the estate of Menstrie in Scotland in 1649. Besides the paintings there is an important collection of English silver and of porcelain of English, continental and oriental origin. The collection of paintings is quite eclectic, for here, rubbing shoulders with Thomas Barker of Bath, are paintings from 17th-century Italy and France together with a group of Dutch, Flemish and German works.

Among the earliest English paintings is an oval *Portrait of a Man* attributed to Cornelius Johnson, Van Dyck's contemporary; then comes a portrait of Laurence Hyde, Earl of Rochester by William Wissing, who was extensively employed by both Charles II and James II—his subject here was one of Charles's chief ministers. Moving on to the 18th century there are several works by Gainsborough: *Portrait of a Lady;* a portrait of Lady Clarges; and another of Dr Charlton, who was his physician in Bath. There is a portrait of Mrs Cussons by John Hoppner; she was by birth a member of the Holburne family. And by Thomas Barker there is a fine portrait of Priscilla Jones—she later became his wife— and several other works, among them *Mishap to Market Eggs, Travelling Gipsies,* and a self-portrait. *The Eagle Tower, Caernarvon Castle* is a landscape by his brother Benjamin Barker. A portrait of Garton Orme is attributed by Joseph Highmore; one of Lady Helen Boyle is by Raeburn; and there are portraits of Rosalind Chambers and her husband John Sargent by Allan Ramsay. A later portrait of their son, also John Sargent, is by Romney. A picture entitled *The Dead Soldier* is ascribed to Joseph Wright. There are several typical works by George Morland, among them *The Deserter Pardoned;* and there is a delightful stylized portrait of Samuel Richardson and his family by Francis Hayman. A portrait of Queen Charlotte formerly attributed to Romney is probably one of the earliest royal portraits of Zoffany, dated 1766-7. Most pleasing of all is a painting by George Stubbs of the Reverend Carter Thelwall and his family.

Most of the Italian paintings derive from the 17th and 18th centuries but there is a work, *Mother and Children,* attributed to the 16th-century Mantuan artist Bartolomme Schedone. There is an *Entombment* by Romanelli, and two works, *St William* and *A Stormy Landscape with Soldiers,* are perhaps doubtfully attributed to Salvator Rosa. Three works, *The Sacrifice of Iphigenia, Sibyl and the Ruins of Carthage* and *Marius amid the Ruins of Carthage,* are by the 18th-century Roman painter Panini, who spent much of his life painting real or imaginary architectural themes.

Of French painting there is a large canvas of *Rinaldo Leaving Armida* by the 17th-century artist Francois Perrier, and *Bacchus and Ariadne* is attributed to Antoine Coypel. Much later comes a landscape by Henri Harpignies. Among Dutch and Flemish works are *Interior of an Alehouse,* attributed to Adriaen Brouwer; *Landscape with Waterfall* by Jan Hackaert; *Courtship* by Hendrick Martensz Sorgh; *Madonna and Child* from the school of Bernard van Orley; *The Wedding Dance,* attributed to Pieter Brueghel the Younger; and *The Cook Shop,* attributed to Jan Brueghel. From the German school there is *The Judgement of Paris* from the early 16th century, possibly by a follower of Cranach; *Adoration of the Magi,* painted on copper, attributed to Rottenhammer; a portrait of Ernest, Count Palatine by a follower of Holbein; and *Adoration of the Shepherds* by the 18th-century painter Christian Dietrich, who was Court Painter to the kings of Poland.

Victoria Art Gallery, Bridge Street

Tel.: 0225 28144

Open weekdays 10-6; closed Sunday, Good Friday, Xmas and Boxing Day

Much of the paintings and drawings to be found in this gallery are, not surprisingly, connected in some way with the social history of Bath, which was, after all, a lively centre of English life at the end of the 18th and beginning of the 19th centuries. Notable among the paintings is a portrait of Mrs Kemble, mother of Sarah Siddons, done by Sir Thomas Lawrence when he was a lad of about 17. Here too are a couple of works of John Opie, known when he first appeared on the scene as the 'Cornish Wonder' (Reynolds' saying of him that he was 'like Caravaggio but finer'), though his promise was not to be fulfilled; the pictures are a self-portrait and a portrait of Samuel Johnson. There is a landscape by George Lambert and *A Fishing Party* by Joseph Farington, who was a pupil of Richard Wilson, but most numerous are those works attributed to Thomas Barker of Bath, a prolific painter who flourished in the last years of the 18th century and the early decades of the 19th and who had considerable success in his own lifetime, though his work depended too much on the example of Gainsborough for his achievement to be very great. Here are *The Woodman at his Cottage Door, The Sand Girl, The Gipsy Girl, The Old Matchwoman, A Distant View of Rome* and *Old Tom Thumb*, a portrait of a man reputed to be 103 years old—as well as many other paintings, drawings and sketches. Among later British paintings in the Gallery are Edwin Long's *Raising of Jairus's Daughter,* John Nash's *The Canal, Sydney Gardens, Bath,* and Rex Whistler's very successful *The Foreign Bloke.*

Of considerable interest is an *Adoration of the Magi* which is probably a contemporary Flemish copy of a work by Hugo van der Goes. Another *Adoration of the Magi* is attributed to the 17th-century Spanish painter Valdes Leal.

There are portraits in the Guildhall and Council Chambers which come under the aegis of the Gallery, among them works by Sir Joshua Reynolds, Sir Godfrey Kneller, James Northcote, Benjamin West and the Swedish-born 18th-century painter Michael Dahl.

BEDFORD
Cecil Higgins Art Gallery, Castle Close
Tel.: 0234 53791

Open weekdays April-September 11-6; October-March 11-dusk; Sunday 2.30-5.30

This gallery was founded by the man who gave it his name, Cecil Higgins, a prosperous brewer and lover of the arts, who bequeathed to it his collection of porcelain and glass, a trust fund for the purchase of other works of art, and his very pleasing Victorian House to contain the collections. Opened in 1949, the Gallery has since been devoted to the acquisition of a collection of English watercolours and drawings of the finest quality, representing as far as possible the history and development of this art form. Also to be found in the Gallery is a diverse selection of prints, woodcuts, lithographs, etchings etc. by artists ranging from Dürer to Josef Albers. There are some 700 pictures in the collection, which is continually being added to; as only a fraction of these can be shown to advantage at any one time the pictures on show are changed frequently in order that all in turn can be exhibited. Those not on show can be seen on request. The one consistent factor is the excellence of the collection as a whole.

One of the earliest works of art in the collection is a pen and wash drawing of a *Hen with Chicks in a Landscape* by the 17th-century artist, Francis Barlow. Better known are the two 18th-century painters, father and son, Alexander and J.R. Cozens; the latter has several watercolours here, *Windsor Castle from the South West* and *The Coast between Vietri and Salerno* being particularly beautiful. Gainsborough is represented by several drawings and William Blake by two watercolours, *The Pardon of Absalom* and *The Good and Evil Angels Struggling for Possession of the Child.* Examples of Paul Sandby's work include *Landscape with Travellers on a Road* and *Rosomond's Pond, St James's Park,* dated 1758. Thomas Rowlandson is represented by several watercolours, *Mr Angelo's Fencing School* of 1787 being among them. Other 18th-century artists to be found here include Edward Dayes, Samuel Hieronymus Grimm, Charles Collins, Michael Angelo Rooker, Francis Towne and Richard Wilson.

The Gallery possesses two watercolours by the short-lived Thomas Girtin, particularly notable being *Jedburgh Abbey from the River,* and two works by Richard Parkes Bonington, a watercolour, *Paris—Tuileries,* and a drawing, *The Pile Drivers.* There are some great watercolours by Turner in the collection; to mention but three: *The Great Falls of the Reichenbach* of 1804; *A First Rate Taking in Stores* of 1818; and *Thun, Lake and Town* of 1838. Constable is less well represented; there is a chalk drawing of *Trees* and a watercolour, *Coal Brigs on Brighton Beach.* The talent of J. S. Cotman is displayed by two studies in sepia and a pencil drawing. David Cox is here with four watercolours, among them

Bolton Abbey and *The Mill;* and there are two by the unfortunate Richard Dadd, *The Flight* and *Hermit in his Cell.* From Samuel Palmer comes *Harvesting the Vineyard* among other works, and other 19th-century artists here are Ruskin, John Linnell, William Henry Hunt, Sir David Wilkie, David Roberts, Edward Lear, Lord Leighton and Whistler. Of the Pre-Raphaelite group Holman Hunt has here two drawings, illustrations to *Peace and War,* a poem by Leigh Hunt; Arthur Hughes has two drawings, Sir John Millais some illustrations for *Great Expectations* and *The Arabian Nights,* and Rossetti a watercolour of *Tristan and Isolde,* a chalk study for *Fair Rosamonde,* and a study for *Paolo and Francesca.* Notable too is a triptych design by Ford Madox Brown for his *Chaucer Reading his Poem at the Court of Edward III* (in the Tate). A number of studies by Burne-Jones include *Lot and his Daughters* done in body-colour.

There is an interesting selection of works by 20th-century artists: *Still Life on a Dinner Table* by Sickert and studies by Wilson Steer, Stanley Spencer and Augustus John. Several watercolours by Wyndham Lewis include a portrait of Sir Stafford Cripps and there are further works by John and Paul Nash, Ben Nicholson, Keith Vaughan, Henry Moore. Here too is a lively watercolour, *The Lobster* by Oskar Kokoschka. Other works which should be mentioned include *Ironbridge* by John Piper, *Vine Pergola II* by Graham Sutherland, *Railroad in the Rockies* by Edward Bawden, *Harlem* by Edward Burra, *Cumberland* and *Piggott's Farm* by David Jones, *Botanical Gardens* by Lucian Freud, *Family Outing* by Josef Herman. There are also works by Ceri Richards, Alan Davie, William Roberts, Alan Reynolds, Lucien Pissarro. Among the prints and engravings, etc. are *Berthe Morisot* by Manet, *Homage to the Square* by Albers, *Le Repas Frugal* by Picasso.

BELFAST
Ulster Museum, Botanic Gardens
Tel.: 0232 668251
Open weekdays 11-6 (Wed. and Thurs. 11-9); Sunday 2.30-5.30

The first public museum in Belfast was opened by the Belfast National History Society in 1831. In 1890 an art gallery was founded by the Corporation to which was added the Grainger collection of antiquities. In the early 20th century it was decided to bring all these collections together and found the Belfast Museum and Art Gallery, the first part of a new building being opened in 1929. In 1961 the name of the Gallery was changed to the National Museum for Ulster, the building was further extended and new galleries were built grouped around an open-air sculpture court. The collecting policy of the Gallery became concentrated upon the acquisition of a representative collection of Irish art, and more recently upon the purchase of works by contemporary British, European and American artists.

Among the older works in the Gallery are a *St Francis* attributed to the late-16th-century Florentine painter Cristofano Allori; a *Landscape with Figures* by Agostino Tassi; *Fortuna* by the 17th-century Lorenzo Lippi; *Pan and Diana* by Filippo Lauri; *St Cecilia* by Romanelli; *The Advent of the Golden Age as Prophesied by the Cumaean Sibyl* by Solimena; *Archimedes at the Siege of Syracuse* by Sebastiano Ricci; *Pastoral Landscape with Figures* by Donato Creti, a late Bolognese painter; *Roman Ruins and Figures* by Panini; *Classical Ruins around a Port* by Michael Marieschi; and *Boy with Dog* and *Boy with Vegetables* by Giacomo Francesco Cipper, called il Todeschini. Paintings from the Dutch school include *St Matthew* by Jan van Bijlert; *Italian Church Interior* by Dirk van Delen; and *Portrait of a Woman* by Nicolaes Maes. From the Flemish school are *St Christopher Carrying the Christ Child* by Jacob Jordaens; *Landscape with Windmills* by Jan 'Velvet' Brueghel; *The Raising of Lazarus* by Cornelis de Vos; and *River Landscape with Figures* by Lucas van Uden. From the 19th century comes a copy by Fantin-Latour of Veronese's *Marriage at Cana* in the Louvre.

Over the years the Gallery has acquired such works as Turner's *Dawn of Christianity,* a group of paintings by Sir John Lavery given by the artist himself, and works by Jack Yeats. British artists represented include Sickert, Stanley Spencer, Paul Nash, Matthew Smith, William Roberts, Edward Wadsworth, Robert Bevan, Edward Burra, Henry Tonks, Mark Gertler, and there are early works by Victor Pasmore, Ben Nicholson and Graham Sutherland. Among more recent paintings by British artists are works by Francis Bacon, William Scott, Bridget Riley, Robyn Denny, Patrick Caulfield, John Hoyland, Terry Frost, Allen Jones. Representing aspects of contemporary American and European art are pictures by Helen Frankenthaler, Sam Francis, Morris Louis, Clement Greenberg, Kenneth Noland, J. R. Soto, Heinz Marck, Otto Piene, Karel Appel, Jean Dubuffet, Victor Vasarely, Gunther Uecker, Julio le Parc.

BERWICK-ON-TWEED
Berwick-on-Tweed Museum and Art Gallery, Marygate
Tel.: 0289 7320
Open Mon., Wed. and Fri. 10-7; Tues., Thurs. and Sat. 10-5

This gallery in the historic border town of Berwick-on-Tweed is to be found in the public library. The collection of paintings was presented to the town in May 1949 by Sir William and Lady Burrell. Paintings by French 19th-century artists predominate. Among them are *Cap Gris Nez* by Daubigny, *Danseuses Russes* by Degas, *On the Tow-path* and *Milking*

Hour by Anton Mauve, *Fête Champêtre* by Adolph Monticelli, *Wounded Cavalry Officer* by Géricault, *Le Moulin* by Georges Michel, and works by Boudin, Bonvin, Ribot, Fantin-Latour. Among the other paintings here are a *Group of Peasants* attributed to one of the Le Nain brothers, and portraits of various ladies by Thomas Hudson, Allan Ramsay, Sir Henry Raeburn and others.

BIRKENHEAD
Williamson Art Gallery, Slatey Road
Tel.: 051 652 4177
Open weekdays 10-5 (Thursday 10-9); Sunday 2-5

The Williamson Art Gallery and Museum, founded through the generosity of John Williamson, a Director of the Cunard Steamship Company, and of his son, Patrick, was first opened to the public on 1 December 1928. It had its origins in an earlier gallery housed in the central library and established in 1912 but the new gallery was specially designed for its purpose, providing in all 14 galleries and a sculpture hall, three of the galleries being specifically designed for the exhibition of the collection of watercolours of which the Williamson Gallery is justly proud. The policy of the Gallery over the years has been well-defined, embracing the collection of English painting, English watercolours, local paintings, and English and oriental ceramics. At the outset, John Williamson endowed the Gallery with his own fine collection of art objects.

Except when certain galleries are being used for temporary exhibitions each room has an established function and group of paintings. In Room I 20th-century works are to be found. Among these are *Interior with Duncan Grant* by Vanessa Bell, *Underground* by Carel Weight, *Kitchen Interior* by John Bratby and *Fruit Trees* by Philip Sutton. Room II, for the most part, is devoted to the works of Wilson Steer, a native of Birkenhead, who when a student in France was profoundly impressed by the works of Degas and the Impressionists, and later, with Sickert, became a founding member of the New English Arts Club. Here are portraits, nudes and landscapes by him. Very interesting are some of his early works such as the portrait of Rose Pettigrew of 1892 (she was his model for a time and they also had a love affair), *Girl at her Toilet*, 1894, and *Miss Ethel Dixon before a Mirror*, also 1894. The portrait of Mrs D. S. MacColl of 1904 should also be mentioned and also the impressive *The Muslin Dress* of 1910. Among the landscapes are *Boats on the Shore, Walberswick, Grove at Bridgnorth*, 1911, *Moonrise at Painswick*, 1915, and *Distant View looking towards Bridgnorth*, 1925. The Gallery also possesses numerous watercolours and several drawings by Wilson Steer.

Room III presents a selection of fine watercolours by the artists in this medium of the 18th and 19th centuries. There are works by Paul Sandby, Alexander Cozens, J. R. Cozens, Gainsborough, de Loutherbourg, George Barret, Francis Towne, Nicholas Pocock, Thomas Girtin, Edward Dayes, John Varley, John Sell Cotman, Peter de Wint and many more. There is a landscape by Richard Bonington, and a number of works by Turner dating from all periods of his life; among them are *Battle Abbey, Castle at Chillon Lake* and *Vesuvius Angry*. There are two works by Samuel Palmer; *Layer Towers*, by Constable, presents three examples of his watercolours in one frame. From the later 19th century come examples of the work of J. F. Lewis, David Roberts, Ruskin and Rossetti—*King René's Honeymoon*, a cartoon for a stained-glass window, and Burne-Jones—*Pyramus and Thisbe*, three works in one frame. These are but a fraction of the Gallery's total possessions in this field and there are also works by 20th-century artists in Room XII.

More oil-paintings, this time by the Liverpool School of Artists, are shown in Room VIII. Perhaps the best-known artist here is W. L. Windus, a painter who was associated with the Pre-Raphaelites and whose work is also well displayed in the Walker Art Gallery. Here are *Morton before Claverhouse*, a scene from Scott's *Old Mortality, The Burial of Sir Thomas More*, and several studies for larger pictures. His painting *Too Late* (in the Tate Gallery) was criticized by Ruskin when exhibited at the Royal Academy in 1859 and this seems to have deterred him from further serious painting.

Room XIII contains a selection of oil-paintings by a variety of artists of all periods. *Portrait of a Gentleman* by Sir Peter Lely; *Portrait of Andrew Buchanan* by Raeburn; two landscapes by Zuccarelli; *Lions and Tigers Fighting over a Dead Stag* by George Stubbs; and *Study of a Horse* by Romney are among the earliest paintings by artists working in England. There are three landscapes attributed to Richard Wilson, two attributed to Turner and two, *After the Storm* and *The Valley of the Spey*, by John Constable. Further landscapes are by John Sell Cotman, John Crome, James Stark, Thomas Barker of Bath, John Linnell and William Müller. Among other paintings which should be mentioned are several works by William Etty, among them *The Toilet Of Venus; The Bride of Venice* by J. R. Herbert; *At Verona* and *The Destruction of Jerusalem* by David Roberts; and *Commerce* by Sir Frank Brangwyn. There is a small group of pictures by European artists, among them a *Virgin and Child* (after Correggio) by Pompeo Batoni; a landscape attributed to Gaspar Dughet; a landscape by Jan Both; and *St Michael's Mount* by Willem van de Velde.

Apart from collections of paintings and watercolours the Williamson Gallery is worth visiting for its extensive collection of ceramics and its tapestry room.

BIRMINGHAM
The Barber Institute of Fine Arts, University of Birmingham
Tel.: 021 472 0962
Open Mon.-Fri. 10-5; Saturday 10-1

This collection, which belongs to the Trustees of the Barber Institute, is intended to serve the purposes of the University and is strictly speaking not a public institution. Fortunately, however, the gallery, in itself a place of great appeal, is normally open to the public at the hours named above. The existence of the gallery is due to the generosity of Dame Martha Constance Hattie Barber, who founded the Barber Institute in memory of her husband Sir Harry Barber, and in order to foster the study of the fine arts and music at the University of Birmingham. It was decided that the Director of the Institute should at the same time hold a Professorship of Fine Arts at the University. The Trust for the implementation of these wishes was founded not long before Lady Barber's death in 1932, the work entailed being carried out by the Trustees. The gallery was opened in 1939 just before the outbreak of the war when the collection only amounted to 13 pictures and 20 drawings with a few examples of sculpture, furniture and art objects. Lady Barber stressed the need to collect 'works of art of exceptional and outstanding merit' and prohibited the acquisition of works dating from after the end of the 19th century. These requirements have resulted in a collection of the highest quality spanning a considerable proportion of the history of art before the 20th century.

The earliest Italian painting in the gallery is a 13th-century *Crucifixion* which has been attributed to Giunta Pisano. From Siena there is a haunting *St John the Evangelist* by Simone Martini, dated 1320—this is a modern inscription but it is possible that it is still correct. Also from 14th-century Siena is a panel representing *St Francis of Assissi* by Ugolino da Siena, a close follower of Duccio, while from the 15th century comes *Madonna and Child with St John the Baptist and St Michael* by Matteo di Giovanni. An example of Sienese 16th-century painting is the Mannerist work *Venus and Cupid* by Domenico Beccafumi.

From Florence comes a *Madonna and Child with the Infant St John* from the studio of Botticelli, and there is also a very good portrait of the tyrant Niccolo Vitelli by Luca Signorelli, whose work was one of the formative influences on Michelangelo. Here too are an *Adoration of the Child Jesus* by Cosimo Rosselli and an interesting landscape drawing, *Hill Town in Tuscany,* by Fra Bartolommeo.

There are some fine examples of Venetian art: two paintings by Giovanni Bellini—a very early work, *St Jerome in the Wilderness,* and a *Portrait of a Boy;* a splendid *Crucifixion* by Cima da Conegliano; a

Portrait of a Young Man, dated 1554, attributed to Tintoretto, and an impressive *Visitation* by Veronese. *A Mythological Scene* is by Paris Bordone and later Venetian painting includes Guardi's *Regatta on the Grand Canal* and an allegorical composition by Sebastiano and Marco Ricci.

Among the Neapolitan paintings in the gallery are Bernardino Cavallino's *St Catherine of Alexandria,* Solimena's *Holy Trinity* and Mattia Preti's *Martyrdom of St Peter,* all three examples of Italian Baroque. The same can be said of the Genoese G. B. Castiglione's crowded composition *Rebecca Led by the Servant of Abraham.* Another Genoese artist, Bernardo Strozzi, is represented here by *Head of an Old Woman. The Flea* is a typical genre painting by the Bolognese artist Giuseppe Maria Crespi. Other Italian paintings include a mythological scene drawn from Virgil's *Aeneid,* Book V, by the Ferrarese Dosso Dossi, and *The Blind Leading the Blind* by the Roman painter Domenico Feti.

Among the earliest Flemish painting is Mabuse's *Hercules and Deianira,* dated 1517. Pieter Brueghel the younger recalls the bizarre realism of his father in the *Two Peasants Binding Faggots.* By Rubens there is a splendid *Landscape near Malines* and a pencil and chalk drawing of his second wife Hélène Fourment, which once belonged to Reynolds and later to Sir William Hamilton. *Ecce Homo* is an example of Van Dyck's religious painting at its greatest; by him also is a beautiful small watercolour, *An English Landscape.*

The 17th century, the great age of Dutch painting, is comprehensively represented. Among the portraits are a sober work by Frans Hals, *Portrait of a Man Holding a Skull; Portrait of a Lady* by Nicolaes Maes; *Portrait of a Dutch Boy,* dated 1640, by Govaert Flinck; and *An Old Warrior* by a follower of Rembrandt. Other modes of Dutch painting are illustrated by Cuyp's *Setting out for the Chase,* Jacob Ruisdael's *A Wooded Landscape,* Jan van de Cappelle's *Boats on a Ruffled Sea,* and Jan van Goyen's *Scene in the Dunes;* and by works on a religious theme such as Jan Lievens's shadowy *Angel Appearing to Hannah,* Aert de Gelder's *Ahasuerus and Haman,* Jan Steen's beautifully detailed *Wrath of Ahasuerus* and Bartolomeus Breenbergh's *Joseph Distributing Corn in Egypt.* The gallery also possesses a beautiful group of Rembrandt's drawings. Moving forward over 200 years one finds here too, Van Gogh's *Old Woman Digging.*

French painters represented include those of the highest rank. *Tancred and Erminia* by Nicolas Poussin, once in the collection of Sir James Thornhill, was inspired by verses from Tasso's *Gerusalemme Liberata;* there is an earlier version of the same subject in the Hermitage Museum, Leningrad. Poussin's powerful influence is evident in the *Classical Landscape with Figures* by his brother-in-law Gaspar Dughet; a *Classical Landscape* by Claude also hangs here. *Ste Julienne de Liège* is a muted

I   Miravan inspecting the tomb of his ancestors   (JOSEPH WRIGHT OF DERBY)
Derby Museums and Art Gallery

2 *A Woman in Bed*
(REMBRANDT)
National Gallery of Scotland

3 *The Adulteress brought before Christ*
(GEORGIONE)
Glasgow Art Gallery
and Museum

work by Philippe de Champaigne, who was much influenced by the austere Catholic sect, the Jansenists, for whom he did a great deal of painting. *Solomon and the Queen of Sheba* is by another 17th-century French painter, Eustache Le Sueur. *The Gamesters,* set in a guardroom, is characteristic of the work of Mathieu Le Nain. There are several delightful works from 18th-century France: *The Hurdy-Gurdy Player* by Watteau, *Les Tourterelles* by Nicolas Lancret, *L'Amour Paternel* by Aubry, and *Le Presbytère* by Hubert Robert. The two adversaries of the early 19th century, Ingres and Delacroix, are both represented, the former by an interesting *Paolo and Francesca,* the latter by *The Burial of St Stephen.* Other 19th-century paintings include *Paysage d'Auvergne* by Théodore Rousseau, *Taliferme en Bretagne* by Daubigny, and *La Roche Percée, Étretat,* by Courbet, painted about 1869. Unfinished is a portrait by Manet of the society painter Carolus-Duran—he was staying near Manet so they agreed to paint each other's portraits. Monet's *L'Église de Varangeville* is one of a series painted in 1882 at different times of the day. Camille Pissarro is represented by *L'Abreuvoir de Montfoucault,* Boudin by *Trouville, 1896,* and Degas by two works, *Jockeys avant le Course* and a pastel portrait of *Mlle Malo. Paysage à Pont Aven* was painted by Gauguin in 1888 and *Baigneuses à Tahiti in 1897*—the latter was once owned by Samuel Courtauld. *La Songeuse* by Toulouse-Lautrec, *La Dinette* by Bonnard and *Femme Se Coiffant* by Vuillard are also here. In a very different vein is Puvis de Chevannes's *La Décollation de St Jean Baptiste.*

Spanish painting is sparsely represented but Murillo's large *Marriage Feast at Cana*—it contains 22 figures—is a very fine example of his work. *St Marina* is from the workshop of Zurbarán.

English painting ranges from a miniature portrait of Henry, Prince of Wales, elder brother of Charles I, by Isaac Oliver to a series of drawings by the famous contributor to *Punch,* Phil May. There is an excellent portrait by Reynolds of the Primate of All Ireland, Dr Richard Robinson, and another one of the Reverend William Beale. By Gainsborough are two late portraits, one of Giusto Ferdinando Tenducci, a celebrated singer and friend of Mozart, the other of the Honourable Harriet Marsham, whose sister is to be found, also portrayed by Gainsborough, in the Sudley Art Gallery, Liverpool. Gainsborough's *The Harvest Wagon,* widely regarded as one of the masterpieces of British painting, is also here. An interesting story attaches to this painting concerning the carrier Wiltshire, a close friend of the artist, who also arranged the transportation of his pictures from Bath to London. Gainsborough grew fond of Wiltshire's old grey horse, which appears as the leader in this painting, and when he moved to London he offered to buy the horse for 50 guineas. Wiltshire instead sent the horse as a parting gift and in return Gainsborough gave him this painting, writing, 'Because I think this is one of my best compositions I send it to a gentleman who has vastly contributed to my happiness.'

There are several other English landscapes: Richard Wilson's *The River Dee near Eaton Hall*, John Crome's *View near Harwich*, and Turner's *The Sun Rising Through Vapour*, painted about 1807. Paintings from much later in the 19th century are Rossetti's *The Blue Bower*, Whistler's *Symphony in White No. III* (a study of two girls in white), Sir William Quiller Orchardson's portrait of his wife, and Sickert's *The Eldorado, Paris*.

The collection of sculptures in the gallery includes several small bronzes by Giovanni Bologna, a bronze by Sansovino, a terracotta relief by Giovanni della Robbia, a bust of Alexander Pope by Roubiliac, a bronze by Géricault and two small works by Degas. In addition there are many interesting drawings, prints and other works of art.

Birmingham City Museum and Art Gallery, Congreve Street
Tel.: 021 235 2834
Open weekdays 10-6; Sunday 2-5.30

Opened in 1867, the Birmingham Art Gallery was originally housed in the library. With extensions to the Council House being planned it was decided to allocate space for the Art Gallery and this was finally opened in 1885. Further galleries were opened in 1912 and 1919. From its inception the Gallery was administered by the Corporation but for over half a century funds for purchase derived from private benefactors, of whom there were a good number, and it was not until 1946 that acquisitions began to be financed from the rates.

Among the earliest Italian paintings in the Gallery is an octagonal panel by Simone Martini of *A Saint Holding a Book* which may derive from the predella of an altarpiece. From the late 14th century comes a *Madonna and Child Enthroned with Eight Saints* by an artist known as the Master of San Lucchese. *The Dead Christ,* a panel by Cima da Conegliano, may have decorated the pinnacle of a polyptych. *The Descent of the Holy Ghost* is attributed to Botticelli and assistants and is probably a late work of 1500-05. Dated about 1512-13 is *Virgin and Child with Saints and Donor* by Boccaccio Boccacciono. An *Adoration of the Shepherds* is the work of Bonifazio de' Pitati (called Veronese), a 16th-century Venetian. From the 17th century come *Rest on the Flight into Egypt* by Orazio Gentileschi; *Woman Holding a Dish* by Guido Reni; *Erminia and the Shepherd* by Guercino, dated 1620; *Adoration of the Kings* by Carlo Carlone; *An Angel Appearing to the Shepherds,* probably painted in Rome about 1640 by Giovanni Castiglione; *St Andrew Praying before his Execution* by Carlo Dolci; and *Portrait of a Genoese*

Nobleman by Bernardo Strozzi. Another *Angel Appearing to the Shepherds* has been attributed to Bartolomeo Passante, a pupil of Ribera. 18th-century works include *The Arrival of the 4th Earl of Manchester in Venice in 1707* by Luca Carlevaris, the first of a series of state arrivals painted by him; *A Girl Holding a Dove* by G. M. Crespi; *Dives and Lazarus* by Luca Giordano; *Miracle of St Vincent Ferrer* by Sebastiano Ricci; *Venetian Capriccio* by Marco Ricci; *Santa Maria della Salute and the Dogana* by Guardi; and *Caesar before Alexandria* by Giovanni Pellegrini. A still life by Giorgio Morandi represents 20th-century work.

Among Dutch paintings to be seen are a triptych, *Noli me Tangere,* of about 1550 by Jan van Scorel; *Winter Landscape* by Jacob Ruisdael; *Harbour Scene* by Salomon Ruisdael; *Landscape with Cattle* by Albert Cuyp; *River Scene,* dated 1642, by Jan Van Goyen; *The Ford* by Barent Gael; and *A Fresh Breeze* by Willem van de Velde. Among other works not to be missed are *Lady Playing a Guitar* by Terborch; *Woman and Child* by Pieter de Hooch; *The Music Lesson* by Jacob Ochterveldt; *Old Woman and a Boy by Candlelight* by Mathias Stomer; *Christ before Caiaphas* by Leonard Bramer; and works by Aert van der Neer, Isaac Ostade, Bartolomeus van der Helst and Philips Wouwerman.

There are a small number of Flemish works of great interest in the Gallery. Among them is a tiny, exquisite *Man of Sorrows* ascribed to Petrus Christus and an equally fascinating *Nativity* by Hans Memling. From Adriaen Ysenbrandt comes a triptych, dated about 1510-12, with three scenes, *Adoration of the Magi, Nativity* and *Circumcision;* and with an *Annunciation* in grisaille on the reverse. From Rubens comes a sketch for the Whitehall ceiling.

Two outstanding works in the collection are by Claude; one, *Landscape with the Ponte Molle,* dated 1645, and the other, one of his last scenes done on copper, *Coast Scene with the Embarkation of St Paul,* dated about 1654-5. Also from the 17th century is a *Classical Landscape* by Gaspar Dughet and here too is Millet's *Regulus Returning to Carthage,* a story found in Livy and Horace. An example of 18th-century painting is Pierre Patel's *Jephthah and his Daughter,* and here also is Pierre-Hubert Subleyras's *Blessed John of Ávila,* the counsellor of St Theresa. Early 19th-century painting includes a portrait of Madame Simon by Delacroix; *The Death of Hippolytus* by Girodet; and *Portrait of a Sculptor* by Thomas Couture. There is an unfinished study for *Venus and Psyche,* a picture he painted in 1863, by Courbet; a *Woodland Scene* by Diaz; and *Sea at Étretat* by Jongkind. From Degas comes *A Roman Beggar-Woman,* painted on a visit to Italy in 1857, and among other works by Fantin-Latour is a portrait of Marie Fantin-Latour, dated 1859. The academic painter Bouguereau is represented by a painting called *Charity,* dated 1865. From Guillaumin comes *Les Environs de Paris,* dated 1874, and from Harpignies *Le Pont de Nevers.* A favourite scene for painting by Camille Pissarro, *Le Pont Boildieu à Rouen, Soleil Couchant,* is here; and by Sisley there is a view which he also painted many times in 1893-4, *La Vieille Église de Moret par la Pluie.* There is an unfinished *Portrait of a Woman* by Mary Cassatt, the American associate of the Impressionists. Later French works include *Notre Dame de Constance, Bormes* by Lucien Pissarro; *Le Repas* by Vuillard; *La Lampe* by Bonnard; *La Route avec Peupliers* by Vlaminck; and *Port of Cette, Marseilles* by Albert Marquet.

In the field of British painting the Birmingham Gallery is famed for its collection of Pre-Raphaelite works but there are many good things from other periods too. A *Portrait of a Woman* by William Dobson is the only picture which certainly bears his signature. From Sir Peter Lely come an early work, *Susannah and the Elders,* a portrait of Oliver Cromwell, dated about 1653, a portrait of Sir John Nicholas, and another portrait of Elizabeth, Lady Monson, who whipped her husband until he promised to behave better politically. Attributed to Michael Dahl is a portrait of the Countess of Sandwich, and from Kneller comes a portrait of Mary, Marchioness of Rockingham. By John Riley is a portrait of Sir Edward Waldo, whom Charles II knighted at his own house in Cheapside in 1677. There are several portraits by Joseph Highmore and a series of five by Arthur Devis. From Reynolds comes come a portrait of Mrs Luther, dated 1766, a group portrait of the Roffey family, and a head of Viscount Keppel. Gainsborough is represented by three portraits, of Thomas Coward, of Matthew Hale, and of Sir Charles Holte, together with a *Landscape with Cottage and Cart,* painted about 1785. Certainly not to be overlooked is Allan Ramsay's portrait of Mrs Martin, dated 1761. *The Distressed Poet* is by Hogarth; from Francis Cotes comes a portrait of Miss Hargreaves; and from Francis Hayman comes *Sir John Falstaff Raising Recruits,* dating from the early 1760s. *The Angry Father, or the Discovery of the Clandestine Correspondence* is by John Opie and there are portraits by Romney and Sir Thomas Lawrence, and a portrait of Matthew Boulton by Lemuel Abbott. There are two landscapes by Richard Wilson: *The Ruins of the Villa of Maecenas at Tivoli* is one of several versions of this subject; *Okehampton Castle* dates from about 1771-4. From Zoffany come a portrait of the Blunt children and two scenes from *Lethe,* a play by David Garrick. Another theatrical scene derives from *The Tempest* and is by Francis Wheatley; and yet another scene derived from Shakespeare is *The Dispute between Hotspur, Glendower, Mortimer and Worcester* from 1 *Henry IV,* by Fuseli, painted about 1784. John Philip Kemble is said to have sat for both Hotspur and Glendower. In a different vein are George Morland's *Shooting Sea Fowl* and *Pigs,* and James Ward's *Sheepshearing.*

The Pass of St Gotthard, uncertainly attributed to Turner, and a small *Study of Clouds* by Constable are both here. There are two views by

John Crome, *The Way through the Wood* and *View at Blofield, near Norwich.* Dated 1824 is *The Champion* by Sir Charles Eastlake—Haydon commented on its 'Titianesque simplicity' when it was first exhibited. From Benjamin Robert Haydon himself comes a work recording a historical scene, *The Meeting of the Union on Newhall Hill, Birmingham, 16th May, 1832.* This was a radical organization which held meetings during the time of the Reform Bill legislation. A portrait of Haydon by George Henry Harlow is also in the Gallery. Of special interest is the collection of paintings by David Cox, who was born and worked in Birmingham and is very well represented here with *Bolton Abbey, All Saints' Church, Hastings, Welsh Funeral, The Skylark, Rhyl Sands, Skirts of the Forest* and *Crossing the Sands,* to name just a few. Other 19th-century landscape artists include Thomas Creswick, Thomas Sidney Cooper, John Linnell and B. W. Leader, whose popular *February Fill Dyke,* dated 1881, is here. From Sir David Wilkie comes *Grace Before Meat;* from William Etty *Gather the Rose of Love while yet 'tis Time,* drawn from Spenser's *Faerie Queene,* Book II, and the unfinished *Pandora Crowned by the Seasons;* and from Edward Calvert come several mythological scenes. William Dyce is represented by a portrait of Mrs John Clerk Maxwell and *The Woman of Samaria,* Robert Martineau by *The Last Chapter,* and Augustus Egg by the splendidly composed *The Travelling Companions* which he painted in 1862 near Menton while travelling in the South of France. These last painters were in some way or another slightly connected with the Pre-Raphaelites and it is in the work of this group that the Birmingham Gallery is particularly rich.

To consider first the original Pre-Raphaelites, there are several works by Holman Hunt; *Two Gentlemen of Verona,* dated 1851 and one of the paintings exhibited at the Royal Academy in that year which inspired Ruskin's defence; *The Finding of the Saviour in the Temple,* begun in Palestine in 1854-5 but finished in England and first exhibited in 1860; and *May Morning on Magdalen Tower,* a study for the larger version in the Lady Lever Gallery. From Millais come his well-known *The Blind Girl,* painted in 1854 and awarded the prize of the Liverpool Academy in 1858; the unfinished *The Poacher's Wife; My Second Sermon,* a replica of the picture in the Guildhall Gallery; *The Enemy Sowing Tares* of 1865; and *A Widow's Mite* of 1870. Works by Rossetti include *The Boat of Love,* which he began in 1874 but abandoned in 1881—it illustrates one of Dante's sonnets; *Beata Beatrix,* painted in 1877 and an unfinished replica of the painting in the Tate—the background view of Florence was added by Ford Madox Brown after Rossetti's death; *La Donna della Finestra,* painted in 1881 and an unfinished version of the picture done in 1879—Jane Morris was the sitter and it illustrates a passage from Dante's *Vita Nuova; Proserpine,* dated 1882, a replica of the version of 1877.

Associated with the Pre-Raphaelites though not strictly one of their group was Ford Madox Brown, who is extensively represented at Birmingham. His original version of *The Last of England*, of which there are replicas in the Fitzwilliam and the Tate, is here. Painted between 1852 and 1855, it depicts the emigration of middle-class people to Australia and was suggested by the sculptor Thomas Woolner's leaving England for Australia. By Brown also is *Pretty Baa-Lambs* (there is also a replica in the Ashmolean), which was begun in 1851 and exhibited in 1852, but retouched until sold in 1859. Of it Brown wrote, 'This picture was painted out in the sunlight; the only intention being to render that effect as well as my powers in a first attempt of this kind would allow.' *An English Autumn Afternoon*, dated 1852-4 and showing a view towards Highgate from Brown's lodgings in Hampstead (Ruskin thought it an ugly subject), is also here. Other works include *Walton on the Naze;* a replica of *Work* (in Manchester City Gallery); *Elijah and the Widow's Son; The Death of Sir Tristram; The Finding of Don Juan by Haidee,* derived from Byron's *Don Juan;* and *Wycliffe on his Trial,* an unfinished replica, begun in 1891, of one of the decorations for the great hall of Manchester Town Hall.

Also very fully represented at Birmingham is Burne-Jones, who was a native of Birmingham. Best known perhaps is the series of panels, *The Story of Cupid and Psyche,* based on William Morris's *Earthly Paradise* and painted for the dining-room of No. 1 Palace Green, the house in Kensington built for the Hon. George Howard by Philip Webb. Also here are *Annunciation;* a series of four paintings called *Pygmalion and the Image; The Feast of Peleus;* and *The Story of Troy.* Among other associates of the Pre-Raphaelites represented are Arthur Hughes with among others *Musidora, The Young Poet, The Lost Child,* and *The Long Engagement,* which was originally intended as a picture of Orlando in the Forest of Arden; Walter Howard Deverell with *A Scene from 'As You Like It',* which Rossetti retouched after Deverell's death in 1854; James Smetham with *Imogen and the Shepherds,* an illustration derived from *Cymbeline;* Frederick Sandys with *Morgan-le-Fay,* and *Medea;* John Brett with several sea pieces; and Henry Wallis with a smaller version of the *Death of Chatterton* in the Tate, and *The Stonebreaker,* which was exhibited in 1858 with a quote from Carlyle's *Sartor Resartus* and of which Ruskin wrote ' . . . on the whole, to my mind, the picture of the year . . . It is entirely pathetic and beautiful in purpose and colour.' The Birmingham Gallery also owns several hundred watercolours and drawings by the Pre-Raphaelite group of artists including some by Ruskin.

Other Victorian painters to be found in the Gallery include J. F. Lewis, among whose works are *The Doubtful Coin* and *The Harem.* Thackeray visited this painter when he was living in Cairo and described him 'living like a lotus-eater—a dreamy, hazy, lazy, tobaccofied life'. Here also are Alma-Tadema with *Autumn-Vintage Festival,* and *Pheidias and the Frieze of the Parthenon;* Lord Leighton with *A Condottiere,* and *The Garden of the Inn, Capri;* Frank Holl with three portraits including one of John Bright; Henry O'Neil with *The Trial of Queen Catherine;* Richard Redgrave with *The Valleys also Stand Thick with Corn;* Abraham Solomon with *A Conversation Piece;* Albert Moore with *Sapphires, Canaries, and Dreamers;* and G. F. Watts with *Britomant, Little Red Riding Hood,* and a portrait of Burne-Jones, dated 1870.

There are a number of works by Sickert at Birmingham including *La Rue Pecquet, Dieppe,* one of his favourite scenes; *The Gallery of the Old Mogul; The Horses of St Mark's,* one of many versions; and *The Miner.* From Wilson Steer come several works also including *The Posy,* dated 1904, *Brill, Bucks,* 1823, and *A Shipyard, Shoreham. Music Hall Audience* is by Therese Lessore, and *The Artist's Family* is by Mark Gertler, painted in 1910 when he was studying at the Slade. There are works by Harold Gilman, Spencer Gore, Roger Fry and Duncan Grant; and from William Nicholson come *The Brown Veil,* dated 1905, and *The Silver Sunset.* David Bomberg, born in Birmingham, is represented by *Bab-es-Siq, Petra,* 1924; C. R. W. Nevinson by *Storm and Steel—an Impression of Downtown New York;* Matthew Smith by *Sunflower,* 1912, *Aix-en-Provence,* 1936, and *Chrysanthemeums in a Jug,* 1952. There are several paintings by Stanley Spencer, among them *The Psychiatrist,* done in 1945, and *The Resurrection: Tidying,* also done in that year. Among the works of Augustus John are *Canadian Soldier* and a *Portrait of King Feisal of Iraq,* 1919, a larger version of the one in the Ashmolean. Here also are a *Landscape near Collioure* by J. D. Innes and *Woman Holding a Flower* by Gwen John. Other 20th-century works to be found in the Gallery include *Girl in a Straw Hat* by Victor Pasmore; *Landscape in the Moon's First Quarter,* 1943, by Paul Nash; *Figures in a Landscape* by Francis Bacon; *La Symphonie Tragique* by Carel Weight; and other paintings by such artists as Graham Sutherland, Ethel Walker, Laura Knight, L. S. Lowry, Ivon Hitchens, John Piper, Keith Vaughan, Philip Sutton, Josef Herman, William Scott.

Among the sculpture in the Gallery is a bust of Cardinal Orazio Mattei by the late Baroque sculptor Lorenzo Ottoni; two busts by Roubiliac, one being of the Earl of Pembroke; a bust by Nollekens; and a large winged sculpture of *Lucifer* by Epstein. The collection of English watercolours is also very fine, including the work of artists such as J. R. Cozens, Paul Sandby, Thomas Girtin, William Blake and Samuel Palmer, as well as numerous others and the Pre-Raphaelite collection already mentioned.

There is only a small selection of Spanish art but of great interest is *The Vision of St Anthony of Padua* by Murillo, which was purchased by the collector John Blackwood in Spain about 1760 and given to his granddaughter. There is also a self-portrait by the same artist.

BLACKBURN
Blackburn Museum and Art Gallery, Library Street
Tel.: 0254 59511

Open Monday-Friday 9.30-8; Saturday 9.30-6

Like many northern provincial galleries Blackburn's collection is firmly rooted in the 19th century. Here are works by artists such as John Linnell, Frederick Goodall, David Roberts, T. S. Cooper, J. F. Herring, Marcus Stone, Richard Redgrave and Richard Ansdell, as well as Lord Leighton's *Cherries* and the well-known *Opera Box* by Henry O'Neil. Of earlier work there are two portraits, *Queen Mary II* and *Lady Mary Wortley Montague,* attributed to Sir Godfrey Kneller, and further portraits are attributed to Reynolds, Romney and Lawrence. Of more recent work there is *Ready to Show* by Dame Laura Knight, *Lords and Ladies* by William Coldstream, and *Solario* by Sir Alfred Munnings. The selection of watercolours contains works by many of the finest artists in this medium: Richard Bonington, Thomas Girtin, J. R. Cozens, J. S. Cotman, Turner, Peter de Wint, George Barrett, Samuel Palmer, John Varley, William Callow, and many others.

BLACKPOOL
The Grundy Art Gallery, Queen Street
Tel.: 0253 23977

Open weekdays 10-5; Sunday 2-5

This collection is centred mainly on the 19th century with works such as *Bolton Abbey* by Thomas Creswick, *Getting in the Sugar Cane* by Frederick Goodall, *Woodland Forest* by John Linnell, *Rouen Cathedral* by David Roberts and *Five Views of Old Liverpool* by Atkinson Grimshaw. From the 20th century an interesting work is a portrait of *Air Mechanic Shaw* (T. E. Lawrence) by Augustus John; also here are *No. 1 Dressing-Room* by Laura Knight and *Girl Writing* by Harold Knight.

BOLTON
Bolton Museum and Art Gallery, Civic Centre
Tel.: 0204 22311

Open Monday-Friday 10-6; Saturday 10-5.30

This art gallery is housed in a fine neo-classical building in Bolton's impressive Civic Centre. It was opened in 1939 but Bolton has had an

Art Gallery since 1890 when Mere Hall was presented to the Corporation by J. P. Thomasson together with a collection of paintings. Other paintings have also been bequeathed to the Gallery, which since the war has also been provided with a grant largely used for the purchase of English paintings and watercolours.

One interesting work to be seen here is *Adoration of the Shepherds* by the Roman Baroque artist Romanelli, who worked on decorative painting in the Louvre for Louis XIV. Also here is a small *Classical Landscape* by Gaspar Dughet; and by Luca Giordano is a very dramatic work, *The Death of Seneca*—it shows the circumstances of his end, bleeding to death into a basin.

Several 19th-century artists are represented. Here are *The Sacristy of Toledo Cathedral* by J. F. Lewis, who gathered so many of his themes from Spain, and a portrait drawing, *The Primate*, done during his ten years' stay in Turkey; and here also are *Sancta Lilias* by Rossetti, *Vespertina Quies* by Burne-Jones, and three large works by Millais: *North-West Passage* (on loan from the Tate); *The Moon is up and yet it is not Night* (inspired by a line in Byron's *Childe Harold);* and his famous work *The Boyhood of Raleigh,* reproductions of which must have decorated many a Victorian home. More recent are a portrait of William McElroy by Augustus John and *The Garden* by Paul Nash.

Many of the famous watercolour artists are here: Gainsborough, Paul Sandby, John Varley, Francis Towne, Nicholas Pocock, Peter de Wint, Edward Dayes, William Callow, David Cox, John Ruskin, Edward Lear and many others.

There are also some fine sculptures. By Epstein *The Slave Hold,* a bust of Einstein, and a maquette for a mourning group carved for the Trades Union Congress. There are also three sculptures by Henry Moor; *Helmet Head No. 5 (Giraffe), Head,* and *Mother and Child; Winged Figure* by Elizabeth Frink; and a maquette for a *Winged Figure* by Lynn Chadwick.

BOURNEMOUTH
Russell-Cotes Art Gallery and Museum, East Cliff
Tel.: 0202-21009

Open weekdays April-October 10-6; Sunday 2.30-5. November-March weekdays 10-5; Sunday 2.30-5

The building which houses this collection was originally designed as a villa for Sir Merton Russell-Cotes. Built in 1894, it is an imposing example of late Victorian domestic architecture. There are a few 18th-century paintings in the Gallery: George Morland's *The Peasants' Repast,* Francis Wheatley's *The Sailor's Return* and Richard Wilson's *View in the Strada Nomentana;* but the majority of the works come from the 19th century. One of the most important is Rossetti's *Venus Verticordia*, painted in 1864-5. About this painting Ruskin wrote to Rossetti the following severe comment: 'I purposely used the word "wonderfully" painted about those flowers. They are wonderful to me, in their realism; awful—I can use no other word—in their coarseness; showing enormous power, showing certain conditions of non-sentiment which underlie all you are doing—now.' Other paintings include *The Dawn of Love* and *Venus and Cupid* by William Etty; *Ramsgate Sands* by W. P. Frith, a version done in 1905 of the original picture of 1854 which was shown at the Royal Academy and bought by Queen Victoria for 1,000 guineas; *Midsummer*, 1887, by Albert Moore; *The Highland Flood* by Landseer; and a number of works by the successful Victorian artist Edward Long. The permanent collection of watercolours includes works by Turner, George Barret, David Cox, J. S. Cotman, Peter de Wint, and John Varley.

BRADFORD
Bradford City Art Gallery, Cartwright Hall, Lister Park
Tel.: 0274 48247

Open Monday-Friday 10-8; Saturday 10-5

Cartwright Hall, the home of this gallery, was built as a memorial to Edmund Cartwright, the inventor of the power loom, and opened in 1904. Always intended as an art gallery and museum, this impressive building is situated in Lister Park, named after Samuel Cunliffe-Lister, 1st Baron Masham, who offered the site of his old home Manningham Hall and bore a large part of the cost of the building. The architecture itself presents a mixture of styles with perhaps a predominance of French Baroque influence. Besides a permanent collection of pictures ranging from the 16th to the 20th century the Gallery also possesses a large library of prints unique outside London. This collection has arisen through the inauguration in 1968 of an International Print Biennale at Bradford which now attracts a considerable number of entries from artists throughout the world. A number of prints are usually on display in the Gallery and others can be seen on request.

The permanent collection contains several Italian works. Two examples of 16th-century Manneristic colouring and composition are a *Madonna and Child* attributed to Rosso Fiorentino and *The Holy Family with St John,* attributed to Giorgio Vasari, renowned for his *Lives of the Painters.* Of 17th-century painting *The Stoning of St Stephen* is ascribed to Domenichino and a large *Flight into Egypt* is by Guido Reni. There is a *Sybil* by Francesco del Cairo and from the 18th century, *St Gregory the Great* by Corrado Giaquinto. *Landscape with Satyrs* and

Coliseum at Rome are attributed to the two 17th-century Flemish painters Paul Brill and Swanevelt respectively. From the Dutchman Godfried Schalken comes a typical scene, *St Peter by Candlelight*. Later European works include *Maria at Moulines* by the Swiss artist Angelica Kauffmann, *Solitude*, attributed to Corot, and works by Maxime Maufra, Fantin-Latour and Lucien Pissarro.

Representing British painting are portraits ascribed to most of the 'masters', Reynolds, Gainsborough, Kneller, Lely, Raeburn, Romney and John Singer Sargent. There are two landscapes attributed to Richard Wilson, and an oil sketch by James Ward for his famous *Gordale Scar* in the Tate. Also here are *The Edge of the Forest* by John Crome, and several small landscapes by Julius Caesar Ibbetson. Other notable paintings from the 19th century are Ford Madox Brown's *Wycliffe Reading his Translation of the Bible to John Of Gaunt, The Rehearsal* by William Mulready, and two nudes by William Etty. There is an interesting theatrical representation by Sickert, *Leslie Banks as Petruchio and Edith Evans as Katherine in The Taming of the Shrew* and works by Therese Lessore and Wilson Steer are also to be found. Spencer Gore is represented by two views, *Suburban Street* and *Panshanger Park*, Harold Gilman by a *Portrait of a Man*, and Charles Ginner by *A Corner of Hampstead* and *Roofs and Chimneys*. From the Bloomsbury Group are *Laughton Castle* by Duncan Grant, *Continental Landscape* by Roger Fry, two works by Vanessa Bell, and three by Mark Gertler. Augustus John's work is illustrated by a portrait of Caspar John and that of J. D. Innes by a Southern French landscape, *'Coullioure'*. *At the Window* is an example of the work of David Bomberg. There is a large group of works, many of them portraits, by Ambrose McEvoy, at one time the protégé of Whistler. Other paintings which should be mentioned include *The Strand at Night* by C. R. W. Nevinson, *The Black Vase* and *The Chinese Vase* by Sir William Nicholson, *The Old Canal, Bath* by John Nash, *Near Southwold, Sussex* by Stanley Spencer, *Troops in the Countryside* by Gilbert Spencer, and works by L. S. Lowry, William Roberts, Christopher Wood, Keith Vaughan, Matthew Smith, Philip Sutton and Ceri Richards.

BRIGHOUSE
Brighouse Art Gallery, Halifax Road
Tel.: 04847 740

This collection consists mainly of paintings by Victorian artists. Here are *The Duke's Blessing* by W. P. Frith; *Faust and Marguerite* by Lord Leighton; *Reflection* by Millais; *The Organ Grinder* by William Mulready; *Queen Elizabeth in a Rage* by Augustus Egg; *My Native Land Goodbye* by Henry O'Neil; *The Orphans* by Philip Hermogenes

Calderon; *The Mitherless Bairn* by Thomas Faed; *Scene in Spain, near Seville* by J. B. Burgess; *Rolling Easter Eggs* by Edward Hornel; and works by Frederick Goodall, Atkinson Grimshaw, William Collins, J. F. Herring, J. B. Pyne and David Wilkie. A collection of watercolours includes work by Whistler, David Cox, Samuel Prout and David Roberts.

BRIGHTON
Brighton Art Gallery, Church Street
Tel.: 0273 63005
Open weekdays 10-7; Saturday 10-5; Sunday 2-5 (Summer 2-6)

The idea of the need for a public art gallery in Brighton originated in 1851 and in that year part of the Royal Pavilion was set aside for annual art exhibitions. In 1868 space for a museum and library was finally decided upon, the Gallery itself being opened in 1873 in buildings that form part of the Royal Pavilion Estate. The Central Gallery was built on the site of what was once intended to be the tennis court (later it was a cavalry barracks), and the other rooms were once part of the royal stables and coach-houses. The rebuilding of the Art Gallery and Museum took place in 1902 and at the same time the Gallery received as a gift an important part of the collection of Henry Willet, a local brewer, which included some impressive early Italian and German paintings; he also donated a fine collection of English pottery and of fossils to the Museum. Recently part of the Edward James Foundation important collection of Surrealist paintings included many works by Magritte and Dali has been loaned to the Gallery.

Most of the British paintings derive from the 18th or early 19th century. There is a small work by Richard Wilson, *View on the Dee near Eaton Hall*, dating from about 1760, of which several versions are known. Two other landscapes are by one or other of his followers. A portrait of Dr Richard Russell, author of a treatise on the treatment of glandular diseases by sea-water, and sometimes called the 'Father of modern Brighton', is by Benjamin Wilson, like his subject a Fellow of the Royal Society. An English painting from the Willet collection is George Stubbs's *Shooting*, painted about 1767-9. From Zoffany come two works, *Mother and Child*, dating from about 1764, and a portrait of his stockbroker John Maddison which is one of his few signed works. Possibly painted for Boydell's Shakespeare Gallery is Romney's *Puck with T. A. Hayley as Model*. A *Portrait of a Young Woman* is by William Hogarth and *Portrait of a Musician* by Sir Nathaniel Dance, son of the architect George Dance. By William Blake there is a small *Adoration of the Kings*, executed in tempera and dated 1799. On loan to the Gallery are two portraits by Joseph Wright of Derby of the Rev. Henry Case and Helen Morewood, whom the former married 11 years after these were painted (he also assumed her name). Hardly to be overlooked is a large portrait by Sir Thomas Lawrence of *George IV, Standing in Garter Robes,* a coronation portrait. Other British paintings here are by Benjamin Barker, William Hamilton, John Frederick Herring, William Hodges (who accompanied Captain Cook on his second voyage to the South Seas), John Hoppner, George Morland, John Opie and James Northcote. There is also a portrait of Mrs Marriott of about 1770, painted by Angelica Kauffmann during the time she was in England. Among more recent British painters represented are Sir Frank Brangwyn, Robert Bevan, Philip Connard, Mark Gertler, Dame Ethel Walker, Duncan Grant, Dame Laura Knight and Ivon Hitchens. There is also a large collection of early English watercolours including works by J. R. Cozens, Paul Sandby, Rowlandson, J. S. Cotman, Copley Fielding, Thomas Girtin, David Cox, Peter de Wint, Samuel Prout, Edward Lear, Constable and Turner.

Of Italian painting in the Gallery there is a *Tobias and the Angel Raphael* now attributed to Francesco Botticini though formerly thought to be by Jacopo del Sellaio. There is also a *St Catherine of Siena,* a fragment from an altarpiece by the Ferrarese artist Lorenzo Costa. Outstanding is a *Madonna and Child* by Bartolommeo Vivarini, a 15th-century Venetian painter; the background landscape is particularly pleasing. There are two works, *Europa and the Bull* and *The Centurion of Capernaum,* from the studio of Veronese; *A Classical Allegory* by Sebastino Conca, *Haman Pleads for his Life before Esther and Ahasuerus* by Sebastiano Ricci; *Hercules and Omphale* and *The Finding of Moses* by the Neapolitan painter Luca Giordano, nicknamed 'Fa Presto' because of his speed of execution; and two pastoral landscapes by Francesco Zuccarelli.

Among the Flemish works *Balthazar, the Moorish King* is attributed to Joos van Cleve or possibly Bernard Van Orley, both born towards the end of the 15th century. *Building the Tower of Babel* is a work now ascribed to Pieter Brueghel the Elder and dated about 1548-50 although it was previously attributed to Joachim Patinir. The *Glorification of the Virgin Mary* is considered to be by Albert Pieter Cornelisz, a Bruges painter who died in 1532 and whose only other known work is in the church of St Jacques, Bruges. Also here are a fine still life by Osias Beert; *Pluto and Persphone* by Hendrik van Balen and Jan Brueghel; *A Winter Landscape* by Denis Van Alsloot; and a small *Rest on the Flight into Egypt* on copper by Pieter van der Borcht.

The Dutch group of paintings includes the very moving *Raising of Lazarus,* dated 1631, by Jan Lievens. Lievens shared a studio with Rembrandt during the 1620s and it is believed that this picture once belonged to Rembrandt. Indeed it is thought that Rembrandt's father acted as one of the models for the painting. From Nicolaes Maes, one of Rembrandt's pupils, comes the lively *A Young Fisherman with his Dog;* and from Aert de Gelder, who also studied with Rembrandt, comes *The Marriage Contract.* Other Dutch paintings include *Still Life with Carnations* by Willem van Aelst; *Landscape with a Farmhouse* by Jan van Goyen; *Skating on a Frozen River* by Aert van der Neer, *Landscape with Tobias and the Angel* by Herman van Swanevelt; and a river scene by Esaias van de Velde.

There are several important German paintings, among them a triptych attributed to Michael Wohlgemut, master of Dürer. This is actually a composite work made up from two different altarpieces with a centre panel depicting *St Jerome and St Gregory.* Two small portraits of Electors of Saxony, Frederick III, 'the Wise', and John I, 'the Constant', are by Lucas Cranach the Elder. Both probably derive from an order of 1533 for 60 portraits of the two Electors. A portrait of Henry VIII derives from the cartoon by Holbein in the National Portrait Gallery.

Of French painting there are two landscapes ascribed to Gaspar Dughet, a version by Greuze of his famous *The Reading of the Bible,* exhibited at the Salon of 1755 and much praised by Diderot, and a pleasant self-portrait by Madame Vigée-Lebrun.

BRISTOL
Bristol City Art Gallery, Queen's Road, Bristol 8
Tel.: 0272 25908
Open weekdays 10-5.30

This gallery, situated in a pleasant district of the city in which are also found the University buildings, owes its origin to the Wills family of tobacco fame, particularly to Sir William Henry Wills, later Lord Winterstoke. The first part of the Gallery, donated by him, was opened in 1905 and there was an enlargement in 1930 which was owed to the generosity of Sir George Wills. Since 1922 the H. H. Wills Fund has provided the means necessary for the purchase of pictures and since 1946 this has been augmented by a grant from the City Council. There have been hopes in recent years for a new building to house the possessions of the Art Gallery apart from those of the Museum, which was damaged during the war, but these aspirations at the moment appear to have been frustrated. Like most provincial, and indeed national galleries, Bristol is hampered by its lack of space from displaying its permanent collection to full advantage. The collection itself has benefited considerably from bequests by numerous Bristol citizens such as F. P. M. Schiller, one-time Recorder of Bristol, who besides giving the Gallery a number of important paintings also presented it with a valuable collection of Chinese porcelain.

There is a large collection of works by local artists at Bristol, one room being devoted to works by such artists or by artists who painted local scenes. There is a painting of *Avon Gorge* by Thomas Barker of Bath, and there are many by W. J. Müller who was of German extraction and the son of the first curator of the Bristol Museum. He is widely represented here, not only by local scenes, among the best of these being *View of Bristol Cathedral in 1835,* and *Eel Bucks at Goring.* Also here is a picture of Bristol in the 17th century by Peter Monomay, and painted about 1830 is a view of *Redcliffe Street and Church* by Thomas Shotter Boys. Particularly pleasing among a group of paintings by Francis Danby all set in the district are *The Snuff Mill, Stapleton* and *Clifton Rocks from Rownham Fields.* There are a lot of pictures also by J. B. Pyne dealing with Bristol and its environs; and more recently there are three works by John Piper on Bristol subjects. Because of its size not exhibited in the room devoted to works of Bristol interest, but of considerable local interest too, is the altarpiece painted by William Hogarth for St Mary Redcliffe, Bristol. This is a vast triptych painted in 1756 when Hogarth was nearly 60; the centre panel depicts the *Ascension;* the right wing *Three Maries at the Tomb;* the left wing *The Sealing of the Sepulchre.* The Gallery also possesses a portrait of Dr Edwin Sandys painted in 1741 by Hogarth.

Turning to paintings of a more general nature there are two portraits by Gainsborough, painted in the early 1760s, of an unidentified lady and gentleman of the Leyborne Popham family. Sir Joshua Reynolds's group portrait, *The Committee of Taste,* of about 1759, was once in the collection of Horace Walpole; by Reynolds also is a portrait of an unidentified youth. From Richard Wilson come a large mythological painting, *Diana and Callisto,* painted between 1763 and 1767, and a small *Ruined Tower with Figure. Landscape, Artist and a Woman Sitter* by Zoffany possibly includes a self-portrait. Other portraits are by Thomas Hudson and John Opie and there is a portrait of Lady Caroline Lamb, painted in 1809 by Sir Thomas Lawrence, and a charming, unfinished *Head of a Young Girl* also by him. Two other works which should be noted are Constable's *Study of Clouds with a Low Horizon* and *The Swineherd,* dated 1810, by James Ward.

Another room hung with William Morris hangings is devoted to Victorian paintings. Among these are two large canvases by Burne-Jones, one *St George and the Dragon,* the other called *The Garden Court,* in which are depicted six graceful female figures in various stages of lassitude. There are two small works by William Etty—*Centaurs and Nymphs,* and *The Water Carrier.* Etty's form of eroticism is overshadowed here by *The Mermaid* by Lord Leighton. There is a late work by Millàis, *The Bride of Lammermoor,* and a romantic fantasy, *The Last Moments of Raphael,* by Henry O'Neil whose declared ambition was to paint incidents of striking character which would appeal to the feelings. *Death and the Pale Horse* and a version of *Love and Death* are by G. F. Watts and among other artists represented are E. J. Poynter, David Roberts, Frederick Goodall and Paul Falconer Poole.

Most of the familiar names of 20th-century British art are here. From Sickert come three works: *Army and Navy; Othello; The Horses of St Mark's, Venice;* and there is a portrait of Mrs Montgomery by Wilson Steer. Other works include *The Old Lady* by Harold Gilman; *Nude Figure on a Bed* by Spencer Gore; *The Pursuit* by Charles Shannon; *Tulips* by Duncan Grant; *Roses in a Vase* by Vanessa Bell; *Lilies* by Roger Fry, *Statue in a Park* by Mark Gertler; another flower picture, dated 1943, by David Bomberg; a war picture, *Dog Tired* by C. R. W. Nevinson, *Mexican Shawl* by Wyndham Lewis; *The Palms Foretell* by William Roberts; and works by Matthew Smith, Victor Pasmore and Ben Nicholson. More recent acquisitions include *Purple Woods* by Ivon Hitchens, *Peonies* by Philip Sutton, and *Harvest Scene* by Josef Herman. Some fine pieces of British sculpture of the 20th century are to be seen: *Kathleen* by Epstein; *Musical Trio* by Ossip Zadkine; *Horace Brodsky* and *The Wrestler* by Gaudier-Brzeska; *Girl* by Reg Butler; and *Moon Figure* by Kenneth Armitage.

Outstanding among the Italian pictures in the Gallery is Giovanni Bellini's *Descent of Christ into Limbo.* This painting has the harshly intense quality one associates with Mantegna and indeed is probably a copy by Bellini of a lost Mantegna—the two painters were brothers-in-law. There is a *Portrait of a Young Woman* possibly by Carpaccio, and certainly possessing the full bland face he sometimes favoured. Another work by a Venetian painter of great interest is a triptych altarpiece by Antonio da Solario, signed and dated 1514, and known as the *Withypool Triptych* after its donor Paul Withypool, the son of a Bristol merchant. The side panels are lent by the National Gallery. Of Florentine work there is a small panel, *The Crucifixion and Lamentation* by Taddeo Gaddi, a close follower of Giotto; from Milan by Ambrogio da Predis, the pupil of Leonardo, there is an extraordinary unchildlike portrait of Francesco Sforza as a child. Seventeenth-century works include *Laban Seeking his Idols* by Pietro da Cortona, a *Sibyl* attributed to Domenichino, *The Return of the Prodigal Son* by Francesco Francanzano, a Neapolitan artist and brother-in-law of Salvator Rosa, and *Christ Supported by Angels* by Francesco Trevisani. Not to be missed is *The Flight into Egypt* of the Milanese artist Giovanni Battista Crespi, known as 'il Cerano'. Here, as Professor E. W. Waterhouse says, 'Cerano's rich and sonorous colour can be seen . . . in its original purity'. From the early 18th century comes Sebastiano Conca's *The Education of the Virgin*

4 *The Guitar Player* (VERMEER)
The Iveagh Bequest, Kenwood, London

5 *The Royal Albert Memorial Museum, Exeter*

and Luca Giordano's *The Rape of the Sabines;* and from 18th-century Venice two works by Michiel Marieschi, *View of the Grand Canal, Venice* and *The Rialto Bridge, Venice,* the latter painting bearing the artist's initials on a barrel on the right.

There is one splendid German painting in the Gallery, a portrait of Martin Luther by Lucas Cranach, signed and dated 1525, one of several which he executed.

Among the examples of Flemish painting is an *Interior of a Tavern, Peasants Carousing* by Adriaen Brouwer, which was once in Rubens's collection—Rubens is known to have admired this painter very much. A large panel of the *Nativity* is by Jacob Jordaens. Earlier works are a portrait of Margaret of Austria by the early-16th-century painter, Van Orley, and two portraits attributed to Corneille de Lyon, *Madame Daubigny* and *A Bearded Man in Brown Coat against a Green Background.* Among the Dutch paintings here are: *River in Spate* by Jacob Ruisdael; *Man Sleeping* by Jan Steen; *River Scene with Figures* by Jan Wynants; *Ferry-Boat Crossing a River* by Jan Asselyn; *The Annunciation to the Shepherds,* dated 1656, by Nicolaes Berchem; *Still Life* by Pieter Claesz; *Nymphs Bathing* and *Venus in a Landscape* by van Poelenburgh; *A Horseman on a Hilly Lane* by Philips Wouwerman; and works by Nicolaes Maes, Karel du Jardin, Jan van der Heyden and others.

The collection of French painting goes back to the early 17th century with a sober genre-piece by Mathieu Le Nain, *A Group of Itinerant Musicians with Two Women in an Apartment.* In a very different tradition is Charles Lebrun's *The Brazen Serpent,* which was a design for a Gobelins tapestry. Attributed to Sebastien Bourdon is *Jacob's Journey and the Pillar of Bethel.* Notable from 18th-century France is Hubert Robert's *A Loggia, Probably at the Villa Albani.* The collection of 19th-century painting is of great interest. There is a portrait of Madame Bruyère by Baron Gros, and from Delacroix *Head of a Woman in a Red Turban.* There are two works by Diaz, a painter of the Barbizon School, and two fine paintings by Courbet, *L'Éternité* and *Landscape, Ornans*—the former was originally in the collection of Puvis de Chavannes. From Eugène Carrière comes *The Pianist,* and from Boudin a *Harbour Scene* and an unusual *Still Life with Oysters.* Camille Pissarro and his son Lucien are both represented, the former by *A Field at Eragny,* the latter by *Snow Scene.* There are works by two women painters: *Mother and Child* by the American Mary Cassatt; and *The Donkey Ride* by Eva Gonzales, the model and pupil of Manet, whose influence is strongly felt in this picture. *Spring Landscape* and *Entrance to a Village* are two lovely works by Alfred Sisley; there is a small *Sunset* by Seurat and a *Portrait of Madame Hessel and her Dog* by Vuillard. The Symbolists, the other stream in French painting, have a token representation with *Perseus and*

Andromeda by Gustave Moreau and a mysterious sketch of *A Rider* by Odilon Redon. A completely different 'Victorian' anecdotal theme is to be seen in the painting *Les Adieux* by James Tissot.

BURNLEY
Towneley Hall Art Gallery and Museum, Towneley Hall
Tel.: 0282 24213

Open weekdays 10-5.30; Sunday 2-5

This museum and gallery is situated in the hall that was once the home of the Towneley family. Many of the paintings in the Gallery derive from the bequest of a considerable sum of money by Edward Massey to the Burnley Corporation to be devoted, among other things, to the purchase of pictures. The majority of the paintings here are British but there is a small representation of French 19th-century art. Among these latter works may be mentioned a landscape by Troyon; *Sunset at Sea* and *River Scene at Sunset* by Daubigny, *Four Nymphs in a Wood* by Diaz, *Chrysanthemums* by Fantin-Latour; *Evening* by Harpignies; *River Scene* by Lépine; and several scenes by Charles-Emile Jacque. There are several paintings among the English group from the 18th century: a landscape ascribed to Richard Wilson; a picture of Charles Towneley and his friends in the Towneley Gallery, Park Street, Westminster, by Zoffany; and a picture of Towneley by George Barret, whose paintings Richard Wilson unkindly described as 'spinach and eggs'. *A Rustic Cottage* is by George Morland. Later works include *Watermill in Derbyshire* by Peter de Wint, exhibited at the Royal Academy in 1814; *The Mountain of Vietry* by Philip Reinagle; *Haymaking, Snowdon,* and *The Vale of Clwyd* by David Cox; *The Hastings Coast* by John Linnell; *Interior of a Cathedral* by David Roberts; *Queen Victoria's Favourite Dog* by Landseer; and *Wood Nymphs* by Burne-Jones. There are also a considerable number of fine watercolours in the Gallery.

BURY
Bury Art Gallery and Museum, Moss Street
Tel.: 061 764 4110

Open weekdays 10-6; Saturday 10-5

Paintings in this gallery are for the most part drawn from the 19th century. There is a small *Hampstead Heath* by John Constable, and among other works are: *Landscape Scene in Norfolk* by John Crome; *The Rising of the River* and *Crossing the Brook* by John Linnell; *Drawing for the Militia* by John Phillip; *The Student* by Daniel Maclise; *The First*

Voyage by William Mulready; *The Crusader's Wife* by J. R. Herbert; *The Random Shot* by Landseer. Also exhibited here are watercolours from the Wrigley Collection; among the artists are David Cox, David Roberts, Peter de Wint, William Hunt, Copley Fielding, Clarkson Stanfield.

CAMBRIDGE
Fitzwilliam Museum, Trumpington Street
Tel.: 0223 50023

Open weekdays 10-5; Sunday 2.15-5

This museum owes its foundation to Richard, 7th Viscount Fitzwilliam of Merrion, who in 1816 bequeathed to the University of Cambridge his library, his art collection (144 paintings) and £100,000 to provide a building to house them. Among his possessions were a Titian, a Veronese, a Rembrandt, a Palma Vecchio, a series of Rembrandt's etchings, many engravings and medieval manuscripts. In 1821 the present site was acquired from Peterhouse College and in 1834 a competition was held for a design for the new building which was won by George Basevi, a cousin of Disraeli and the favourite pupil of Sir John Soane. Basevi died in 1845 and the building was completed by C. R. Cockerell and E. M. Barry, being finally opened in 1848. In 1834 David Mesman presented a large bequest of 17th-century Dutch and Flemish paintings and further munificent gifts enlarged the collection so that its scope embraced priceless works of antiquity, coins, manuscripts and other works of art. At the same time the Museum received several large financial bequests enabling further galleries to be opened and purchases to be made. In 1893 a number of very important early Italian works were acquired and in the first decades of this century Charles Fairfax Murray presented the Museum with Titian's *Tarquin and Lucretia* and paintings by Hogarth, Reynolds and Gainsborough as well as some works by the Barbizon School. Since that date there have been further gifts of French and English paintings. Ruskin's presentation in 1861 of 25 works of Turner, which laid the foundation of a collection of Turner's drawings and watercolours, should also be mentioned.

The gallery possesses an outstanding group of early Italian painting, mainly Sienese, Florentine and Venetian. The earliest Sienese work is a *Crucifixion* of the 13th century; then by Simone Martini there are three splendid panels belonging to a polyptych which was probably originally in an Augustinian convent at San Gimignano. The panels depict *St Michael, St Augustine* and *St Geminianus*. Two paintings of *The Virgin and Child* are by Luca di Tomme and Andrea Vanni and are also 14th-century Sienese works; from the 15th century are two works by Giovanni di Paolo, *St Bartholomew* and *The Entombment of the Virgin*.

From Florence comes the masterly *Madonna and Child Enthroned between two Adoring Angels* by Lorenzo Monaco, one of his earliest known works; even more noteworthy are two small paintings by Domenico Veneziano, by whom there are very few authentic works extant. These two are predella panels from the St Lucy Altarpiece, the main panel of which is in the Uffizzi (Florence), and represent *The Annunciation* and *The Miracle of St Zenobius. The Annunciation,* a rare combination of purity of colour, line and feeling, was the central predella panel; the scene takes place in an enclosed garden *(hortus conclusus)* with its closed gate a symbol of the Immaculate Conception. *The Miracle of Zenobius,* set in a Florentine street, depicts the restoring to life of a child run over by an ox-cart by Zenobius, Bishop of Florence. Later examples of Florentine art include Cosimo Rosselli's *Madonna and Child Enthroned with Four Saints,* Lorenzo di Credi's *Martyrdom of St Sebastian,* Francesco Botticini's *Virgin Adoring the Child* (the scene here is set in a meadow, which was uncommon for this subject in Florentine art at this time) and *cassone* panels by Bartolommeo di Giovanni and Jacopo del Sellaio.

From the Umbrian school comes a *Virgin and Child with St John the Baptist* by Pintoricchio, and from Ferrara a *Crucifixion* by Cosimo Tura who was Court Painter for the Este family there. Two of the earliest works of Venetian art are the altarpiece *St Lanfranc of Pavia Enthroned between Saints* by Cima da Conegliano, painted between 1495 and 1518, and *Virgin and Child with Saints and Donors,* considered to be one of the best works of Marco Basaiti, a pupil of Giovanni Bellini. The greatest aspect of Venetian painting is illustrated here by the two works by Titian already mentioned—*Tarquin and Lucretia* and *Venus and Cupid with a Lute Player.* The former picture was sent by Titian to Philip II of Spain in 1571; the latter formerly owned by Queen Christina of Sweden and then in the Orléans collection before it came into the possession of Viscount Fitzwilliam, was cleaned in 1949-50 and its full quality revealed. Sebastiano del Piombo's *Adoration of the Shepherds,* thought once to be by Giorgione, must not be missed, nor must Palma Vecchio's *Venus and Cupid* and a fine work by Jacopo Bassano, *The Journey to Calvary.* Ovid provided the theme for a magnificent work by Veronese, *Hermes, Herse and Aglauros,* the story being that Hermes, the lover of Herse, transformed her jealous sister Aglauros into a lump of stone. By Tintoretto there is *The Adoration of the Shepherds,* painted early in his career, and *Portrait of a Young Man.*

Italian painting of the Baroque period is represented mainly by painters originally from Bologna. There are two works from the Carracci: *St Roch and the Angel* by Annibale, and *Christ Appearing to the Virgin* by his cousin Lodovico. *Landscape with St John Baptizing* is a beautiful classical landscape by Annibale's pupil Domenichino; *Ecce*

Homo is a remarkable work by Guido Reni and equally noteworthy is *The Betrayal of Christ* by Guercino, a companion work to *The Incredulity of St Thomas* in the National Gallery. Of considerable interest is *The Calling of St Peter and St Andrew* by Pietro da Cortona which was a preliminary study for a series of frescoes executed early in his career. *L'Umana Fragilità* by Salvator Rosa is the strangest work, a sombre painting replete with symbols of the variety and transience of life and the omnipresence of death. A portrait of Cardinal Jacopo Rospigliosi by Carlo Maratta is a late 17th-century Roman work. The 18th-century Italian paintings are much concerned with views: there are three good examples of these by Bernardo Bellotto; two small works by Canaletto, four by Guardi; a late one by Marieschi; and two by Panini.

The collection of Italian drawings in the Fitzwilliam must not be forgotten; among others there are works by Raphael, Leonardo and Michelangelo.

Flemish painting in the Museum begins with the *Transfiguration* by Albrecht Bouts, second son of Dieric Bouts, and is followed by the *Virgin and Child* by Joos van Cleve. *Couple Embracing* is by the Antwerp Mannerist painter Frans Floris, and *Village Festival in Honour of St Hubert and St Anthony* is a lively scene by Pieter Brueghel the Younger deriving from one of his father's works. From Rubens there is a fascinating series of oil sketches on the theme of the Eucharist, designs for tapestries commissioned by the Infanta Clara Eugenia, Governor of the Netherlands. Also interesting are his *Achilles among the Daughters of Lycomedes* and *The Union of Earth and Water,* a sketch for a large painting which is in Leningrad. By Van Dyck is a painting of an *Old Woman* as well as a number of drawings, and from Rubens's other assistant Frans Snyders *The Larder Woman* overflowing with the depiction of fruit and game.

Dutch painting is richly represented. There are a number of drawings by Rembrandt and a *Portrait of a Man in Military Costume,* dated 1650 and possibly a self-portrait. A remarkable *Portrait of a Man* is by Frans Hals and noteworthy also are portraits by Marten van Heemskerck, Bartholomeus van der Helst, Barent Fabritius, Gerrit Dou and Michiel van Miereveld. There are landscapes by numerous Dutch painters; among four by Jacob Ruisdael notice particularly *View on the Amstel looking towards Amsterdam.* Others are by Meindert Hobbema, Salomon Ruisdael, Jan van Goyen, Wouwerman, Jan Both, Adam Pynacker, Karel Dujardin, Swanevelt, Breenbergh and van Poelenburgh—four delightful small works by the latter. Flower pieces, which formed a genre of their own in 17th-century Holland, are also liberally represented.

There are only a few paintings from France before the 19th century but among these is an exquisite octagonal work on copper by Claude, *Pastoral Landscape with a view of the Castel Gandolfo.* It was one of a series painted for Pope Urban VIII and is datable about 1639; it remained with Urban's descendants the Barberini family until 1962. There are a number of landscape drawings by Claude in the Museum as well as a group by Nicolas Poussin. *Landscape with Travellers and an Imaginary View of a Town* is by Gaspar Dughet; two other 17th-century works are *The Entombment* by Simon Vouet and *The Holy Family* by Charles Lebrun. From the 18th century there are several small works by Nicolas Lancret and Greuze, drawings by Watteau, and a Beauvais tapestry of *Apollo and Clytie* executed from the designs of François Boucher. Early 19th-century painting includes several works by Delacroix, three studies for decorative paintings he was commissioned to execute in the Palais Bourbon, the Hôtel de Ville, and the library of the Palais de Luxembourg, and also an exotic *Odalisque*. Besides drawings by Ingres and David there are paintings by Decamps and Thomas Couture. Then come the landscape artists. There are several small sketches by Corot including one of the Roman Campagna and another called *The Dyke*, and a fine *Landscape with a Windmill* by Georges Michel, who was much influenced by a 17th-century Dutch painting. There are four landscapes by Daubigny and two by Diaz including *Storm in the Forest of Fontainebleau*; an early work by Rousseau, *Paysage Panoramique*, and other works by Chintreuil, Harpignies and Courbet—*The Glade* by the latter artist should not be missed. Many of the Impressionists are represented. Among works by Camille Pissarro are the early *Les Bords de la Seine à Bougival* and the beautiful, sunshiny *Garden at Pontoise* of 1882. From Monet come *Le Printemp* of 1886 and *Les Peupliers*, and from Sisley *L'Inondation, Port-Marly, 1876*. From Renoir there is an exciting landscape, *Le Coup de Vent*, and a *Study of a Girl* painted near the end of his life; and from Degas an unfinished work, *Au Café*. There are several scenes by Boudin, among them one of his favourite subjects, *The Beach at Trouville*, and a very early landscape, painted in 1873, by Gaugin, Cézanne is represented by a number of works, among them *L'Église au Village* and *La Forêt*, painted about 1900. Seurat is also here with a small panel, *La Rue St Vincent, Printemps*. Painters born later in the 19th century include Bonnard with a *Still Life*, first exhibited in 1923, and a painting of the house at Vernonnet which he bought in 1912; and Vuillard with the superbly coloured *Dame avec un Chien*, the lady in the picture being Princess Marguerite Caetani, editor of several international reviews including the famous *Botteghe Oscure*. Matisse with *L'Atelier sous les Toits* and *Barques sur la Plage, Étretat;* Modigliani, Rouault, Derain, Braque, Picasso, and de Chirico are all also represented.

There are few Spanish paintings in the Fitzwilliam, the earliest being a 15th-century work, *The Road to Calvary* by Anton and Diego Sanchez of the Andalusian School but much influenced by Flemish art. From the

17th century come *Adoration of the Shepherds* by Luis Tristán and two works by Murillo, *The Vision of Fra Lauterio* and *St John the Baptist with Scribes and Pharisees,* one of five paintings formerly in a convent in Seville.

German painting is even sparser but the two small works on copper by Adam Elsheimer, *Venus and Cupid* and *Minerva as Patroness of the Arts and Sciences,* are of the highest interest and quality. Elsheimer, who settled in Rome in 1600, dying there ten years later at the age of 32, had extensive influence on many painters including Rubens and Rembrandt. These paintings formed part of a set portraying the life of man in three different aspects: Venus represented the instinctive life, Minerva the life of the mind, and one of Juno, now lost, illustrated the active, practical life.

English painting is comprehensively represented from the early 16th century to the 20th century. An early portrait of William Herbert, Earl of Southampton is by a follower of Hans Holbein, and there is an excellent example of Hans Eworth's work, *Queen Mary I when a Princess. Portrait of an Unknown Woman* is attributed to Marcus Gheeraerts the Younger and other outstanding works of the Elizabethan period are miniatures painted by Nicholas Hilliard, among them a likeness of Queen Elizabeth. Later he has a miniature of Anne of Denmark; by his pupil Isaac Oliver are portraits of Henry, Prince of Wales and Richard Sackville, 3rd Earl of Dorset. From the 17th century come a *Portrait of a Lady* by Sir Peter Lely, a self-portrait by Jonathan Richardson and miniatures by Samuel Cooper. From the 18th century come a number of works by Hogarth including *A. Musical Party,* portraits of George Arnold and his daughter Francis Arnold, and two characteristic panels of *Indiscretion - Before and After.* By Joseph Highmore are illustrations to Samuel Richardson's novel *Pamela.* Of great interest is a portrait of the Museum's founder Lord Fitzwilliam at the age of 19 by Joseph Wright of Derby, by whom there is also a landscape painting, *View in Dovedale.* From Sir Joshua Reynolds come two early portraits, *Mrs Angelo,* dated 1759-60, and *Henry Vansittart,* 1767, as well as the unfinished *Edmund Burke and the Marquess of Rockingham.* Gainsborough is represented by several works, among them the charming double portrait of *Heneage Lloyd and his sister in a landscape,* and the late portrait of the Hon. W. Fitzwilliam. Further portraits are by Raeburn (of W. Glendonwyn), Sir Thomas Lawrence (of Samuel Woodburn, the picture dealer), and Romney *(Portrait of a Young Man).* By Romney too are a number of designs for history pictures, a sphere of painting in which he had no success. Historical designs by William Blake are also to be found in the Museum together with numerous watercolours, engravings and writings. *Death on a Pale Horse* is one of his paintings here. Worth noting also is a painting of the horse *Gimcrack* by George Stubbs. Eighteenth century landscape painting is further illustrated by Richard Wilson's *Landscape with Apollo and the Nymphs* and *Italian Landscape with a River.* From the turn of the century comes Turner's *The Trossachs,* the only oil by him in the Fitzwilliam although there is a fine collection of his watercolours originating from Ruskin's gift. *Hampstead Heath* and *Hove Beach* are examples of Constable's approach to two favourite themes; there are also a number of oil sketches and a group of watercolours and drawings. The Museum possesses many fine examples of the English Watercolour School, among them Alexander Cozens, J. R. Cozens, Thomas Girtin, John Sell Cotman, Bonington and many more.

Victorian art also has a niche. There are works by Alma-Tadema, Lord Leighton, Albert Moore, William Mulready and by a number of the Pre-Raphaelites. There is a version of Ford Madox Brown's *The Last Of England* and also his *Death of Tristram;* and by Millais there is a study for the *Lorenzo and Isabella* in the Walker Art Gallery. Numerous studies and drawings by Rossetti include portraits of Elizabeth Siddal, Jane Morris, Robert Browning and Swinburne. A little-known work by Holman Hunt is a portrait of his son by his first wife, Cyril Holman Hunt, and the gallery also possesses a study for the *Claudio and Isabella* in the Tate Gallery and a small *View on the Thames* which Hunt did during the day while working at night on *The Light of the World* and which he gave to Millais.

Later paintings include Sickert's *The Lion of St Mark* and Wilson Steer's *Children Paddling, Walberswick,* dated 1894 and included in his one-man exhibition of that year where it was much praised by George Moore. Spencer Gore, Harold Gilman, Charles Ginner and Robert Bevan are all represented and there are several works by Augustus John including portraits of Bernard Shaw, Thomas Hardy and Sir William Nicholson, whose works are also to be found in the Fitzwilliam, as are paintings by Vanessa Bell, Duncan Grant, Roger Fry and Henry Lamb—his portrait of the critic Lytton Strachey is here. Among painters of a more recent generation are Graham Sutherland *(Descent from the Cross),* Stanley Spencer, Christopher Wood and Ivon Hitchens.

CARDIFF
National Museum of Wales, Cathays Park
Tel.: 0222 26241
Open weekdays 10-5; (April-September 10-6); Sunday 2.30-5

The Department of Art of the National Museum of Wales has grown up as an integral part of the Museum which was founded in 1912. At that time the Department took over the collections of the old Cardiff Museum, the home of a diverse group of paintings bequeathed by

William Menelaus and James Pyke Thompson. The Museum has continued to gain from the generosity of certain benefactors (Pyke Thompson also bequeathed money which was used to purchase paintings up to World War I) and to pursue a policy of acquiring works by Welsh artists whether living or dead. The policy has equally been to obtain paintings illustrative of the Welsh culture and landscape and also to form a portrait gallery of eminent Welsh men and women. But a wider outlook has by no means been eschewed and the gallery has an excellent representation not only of British but even more so of European painting. The gallery owes its outstanding collection of French 19th-century painting to the generosity and acumen of two sisters, Miss Gwendoline and Miss Margaret Davies, daughter and granddaughter of coal owners. Advised by Hugh Blaker, brother of their former governess, they began collecting in 1908 and their collection was virtually complete by 1924 although Margaret Davies made further purchases later in life. For a time they were alone in the collection of late 19th-century French painting in Britain; their collection of works by Daumier remains one of the largest made of that artist; Millet, the Impressionists and Post-Impressionists are also remarkably well represented. But the Misses Davies's interest also extended to the purchasing of contemporary British painting and certain older works, and here too the Museum has been the beneficiary.

In the collection of British painting at Cardiff there are first several portraits of the 16th century, all by unknown artists; among them are likenesses of Catherine of Aragon and the Earl of Pembroke. Similarly there are a number of anonymous 17th- and 18th-century portraits, including one of Oliver Cromwell and another purporting to be of Judge Jeffreys. Here too is a portrait of Sir Thomas Hanmer by Cornelius Johnson, and there are two interesting portraits of Robert Davies and Mrs Mutton Davies of Gwysaney by Thomas Leigh, a painter somewhat in the style of Cornelius Johnson who flourished in the middle of the 17th century. Even more interesting is a selection of miniatures (some of them on loan); for example there is an *Unknown Lady* by Nicholas Hilliard and a portrait of Henry, Prince of Wales, elder brother of Charles I, by Isaac Oliver.

Richard Wilson, being a Welshman, is naturally one of the most copiously represented 'Old Masters' at Cardiff. His impact on British landscape painting, though delayed, was immense, combining as he did the Italianate classical tradition with a genuine feeling for nature. Even Ruskin, who had no great sympathy with his work, stated that 'with Richard Wilson the history of sincere landscape art founded on a meditative love of nature begins in England.' And Constable wrote, 'I recollect nothing so much as a large, solemn, bright, warm, fresh landscape by Wilson, which still swims in my brain like a delicious dream.' There are a number of portraits by Wilson, among them the rather stiff *Maid of Honour* and *Sir Edward Lloyd,* done in 1750, the year he went to Italy. A *View of Dover* was also possibly painted, though this is disputed, before his visit to Italy, and may indeed have been influenced by seeing the work of Canaletto who was in England from 1746. Two romantic paintings, ordered by an English patron while Wilson was in Rome, are *Landscape with Banditti round a Tent* and *Landscape with Banditti: The Murder.* A painting emulating the compositional powers of Claude is *Rome and the Ponte Molle,* dated 1754. Other works from the Italian period include *The White Monk, View at Tivoli* and *The Garden of the Villa Madama, Rome.* Then there are several scenes set in Wales, some, like *Dolbadarn Castle, Valley of the Mawddach with Cader Idris,* and *Caernarvon Castle,* observant of classical precepts; others like *Penn Ponds, Pistyll Cain,* and *Pembroke Town and Castle* evidence of his bolder use of those precepts to convey his own particular vision. Also in the Museum are numerous drawings and studies by Wilson, many of them executed while in Rome, and here too is his portrait, done in Rome in 1752 by Anton Mengs. Another landscape in the gallery—of *Lake Albano*—was at one time attributed to Wilson but is now thought to be by Joseph Wright of Derby.

Wilson's contemporaries, Reynolds and Gainsborough, are also represented though on a much smaller scale. By the former there are two portraits, of Colonel George Catchmaid Morgan and of the 2nd Baron Ducie; by Gainsborough are also two portraits—of Sir Richard Lloyd and Thomas Pennant—and two landscapes, *A Wooded Landscape with Hagar and Ishmael* and *A Wooded Landscape with Market Cart* (on loan). There are a number of landscapes by Thomas Barker of Bath, who was actually born in Pontypool, and there are three views of Glamorgan by the Preston-born painter Anthony Devis. Sir Henry Raeburn is represented by two portraits of ladies, *Mrs Douglas* and *Mrs Tod,* and there are two pleasing studies of girls by Sir Thomas Lawrence. On loan from the Tate are several Turners including *A Thames Backwater with Windsor Castle* and *A Mountain Stream;* there are also several paintings in the Museum attributed to Turner which, it has been said, were originally given by him to his housekeeper in Chelsea, Mrs Booth. From Constable come *Landscape near Dedham* and *A View of Hampstead Heath,* which is also on loan. David Cox, whose favourite scenery for painting was North Wales, is represented by a number of small works, among them *Cardigan Bay* and *The Return of the Flock.* Other Welsh scenes are by Julius Caesar Ibbetson and there is a *Landscape in Normandy* by J. S. Cotman. Later 19th-century painting is represented by *The Tenby Prawnseller* by W. P. Frith, two works by Alma-Tadema, *Poetry* and *Prose,* and several works by Burne-Jones including a large portrait of Alberta, Countess of Plymouth, a small study of a head, *Venus*

Discordia, and *The Wheel of Fortune,* a design for part of a triptych, *The Story of Troy.* A version of Rossetti's *Fair Rosamund, Jeptha* by Sir John Millais, and *King Rene's Honeymoon* by Ford Madox Brown are also here. There are three nocturnes by Whistler: one with simply that title, another of a *Snowstrom,* and the third of *St Mark's, Venice.* There are two Sickerts, *Camden Town* and *Venice, Palazzo Eleanor Duse;* three by Wilson Steer, *The Schoolgirl, Chirk Castle: Stormy Sunset,* and *Distant View of Bridgnorth;* and two works by Harold Gilman, *The Kitchen* and *Mornington Crescent,* the latter title also being given to a canvas by Spencer Gore. By Robert Bevan is a painting titled *Maples at Cuckfield.* The Museum owns a great many works by Augustus John. Particularly notable are his portraits of Dylan Thomas (1936) and W. H. Davies (1920), a self-portrait, and *Dorelia at Alderney Manor.* There are several works by his friend J. D. Innes and a number of studies by his sister Gwen John, including the portrait of *Mère Poussepin.* Dylan Thomas is also portrayed by Alfred Janes whose portrait of the composer, Daniel Jones, has recently been acquired. Sir Frank Brangwyn is another Welsh artist with many works at Cardiff, among them two very large works done in tempera and watercolour, *A Heavy Gun in Action* and *A Tank in Action.*

Other modern British paintings include David Bomberg's *Flowers and Silk,* Matthew Smith's *Carved Figure and Shell,* dated 1955, William Scott's *Still Life,* dated 1957, Stanley Spencer's *Snowdon from Llanfrothen,* Victor Pasmore's *Girl with a Curtain,* John Nash's *Frozen Ponds,* Ivon Hitchens' *Landscape* and *Trees from a House Roof: Autumn,* dated 1947. Of contemporary Welsh painting there are a number of works by Ceri Richards—*Cycle of Nature, Homage to Beethoven,* and *Self-Portrait* among them; a number of Kyffin Williams—*Duffryn Camwy, Patagonia,* and *Farmers, Cwm Nantlle;* and works by Morland Lewis, Evan Walters and Brenda Chamberlain; while the Polish painter Josef Herman who lived for years in the village of Ystradgynlais has here *Pruning the Vine* and a recent portrait of the poet Dannie Abse.

Among the works of European masters in the Museum are many of the highest quality and interest. Italian 15th- and 16th-century painting is represented by two works by followers of Botticelli, a *Virgin and Child with Saints* by Alessandro Allori; and a predella panel, *The Adoration of the Shepherds* by Signorelli (lent by the National Gallery, London). From the 17th century come *St Francis* by Bernardo Strozzi; *Hagar and Ishmael in the Wilderness* by Andrea Sacchi; and *Rocky Landscape with Cattle* by Salvator Rosa. Representative of the 18th century are Canaletto's *Venice, the Bacino di San Marco;* Guardi's *The Dogana, Venice;* two works by Giandomenico Tiepolo—*Christ at the Pool of Bethesda* and *Christ and the Woman taken in Adultery;* and *Roman Ruins* by Panini.

On loan is a portrait by Rembrandt of Catrina Hooghsael; another loan (by Viscount Boyne) is a *Family Portrait in a Landscape* by Frans Hals, thought to be only part of an original picture the rest of which is probably in the Royal Museum at Brussels. There is a *Portrait of a Man* by Van Dyck and a painting jointly executed by Rubens and Frans Snyders, *Figures and Dead Game*, in which the game is particularly finely painted. Apart from the Rembrandt and Hals there are several other splendid Dutch paintings. *Ubbergen Castle* and *A River Landscape with Horses and Peasants* (lent by the Marquess of Bute) are by Albert Cuyp. Here too on loan are a landscape by Jacob Ruisdael and another by Aert van der Neer. An *Italian Landscape with the Church of SS Giovanni e Paolo* by Jan Asselyn and *Pilate Washing his Hands* by Jan van Bylert should not be overlooked.

An outstanding work now in the Museum is *Landscape with the Body of Phocion Carried out of Athens* by Nicolas Poussin (on long loan from the Earl of Plymouth). This is one of Poussin's great 'heroic' landscapes painted in 1648. There is also a small landscape by his brother-in-law Gaspar Dughet. *A Tavern Quarrel* is attributed to Mathieu Le Nain Representation of French 18th-century painting is non-existent but the late 19th century is superbly displayed. There are four works by Corot, among them a *View of the Castel Gandolfo* and a *Distant View of Corbeil*. There is one work by Daubigny, *Morning on the Oise*, one, *A Country Fair*, by Diaz, and two by Monticelli. Among the important group, some of them quite small, by Daumier are *Don Quixote Reading*, formerly in the collection of Degas, *The Third-Class Railway Carriage*, *Les Avocats*, *Workmen in a Street*, *The Watering-Place* and *The Moonlight Walk*. Almost equally interesting are a group of works by Jean-Francois Millet. *The Sower* was a preliminary version of the famous picture exhibited at the Paris Salon in 1850-51. Also here are *Peasant Family*, *The Faggot-gatherers*, begun in 1868 and left unfinished when he died, *The Good Samaritan*, *The Little Goose-girl*, and *The Storm*, probably his last work, painted in 1873, the year of his death: Sickert suggested that this painting shows a foreboding of death's approach. There are a few works by Boudin, among them *Port of Fécamp* and *Beach at Trouville*, and several painters working outside the Impressionist tradition are also here: Meissonier with *A Game of Picquet;* Isabey—*The Norman Port;* James Tissot—*The Parting;* and Eugène Carrière, whose pictures of motherhood and grief are certainly individual.

To turn to the Impressionists and their associates there are three works by Manet: *The Rabbit; Argenteuil;* and *The Church of the Petit-Montrouge, Paris,* the latter painted during the Franco-Prussian War in 1870 when Manet was a lieutenant in the Garde Nationale and Meissonier was his superior officer. The group of Monets are all later works: there is one of his great studies of *Rouen Cathedral* done in the early 1890s; there are three studies of *Waterlilies*, each from a different series done in 1905, 1906, 1908; a painting of *Charing Cross Bridge,* done from a balcony of the Savoy Hotel where Monet worked for brief periods on views of the Thames in 1899, 1900 and 1901; two views of Venice, *The Palazzo Dario* and *S. Giorgio Maggiore,* done in 1908; and a *Sunset* done in the same year. From Berthe Morisot comes *In the Garden at Bougival,* dated 1882. There is a beautiful, full-length picture of a girl by Renoir, *La Parisienne,* one of his paintings shown at the first Impressionist exhibition in 1874; by him also is a *Head of a Girl* and a *Seated Couple,* dated 1912. By Camille Pissarro there is a *Sunset at Rouen,* painted in 1898, and *Pont Neuf, Paris,* painted in 1902, the year before his death. Alfred Sisley, who for a short time in 1897 painted in Cardiff and Penarth, is represented by *Street in Moret,* dated 1892. The Misses Davies and their advisors were particularly perspicacious in their espousal of Cézanne's work. His *Montagnes, L'Estaque* which is here was first bought by Gauguin and later sold by Madame Gauguin. Roger Fry wrote of it: 'it seems to me one of the greatest of all Cézanne's landscapes.' Also here are his *Still Life with Teapot* and *Edge of a Wood in Provence.* There is one painting, *La Pluie,* by Van Gogh, painted at Auvers in 1890, and there is also a small work by his one-time teacher Anton Mauve, *The Shepherdess.*

Painters of later generations are also in evidence. There are three fine works by Maurice Vlaminck: *Trees; The Bridge; The Village Street;* another *Village Street* is by Utrillo; *Sunlight at Vernon* by Bonnard; *La Ciotat* by Othon Friesz; and a portrait of *Madame Zborowska* by André Derain. On loan is a striking work, *The Sermon on the Mount* by the Belgian artist James Ensor; also on loan is an interesting group of paintings by the Italian Futurists Morandi, Carrà, Sironi and Fattori. *Breton Peasant Women at Mass,* formerly thought to be a Gauguin, is now attributed to Armand Séguin. Recent purchases include a Magritte—*The Empty Mask,* Erich Heckel's *Lake near Maritzburg,* and *Coast Scene with Red Hill* by Jawlensky.

The Museum also possesses a collection of sculpture ranging from a bust by Sir Francis Chantrey and works by John Gibson to figures by Epstein, including heads of Augustus John and Lloyd George, bronzes by Rodin and Degas, and other works by Gaudier-Brzeska, Archipenko, Henry Moore and Lyn Chadwick.

CARLISLE
Carlisle Museum and Art Gallery, Tullie House, Castle Street
Tel.: 0228 24166
Open weekdays 9-8 (October-March 9-5); Sunday 2.30-5, June, July and August

The collection in this gallery provides an interesting sample of the work of certain Victorian painters. Many of the paintings were included in a generous bequest of over 600 works received in 1949 from the poet and playwright, Gordon Bottomley, whose collection also extended to embrace the work of a number of 20th-century artists. Another interesting aspect of the Carlisle Gallery collection is that under an arrangement initiated in 1933 over 100 works were purchased for it by Sir William Rothenstein between 1933-42 which constitute a wide selection ranging from the turn of the century until the Second World War. In addition the Gallery received a gift of works in 1960 from Professor C. Collier Abbott, some of which had at one time been in Bottomley's collection.

Among the earliest works in the Gallery are a small oil by John Linnell, *The Baptism of the Eunuch,* and several drawings and water-colours by Samuel Palmer. These are followed by a small painting, *Fortune,* after Veronese by William Etty, dated about 1822-3, and the earliest known oil-painting by the Irishman Daniel Maclise, *First Steps.* In addition there are studies by John Phillip, Lord Leighton, Albert Moore and G. F. Watts, including a small landscape by the latter. There are several drawings by Rossetti; a gouache, *The Borgia Family,* inscribed on the back of which are the words: 'To caper nimbly in a lady's chamber to the lascivious pleasing of a lute'; and the first oil study, dated 1859-61, for *Found,* Rossetti's only attempt at a modern subject, the final version of which is in Wilmington, Delaware. Here also is a small drawing, *St Agnes' Eve,* by his wife Elizabeth Siddal. *The Baptism of St Edwin* is by Ford Madox Brown done in 1879 as a preparatory study for one of his wall paintings in Manchester Town Hall. There are several drawings by Arthur Hughes and two oils, *The Rift in the Lute* derived from lines in Tennyson's *Idylls of the King* and *Madeleine,* inspired by a poem of Keats. Burne-Jones is represented by drawings and watercolours, most notable a study for *The Wheel of Fortune* and *The Goldfish Pool;* and there is a cartoon design for tapestry, *Artemis* by William Morris. Also noteworthy are two watercolours by Simeon Solomon. There are a few small French 19th-century paintings by Monticelli, Diaz and Fantin-Latour, drawings by Alphonse Legros and woodcuts by Lucien Pissarro.

English Impressionism is represented by artists such as Dame Ethel Walker, Charles Conder, Sir William Nicholson and Sir William Rothenstein himself. *Allotments* is a painting by Duncan Grant; *Flowers in a Glass Vase* is by Vanessa Bell; *Through a Cottage Window, Shipley, Sussex* by Charles Ginner; a nude by Malcolm Drummond; and other works, mainly drawings, are by Sickert, Harold Gilman, Spencer Gore, Augustus John. Not to be missed are *Pensive Head,* a portrait by Wyndham Lewis of his wife—it was her favourite painting of herself —and a small work, *Washing Peter's Feet* intended as part of a predella by Stanley Spencer, by whom there are also two other small works. There are many watercolours and drawings by Paul Nash, a close friend of Gordon Bottomley; and also of considerable interest are a number of drawings by the poet Isaac Rosenberg, who was killed in 1918.

CHELTENHAM
Cheltenham Art Gallery and Museum, Clarence Street
Tel.: 0242 22476
Open weekdays 10-6 (Wednesday 10-7); closed Sunday

Much of this collection is owed to the generosity of Baron de Ferrières who in 1898 presented the town of Cheltenham with a group of 43 paintings. He was of Dutch extraction and quite a number of the works here are from the Dutch and Flemish 17th-century schools. Among the finest are *The Lean Kitchen* and *The Fat Kitchen* by Jan Steen; *Man and Woman at Wine* by Gabriel Metsu; a *Portrait of the Artist* by Gerard Dou; and *An Old Woman Reading* by Adriaen Brouwer, whose works were admired and collected by Rubens. Other works include a *Tavern Scene* by Adriaen van Ostade, who was a pupil of Hals and is estimated to have painted over 1,000 pictures; *Dutch Horse Fair* by Philips Wouwerman, also a very prolific painter; *Christ with Martha and Mary* by Hendrick Martinesz Sorgh; and a *Portrait of Rachel Ruysch* by Godfried Schalcken. There is a flower-piece here by Rachel Ruysch herself, and another *Fruit and Flowers* ascribed to Jan Davidsz de Heem. A very good painting of *Poultry* is by Melchior de Hondecouter; there is also a *Landscape with Cattle* by B. C. Koekkoek. Three small pictures framed together depict *The Barber Surgeon* by William van Mieris and *Hurdy Gurdy Player in a Tavern* is also by him.

There is also an 18th-century French work, *River Scene* by Claude-Joseph Vernet, and among British painters represented are George Morland with a painting of *Pigs*, J. F. Herring, T. Sidney Cooper and Thomas Baker.

COOKHAM-ON-THAMES
Stanley Spencer Gallery, King's Hall
Open Easter-October daily 10.30-6.30; November-Easter open Saturday and Sunday only 11-5

This gallery is devoted entirely to the works of Stanley Spencer and is housed in a chapel where the artist attended Sunday School. It was opened in 1962 and besides paintings and drawings contains a variety of objects associated with Spencer's working life. Nearby, in the old church of Holy Trinity, Cookham, hangs his painting of *The Last Supper,* dated 1922. In the Gallery the following works are to be found: *St Veronica Unmasking Christ,* 1921; *Christ Overturning the Money Changers' Table,* 1921; *Sunbathers at Odney,* 1935; *High Street, Cookham,* 1936; *Looking at a Drawing,* 1936, *The Garden; The Beatitudes of Love v. Contemplation,* 1937; *Listening from Punts; Lilac and Clematis at Englefield,* 1955; *The Dust Bin, Cookham,* 1956; two paintings of *Shipbuilding on the Clyde* (lent by the Imperial War Museum); and his very large, last, unfinished painting, *Christ Preaching at Cookham Regatta.* This was exhibited at the Royal Academy in 1960 after Spencer's death.

COVENTRY
Herbert Art Gallery and Museum, Jordan Well
Tel.: 0203 25555
Open weekdays; Monday, Thursday, Friday and Saturday 10-6 (Tuesday and Wednesday 10-8); Sunday 2-5

The Herbert Art Gallery and Museum was opened in 1960, a large part of the cost of the building being defrayed by two large benefactions donated to the city for this purpose by Sir Alfred Herbert. A major feature of the Gallery is the Iliffe collection of studies by Graham Sutherland for the tapestry of *Christ in Glory* in Coventry Cathedral; these include studies in oil, gouache, watercolour, chalk, pencil, etc.

Other paintings in the Gallery include *Dahlias and Pears* by Matthew Smith; *Summer in the Downs* by C. R. W. Nevinson; *Portrait of Miss Ashwanden* by Stanley Spencer; *Oxfordshire Landscape* by Gilbert Spencer; *Two Forms* by Ben Nicholson; *Glasgow Boy with Milk Bottle* and *Seated Boy* by Joan Eardley; *A Group of Fishermen* by David Bomberg; *Factory at Sheffield* by Robert Medley; *Haystacks* by Paul Nash; and works by other artists such as L. S. Lowry, Lawrence Gowing, Henry Lamb, Anne Redpath, Fred Uhlman, Julian Trevelyan, Keith Vaughan, Carel Weight, Kyffin Williams, John Bratby, Prunella Clough.

Sculpture includes a bust of Rabindrinath Tagore by Jacob Epstein; *Figure in Walnut* by Barbara Hepworth; a bust of Elizabeth Frink by F. E. McWilliam; and two works by Frank Dobson which are on loan.

Also of considerable interest among the Gallery's possessions are a collection of watercolours associated with Warwickshire and a group of figure drawings by 20th-century British artists.

DERBY
Derby Museum and Art Gallery, Strand
Tel.: 0332 31111
Open Monday to Friday 10-6; Saturday 10-5; Sunday 2.30-4.30

Among the attractions of this gallery is a magnificent collection of
porcelain, but of outstanding interest is the major collection of the works
of Joseph Wright of Derby who, as his name implies, was a native of the
town. These consist of oil-paintings and a considerable number of
pen-and-wash and chalk drawings. Several portraits here give evidence
of Wright's skill in that field. Among the earliest are a portrait of the
Derby attorney, *Thomas Bennett,* painted about 1760, and two companion pieces, *Thomas Borrow* and *Anne Borrow,* coming from the early
1760s. There is a charcoal self-portrait in a fur cap of about 1767-70, a
quite romantic image, and the realistic image of *Sarah Carver and her
daughter* of 1769-70). The portrait of *The Reverend d'Ewes Coke, his wife
Hannah, and Daniel Parker Coke, M.P.* has been called his 'masterpiece
of group portraiture'. From the 1780s come *Samuel Ward* and *The Wood
Children,* and a portrait of his daughter Harriet, aged about 11, is dated
about 1790.

Landscapes, especially those with an interesting effect of light, are also
prominent among Wright's works. *The Earthstopper on the Banks of
the Derwent* shows an agitated light, the subject being a man filling up
foxholes. There are two pictures done in Italy in the early 1780s, *The
Colosseum, Daylight,* and *The Colosseum, Moonlight. View of Tivoli* is
from the same period, and on loan is *The Convent of S. Cosimato,* dated
1789. Two English landscapes are *Bridge through a Cavern, Moonlight,* and
Landscape with a Rainbow, near Chesterfield of 1794-5.

A Philosopher Giving a Lecture on the Orrery illustrates Wright's
fascination with light and shadow in the depiction of indoor scenes.
Hermit Studying Anatomy was painted in the late 1770s before Wright
went to Italy. *Miravan Opening the Tomb of his Ancestors* is signed and
dated 1772. In his account book Wright described his literary source for
the painting, 'The young nobleman who read the inscription that the
tomb contained "a greater treasure than Croesus ever possessed" and
hoped to find treasure in the tomb finds that the treasure was in fact
"eternal repose".' *The Captive* and *Maria* are both portrayals of
characters from Laurence Sterne's *Sentimental Journey. The Indian
Widow,* a companion picture to *The Lady in Milton's Comus* in the
Walker Art Gallery, reveals a certain sympathy for the American Indian,
the 'noble Savage'. A very interesting work dated 1795 is *The Alchemist
in Search of the Philosopher's Stone Discovering Phosphorous.* It possesses
the element of scientific investigation to be seen in the Tate's *Experiment
with a Bird in an Air Pump* of an earlier date.

DONCASTER
Doncaster Museum and Art Gallery, Chequer Road
Tel.: 0302 62095 and 60814
Open daily 10-5.30

The Doncaster Art Gallery contains a number of oil-paintings and an even greater collection of watercolours and drawings. Amongst the oils are works by William Etty, J. B. Pyne, J. F. Herring, Sir Frank Brangwyn and Bernard Meninsky. The watercolour section includes works by Thomas Rowlandson, Peter de Wint, John Crome and Samuel Prout, and innumerable sketches and drawings by Sir Frank Brangwyn. There is a bronze by Epstein, *Sybil Thorndike as St Joan, Head of Sir Edward Marsh* by Frank Dobson, and a marble plaque—*Two Figures*—by Gaudier-Brzeska.

DUBLIN
Municipal Gallery of Modern Art, Parnell Square
Tel.: 0001 41903
Open Tuesday-Saturday 10-6; Sunday 11-2; closed Monday.

This gallery, opened in 1908 exclusively for the exhibition of modern works of art, was temporarily housed for 25 years until in 1933 it was opened in Charlemont House, Parnell Square, built in 1762-3 for the Earl of Charlemont by Sir William Chambers. This was the only town house built in Ireland by Chambers. The collection of pictures owes its existence principally to Sir Hugh Lane and since 1933 a room has been reserved for the return of the Lane pictures held in London following a dispute over his will. An agreement reached in 1959 between the Irish Government and the Trustees of the National Gallery in London provides that for 20 years at least half of the Lane collection may be seen in the Municipal Gallery. The pictures are divided into two groups, and each group is loaned to Dublin alternately for five-year periods. Among the pictures involved are works by Boudin, Corot, Daumier, Ingres, Renoir and Manet. Since 1970, when an agreement was reached with the National Gallery of Ireland, the Municipal Gallery exhibits only works by artists born after 1860; many of these are now on loan from the National Gallery and in return the National Gallery has received on loan the Municipal Gallery's older works.

Among the Gallery's more interesting possessions are the portraits of Irishmen and women which W. B. Yeats praised in his poem, *The Municipal Gallery Revisited:* 'And say my glory was I had such friends'. These people were portrayed by Sir John Lavery, John Singer Sargent, Antonio Mancini, Charles Shannon, John Keating, and John Butler Yeats, father of the poet.

National Gallery of Ireland, Merrion Square
Tel.: 0001 67571
Open weekdays 10-6 (Thursday 10-9); Sunday 2-5

In 1766 the Irish Society of Artists began to seriously consider the question of bringing a national gallery into existence. It took 21 years, until 1787, for plans to be drawn up but these in the event proved abortive, when it was proposed instead to set up a joint Academy of Arts and Manufactures. This plan also failed and the founding of a National Gallery was delayed until 1864. It came about then after a large and successful exhibition was held in Dublin in 1853 which resulted in the setting up of a Testimonial Fund to commemorate the services of William Dargan, a wealthy railway owner, who had defrayed the costs of the exhibition. A sum of £15,000 was voted in 1854 towards the setting up of a Gallery of Art to be known as the Dargan Institute, and in the same year an Act of Parliament was passed to provide for the setting up of a National Gallery, Library and Museum. A site for the building was obtained on Leinster Lawn and the building was finally opened by the Lord Lieutenant, the Earl of Carlisle, in January 1864. The title 'Dargan Institute' was waived in favour of 'National Gallery of Ireland' on condition that a memorial tablet and a statue of Dargan were placed in a prominent position to acknowledge his instrumental services. Sums voted by Parliament and private donations provided for the purchase of pictures during the next few decades and at the beginning of the 20th century the gift of the Milltown collection was received. In 1914 Sir Hugh Lane was appointed Director of the Gallery. He gave 21 pictures to the Gallery in his lifetime, and on his tragic death 15 months later in the Lusitania disaster the Gallery received all his property, apart from the modern paintings; some paintings were sold (under the terms of his will) to enable the Gallery to purchase other works. The Gallery also received the gift of a splendid collection of paintings in 1950 from Sir Chester Beatty; another benefactor was Bernard Shaw, who left a sum to aid the purchasing power of the Gallery.

The Dublin Gallery is rich in Italian painting. Among the earliest Florentine works is a *Madonna and Child with Angels* by the 14th-century artist Giovanni del Biondo. Then comes a small panel by Fra Angelico, *The Attempted Martyrdom of the Physicians Saints Cosmas and Damian*. This is one of six panels forming the predella of the altarpiece of San Marco; the main picture is still there. Of it Vasari wrote: 'The predella, in which are stories of the martyrdom of San Cosimo, San Damiano, and others, is so perfectly finished that one cannot imagine it possible for anything to be executed with greater care, nor can figures more delicate, or more judiciously arranged be conceived.' Formerly attributed to Uccello but now thought to be by the Prato Master is a

Madonna and Child. A *Holy Family* comes from the school of Fra Bartolommeo; *Portrait of a Musician* is by Filippino Lippi; and there is a small work by Franciabigio, the *Canonization of St Bernardino of Siena*. Attributed to Ghirlandaio is a presumed portrait of Clarice Orsini, wife of Lorenzo the Magnificent, and to a painter of the school of Verrocchio, a *Madonna and Child with Angels*. A *Holy Family with St John in a Landscape* painted about 1494 has been variously attributed to Michelangelo, Granacci, and Mainardi. From 16th-century Florence come a *Pietà and Eight Figures of Kneeling Saints*, panels making up the predella of an altarpiece in the Church of San Michele Visdomini by Pontormo, painted about 1518 and arguably one of the first Mannerist pictures. A *Portrait of a Lady* by a member of Bronzino's school is also to be seen as is *St John the Baptist* by Alessandro Allori. From 17th-century Florence comes Carlo Dolci's *St Agnes*.

The *Crucifixion* by Giovanni di Paolo is the major work of the Sienese school but also to be seen are *The Prophet Isaiah*, attributed to Ugolino of Siena, and *St Galganus* by Andrea di Bartolo. *The Sacrament of Baptism* is by Beccafumi. Of Venetian painting there are several works attributed to Bonifazio de' Pitati who ran a large workshop in Venice in the first half of the 16th century. More important are *Head of a Man* and *Portrait of Two Venetian Personages* by Giovanni Bellini. One of his pupils was Jacopo Bassano, whose *Holy Family with Donors* is here, as some works by his son, Leandro, among them *Visit of the Queen of Sheba to Solomon*. Another pupil of Bellini's was Palma Vecchio, who is represented by a *Holy Family*, but on a much grander scale is *Madonna and Child with Saints and Angels* by his great-nephew Palma Giovane. From Titian come three works, *Ecce Homo*, *The Supper at Emmaus*, and a portrait of *Baldassare Castiglione*, diplomat and author of *The Courtier*. And from Tintoretto are *A Venetian Senator*, *Diana and Endymion*, *The Miracle of the Loaves and Fishes*, and *Portrait of a Venetian Gentleman*. By his son Domenico is *Venice, Queen of the Adriatic, Crowning the Lion of St Mark*. *Portrait of a Man* by Paris Bordone is here and there are two works by Veronese, *Portrait of a Lady* and a large canvas depicting *St Philip and St James the Less*. A picture of the greatest interest is Sebastiano del Piombo's portrait of Cardinal Antonio Ciocchi del Monte Sansovino, allegedly painted between 1511 and 1516 after he had gone to Rome and come under the powerful influence of Michelangelo.

Later Venetian painting includes *Archimedes and Hiero of Syracuse* by Sebastiano Ricci, and *Bathsheba* by Giovanni Pellegrini, the first Venetian painter to visit England to work on decorative projects. Eighteenth-century views of Venice itself include Michiel Marieschi's *Piazza San Marco*, the same subject rendered by Canaletto and Guardi's *Doge Wedding the Adriatic*. There are two views of Dresden by Bernardo Bellotto; two portraits by Pietro Longhi and two works by G. B.

Tiepolo, *Allegory of the Incarnation* and *Christ in the House of Simon the Pharisee* (after Veronese).

Roman painting begins with a self-portrait by Gian Francesco Penni, an assistant of Raphael. A *Coast Scene* comes from the school of Agostino Tassi. *David and Goliath* is by Orazio Gentileschi, one of the most notable followers of Caravaggio at one point in his career. Two works by Lanfranco come from a series of eight Biblical paintings he did for the church of S.Paolo fuori le Mura; the other six are also now dispersed throughout Europe as by 1668 they had been affected by damp and were replaced in the church by copies. *Jupiter and Europa* is by Carlo Maratta, and *Party Feasting in a Garden* is by Giovanni Passeri, distinguished for his biographies of contemporary artists. *The Parable of the Lord of the Vineyards* is by Domenico Feti; there are several portraits by Pompeo Battoni and scenes with ruins by Panini.

Among other notable Italian works in the Gallery are Andrea Mantegna's *Judith with the Head of Holofernes,* a companion picture to his *Samson and Delilah* in London's National Gallery; *Pietà* by Perugino; *Feast in Simon's House* by Signorelli; *The Holy Family* by Lorenzo Costa; *Lucretia* by Francesco Francia, who for a period was in partnership with Costa in Bologna; *St Cecilia,* attributed to Domenichino; *St Jerome,* attributed to Guido Reni; *St Joseph with the Holy Child* by Guercino; *Adoration of the Shepherds* by Girolamo da Carpi; *Shepherdess Finding the Infant Cyrus* by Castiglione; *Portrait of a Bishop* and *The Decollation of St John* by Mattia Preti; *St John in the Wilderness* and *Landscape with the Baptism in the Jordan* by Salvator Rosa; *St Paul* by Solimena; and other paintings by Bernardo Strozzi, Giuseppe Crespi, Luca Giordano, Sassoferrato, Alessandro Magnasco, Pier Mola and Giovanni Pordenone.

The great era of Dutch painting is well represented here. There are four Rembrandts: *Rest on the Flight into Egypt,* dated 1647; *Head of an Old Man,* 1650; *Portrait of a Young Man;* and *Portrait of a Young Woman,* 1633. By Rembrandt's friend Jan Lievens is *Portrait of an Old Man*—possibly Rembrandt's father; and from the teacher of both of them, Pieter Lastman, comes *Joseph Selling Corn in Egypt,* dated 1612. Several of Rembrandt's pupils are also represented: Ferdinand Bol by *David's Dying Charge to Solomon, The Holy Women at the Tomb,* and *Portrait of a Lady;* Govaert Flinck by *Bathsheba's Appeal* and *Head of a Rabbi;* Nicolaes Maes by a late work, *Vertumnus and Pomona,* dated 1673, and *Portrait of a Lady. A Wooded Landscape,* dated 1678, and *A Stormy Sea* are by Jacob Ruisdael; there are two works by Salomon Ruisdael; and *Milking Cows* by Albert Cuyp. From Frans Hals comes *A Fisherman of Scheveningen;* from Hobbema *The Ferry Boat;* from Pieter de Hooch *Players at Tric-Trac;* from Mathias Stomer *The Betrayal of Christ.* Other Dutch painters represented include Paulus Potter, Avercamp, Wouwerman, Jan Both, Berchem, Breenbergh, Jan Steen, Bakhuysen, van de Cappelle, Van Goyen, Heda, de Heem, Van der Neer, Ochtervelt, Schalcken, Frans Post, Bartholomeus van der Helst, and Terborch.

Among works by early Flemish masters are *The Miracles of St Nicholas of Bari* by the Master of the St Barbara Legend; *Madonna of the Prophecies* by van Orley; and *Madonna and Child in a Landscape* by the obscure artist Adriaen van Ysenbrandt. *Christ Bidding Farewell to his Mother* is by Gerard David and there are two works by Pieter Pourbus, *The Golden Calf* and *The Annunciation. Portrait of a Lady* is by his grandson Frans the Younger, the most illustrious member of the family, who ended his life working for Marie de' Medici. *Moses Striking the Rock* is the work of Abraham Janssens. Rubens is represented by three works, *The Annunciation, St Francis of Assisi,* and *St Dominick.* Other canvases come from his school and another work, *Christ in the House of Martha and Mary,* was painted by him in association with Jan van Kessel and Jan 'Velvet' Brueghel. *A Boar Hunt* and *A Breakfast* are by Frans Snyders. Examples of Van Dyck's work are *Portrait of the Diplomat Frederick Marselaer,* and a *Study for a painting of St Sebastian.* There are two large works by Jacob Jordaens, *The Church Triumphant* and *The Supper at Emmaus;* from Adriaen Brouwer comes *The Corn Doctor* and other works are by Hendrik van Balen and David Teniers the Younger.

One of the earliest works in the collection is an *Annunciation* from the school of Avignon, dated about 1410, but French painting of the 17th century is most notable at Dublin. It includes several fine works by Poussin: *The Lamentation over the Dead Christ,* datable to the mid-1650s; *The Holy Family with Ten Figures,* painted in 1649; *Bacchante and Satyr;* and *Acis and Galatea,* sometimes called *The Marriage of Thetis and Peleus.* From Claude comes *Landscape with Juno Confiding Io to the Care of Argus,* the story derived from Ovid's *Metamorphoses,* and painted in 1660. Other 17th-century works not to be missed include a landscape by Gaspar Dughet; *The Four Seasons* by Simon Vouet; *Christ in the House of Martha and Mary* by Lesueur; *Adoration of the Shepherds* by Louis Le Nain, dated 1644; and *The Image of Saint Alexis* by Georges de la Tour. Some of the great names of the 18th century are also represented. There are three works by Chardin: a still life, *Les Tours de Cartes,* dated 1736, and *The Young Governess. The Capuchin Doll* is by Greuze; *Young Girl in a Park* is by Boucher; *La Malice* by Lancret; *A Rural Scene* and two *Fêtes Champêtres* by Pater; and there are further works by Hubert Robert, Prud'hon and Nattier.

From the beginning of the 19th century comes *A Horse* by Géricault and two landscapes by Georges Michel, who once declared that a painter needed no more than four square miles in which to find all the subjects he desired. There is a Delacroix, *Demosthenes on the Seashore,* dated

1850, and a landscape, *Willows,* by Corot together with another done jointly by Corot and Daubigny and dated 1853. Two more landscapes are by Daubigny and there is a portrait of Adolphe Marlet by Courbet. In a different vein is *The Arrest of Charlotte Corday* by Ary Scheffer. The representation of Impressionism is fairly sparse, there being only one Monet, *River Scene, Autumn;* one Berthe Morisot, *Le Corsage Noir;* one Sisley, *The Canal du Loing at St Mammes,* dated 1885; and a landscape by Henri Harpignies. Other painters include Bastien-Lepage; Forain, represented by *Scene in the Law Courts;* Vlaminck; Albert Marquet with *Porquerolles,* painted in 1938; and Jacques-Emile Blanche with a portrait of James Joyce dated 1934.

Among the earlier examples of Spanish painting at Dublin is a portrait of Prince Alexander Farnese by Alonso Coello; *Abraham and the Three Angels* by Juan Fernandez de Navarrete; and most notably *St Francis in Ecstasy* by El Greco (one of several versions). A *Portrait of a Man* is attributed to Velazquez; a large *St Rufina* is by Zurbarán; a *Legend of St Anthony* by Ribalta; and from Ribera comes *St Procopius,* signed and dated 1630. There are four works by Murillo: *St Mary Magdalen; The Holy Family; The Infant St John Playing with a Lamb;* and *Portrait of Joshua van Belle,* dated 1670. Other pictures include *The Musicians* by Velazquez's son-in-law and assistant Mazo; *The Liberation of St Peter* by José Antolinez; *Jael and Sisera* by Antonio Pereda; *The Madonna of the Rosary* by Llanos-y-Valdes. There are also four works by Goya: *Lady in a Black Mantilla; Portrait of El Conde del Tago,* painted about 1795; *Woman in a White Fichu;* and *El Sueño.*

A few German, Austrian, and Swiss works should not be overlooked. Among the German works are *Judith with the Head of Holofernes, St Christopher* and *Christ on the Cross,* dated 1540, by Lucas Cranach, and *Adoration of the Kings* by Hans Rottenhammer. From Wolfgang Huber, an important member of the Danube School, comes a portrait, *Anthony Hundertpfundt,* signed and dated 1526, and also from Austria is a *Portrait of a Lady,* presumed to be a daughter of the Emperor Charles V, by Jacob Seisenegger, who was supplanted by Titian as painter of the Emperor's portraits. Swiss painting is represented by several portraits by Angelica Kauffmann.

Among the earliest English paintings in the Gallery are two portraits by William Dobson and two by Sir Peter Lely, one of the latter being a portrait of Van Dyck's mistress Margaret Lemon. Works by Sir Godfrey Kneller include a portrait of Richard Steele, and a scene, *King William returning from the Peace of Ryswyck, Margate, 1697.* There are two portraits by Thomas Hudson including one of Diana, Countess of Mountrath; and a *Scene from Henry IV, Part II* by Francis Hayman. Francis Cotes has two portraits of aristocratic ladies and there are several portraits by Reynolds, among them *Captain George Edgcumbe; Charles*

Coote, Earl of Bellamont; Robert Henley, 2nd Earl of Northington; Mrs Francis Fortescue; and *Portrait Group of George Greville and his Family.* Also by him are three sets of caricatures and *A Parody on Raphael's School of Athens.* From Hogarth come several portraits also: a group portrait of George II, King of England and his family; *The Mackinnon Family; The Western Family; Benjamin Hoadley; George Wade;* and another work entitled *The Denunciation.* Gainsborough is represented by several landscapes, notably *Landscape with Cattle* and *A View in Suffolk;* but the majority of his works here are portraits including: *James Quin,* the actor; *Hugh Smithson, Duke of Northumberland; General James Johnston; Mrs Horton,* later Duchess of Cumberland; *Mrs King; John Gainsborough; A Gamekeeper.* By Richard Wilson are *Solitude; View from Tivoli over the Campagna; View near Rome.* Further portraits come from George Romney, among them a portrait of his wife and another of Mary Tighe. Another work by him is *Titania, Puck and the Changeling.* Also of theatrical interest are two portraits by Zoffany—of David Garrick, and of *Charles Macklin in the Part of Shylock.* Francis Wheatley, who from 1779 to 1784 worked in Dublin, has one work evidently set there, *The Volunteers in College Green,* dated 1779, in addition to three others, *Portrait of a Child with a Dog, Mary's Dream* and *Mr and Mrs Richardson.* The skill of that prolific portraitist Sir Thomas Lawrence is shown in several works, among them *John Philpot Curran* and *Lady Elizabeth Foster.* From John Constable come two works, *Landscape near Salisbury* and *Portrait of a Child with a Dog.* Other British painters represented include George Stubbs, David Roberts, David Wilkie, John Opie, George Morland, John Linnell, Richard Bonington, John Crome, Landseer, Augustus John.

The collection of Irish painting is considerable. There are numerous works by the landscape painter George Barret and also by his son. A large *Adam and Eve, The Death of Adonis* and other works are by James Barry who was patronized by Edmund Burke. A portrait of him by Barry, as well as a self-portrait, are here. Sir Martin Archer Shee, Lawrence's successor as President of the Royal Academy and holder of that office for twenty years, has a number of portraits here, among them one of the poet Thomas Moore. There is a large collection of the works of both Nathaniel Hone the Elder and the Younger; and several interesting little works illustrate the bizarre career of George Chinnery, who spent much of his life in the Far East. From Francis Danby comes *The Opening of the Sixth Seal.* William Mulready, the successful painter of genre scenes whom Thackeray, writing in 1838 and surveying the current art scene, rated the very highest, is substantially represented by a number of characteristic works. Also here are several works by Daniel Maclise, one of them being *The Marriage of the Princess Aoife of Leinster with Richard De Clare, Earl of Pembroke,* which the artist refused to sell to the Houses of Parliament when it was exhibited in 1854. Other Irish painters shown here include Henry O'Neil, William Orpen, Roderic O'Conor and Walter Osborne. An interesting and important group includes the works of John Butler Yeats and Jack B. Yeats, father and brother of the poet—among those of the former are portraits of W. B. Yeats and the novelist and critic George Moore.

DUNDEE
Dundee City Art Gallery, Albert Square
Tel.: 0382 25492/3
Open weekdays 10-5.30

The Dundee Art Gallery was first opened in 1873 as an extension of the Albert Institute originally designed by Sir George Gilbert Scott. In 1887 £10,000 was donated to build further extensions to be called the Victoria Art Galleries in commemoration of the Queen's Jubilee and this project was completed in 1889-90. The present collection is the result of various bequests and donations of paintings and money.

Most of the paintings are by artists of the Scottish school, the earliest being by Allan Ramsay, a portrait of Edward Harvey, dated 1747, and its pendant portrait of William Harvey. By Ramsay's assistant David Martin is a portrait of his brother the Reverend Samuel Martin. Martin taught Sir Henry Raeburn, by whom there is another portrait, *Mrs Moir of Leckie.* By David Allan, who was one of the products of the Glasgow printer Robert Foulis's attempt to establish a Scottish Academy of Art, there is a charming portrait dated 1782 of Charles Watson and his wife Lady Mary with their two children in a landscape. Also to be noted are two works by Sir John Gordon, the leading portraitist after Raeburn's generation. There are several small works by Sir David Wilkie and some portraits by Sir Daniel MacNee. Several works by the quasi-Impressionist William McTaggart are also here, among them *Wind and Rain, Carradale,* and *A Message from the Sea.* Other portraitists to be noted are Sir William Quiller Orchardson and John Zephaniah Bell, the latter for a fine portrait of the surgeon John Crichton.

Other 19th-century Scottish painters include John Phillip, George Johnstone and Sir Noel Paton; members of the Glasgow School—William York MacGregor, Sir James Guthrie, George Henry, Sir David Cameron, Edward Hornel—are also represented. Paintings by the 'Scottish Colourists' are also of importance: two still lives by Leslie Hunter; three works by J. D. Fergusson, among them *A Lowland Church;* two paintings by S. J. Peploe and two by Francis Cadell. Representative of a later generation are works by Sir William Gillies and

Anne Redpath, and more recently there are paintings by Joan Eardley, William Gear, Alan Davie.

There is a scattering of English painting in the Gallery: two paintings by George Morland, some watercolours by Paul Sandby and drawings by David Cox; *Puss in Boots* by Millais and an important work by Rossetti, *Dante's Dream on the Day of the Death of Beatrice*. This is a large painting with two small predella pictures and is a smaller replica, done in 1880, of the version painted in 1871 which is in Liverpool's Walker Art Gallery. Also of interest is a large collection of watercolours and drawings by Sir Frank Brangwyn. In addition there are works by Burne-Jones, Frank Holl, Sickert *(La Scierie de Torqueville)*, Wilson Steer, Laura Knight, Edward Burra and Stanley Spencer.

Also at Dundee are a number of European paintings; from Italy come *The Sacrifice of Abraham*, attributed to the Caravaggesque Neapolitan painter Caracciolo; a *Pietà* ascribed to Lodovico Carracci; *Rest on the Flight into Egypt* by Pompeo Batoni. From France are Boudin's *Le Bassin de L'Eure au Havre* and *The Flower Girl* by the popular 19th-century portrait painter Carolus-Duran, and a landscape by Stanislas Lépine; from 19th-century Holland there are several works by Josef Israels and Jacob and Willem Maris.

Among the sculpture there is a bronze by Rodin of Victor Hugo, two portrait bronzes by Epstein and works by Eduardo Paolozzi and William Turnbull, a native of Dundee.

EASTBOURNE
Towner Art Gallery, Manor House, Borough Lane
Tel.: 0323 21635
Open weekdays 10-6 (Oct.-March 10-5); Sunday 2-6 (Oct.-March 2-5)

The collection of paintings here consists of a small group of 19th-century oils and watercolours from the Towner bequest and a much larger group of acquisitions. Included in the first group are works by J. F. Herring, Frederick Goodall, T. S. Cooper, William Müller. Among paintings in the second group are *Negro Head* by Alma-Tadema; *The Painter and his Muse* by Sickert; *8 Fitzroy Street* by Vanessa Bell; *The Glade, Firle Park*, and *Still Life* by Duncan Grant; *Evening Sky over Hills* by Ivon Hitchens; *Poisson d'Or* by Ceri Richards; a portrait of Constant Lambert by Christopher Wood; and works by Carel Weight, Keith Vaughan, Robert Medley, Matthew Smith, Bernard Meninsky, Julian Trevelyan, Ruskin Spear, Alan Davie and William Gear. There is also a collection of watercolours, gouaches and drawings.

EDINBURGH
National Gallery of Scotland, The Mound
Tel.: 031 556 8921
Open weekdays 10-5; Sunday 2-5

The National Gallery of Scotland, though given official blessing by the National Galleries of Scotland Act of 1906, originated in what remains basically its present form in 1859 and drew what was to be its permanent collection from several different sources. The building, designed by W. H. Playfair, in which the collection was to be housed was provided by the Honourable Board of Manufacturers, a body set up in 1727 to administer the Annuity paid to Scotland under the Act of Union. (In 1906 this body was replaced, in connection with the Gallery, by a smaller group of Trustees). The collection of pictures, however, originally derived from three other main sources, namely, the Royal Institution, the Royal Scottish Academy and the University of Edinburgh. The Royal Institution, which began as the Institution for the Encouragement of the Fine Arts in Scotland, had in 1830-31 added to their collection of works by living Scottish artists a group of 'Old Masters' including three large works by Van Dyck. The Royal Scottish Academy, founded in 1826, also acquired a considerable number of paintings mainly by contemporary artists including a group of large works by William Etty. Both these institutions deposited their collections with the new Gallery and Edinburgh University contributed on loan the collection bequeathed to it by Sir James Erskine of Torrie, consisting mainly of small 17th-century Dutch works but including an important large work, *The Banks of a River* by Jacob Ruisdael. Also given to the Gallery at an early date was another great work, *The Finding of Moses* by Tiepolo. Thus with these and other valuable gifts the national collection of Scotland was built up but it was not until recent decades that the Gallery reached its present position of the highest national and international importance. In 1946 the Gallery was fortunate enough to receive on long-term loan 30 pictures from the collection of the Duke of Sutherland. A large number of these were originally acquired by the 3rd Duke of Bridgewater—he who built the Bridgewater Canal to carry coal from his collieries at Worsley to Manchester—from the great collection of the Duc d'Orléans. The Duc d'Orléans was forced to sell his collection in 1791 and after some years the majority of them were bought by a syndicate of three Englishmen, among them the Duke of Bridgewater. William Hazlitt wrote of seeing this collection, 'I was staggered when I saw the works there collected and looked at them with wondering and with longing eyes ... A new sense came upon me, a new heaven and a new earth stood before me.' Outstanding among these paintings are works by Raphael, Titian and Poussin which will be named later. In 1960 the Gallery received its as yet most valuable gift in the shape of 21 19th- and 20th-century French paintings, given in memory of his wife by Sir Alexander Maitland. These raised the Gallery's representation of French painting of this period to an altogether new level.

Early Italian painting is not extensively represented in the Gallery but among the few works are to be found a fine triptych with the *Crucifixion* by Bernardo Daddi, a pupil of Giotto, and a *Madonna and Child* by Lorenzo Monaco, a Sienese painter who settled in Florence and became a monk there; the Madonna is depicted seated on the lion-headed throne of Solomon. By another Sienese, Matteo di Giovanni, is *Madonna and Child with St Sebastian and St Francis.* This painting was bought by Ruskin in Siena. There is a predella panel, *The Nativity with Two Angels* by Filippino Lippi, and two panels attributed to Jacopo del Sellaio. A strange mystical work, *St Catherine of Siena as Spiritual Mother of the Second and Third Orders of St Dominic* is by the usually rather uninspired painter Cosimo Rosselli. From 15th-century Ferrara there is a painting of the *Madonna and Child* with an illusionistic frame with torn strips of vellum. From Perugino there is a somewhat puzzling fragment of four nude male figures possibly from a large mythical composition.

Italian High Renaissance painting is richly represented owing to the Duke of Sutherland loan. There are two works by Raphael, both painted in Florence about 1507 before he left for Rome, *The Bridgewater Madonna,* a masterpiece of design and sensitive handling, and *The Holy Family with a Palm Tree,* equally masterly in execution. Another work, *The Madonna with the Veil,* is a good version of a Raphael design of which there is no known version by Raphael himself; and there is dispute about the *Madonna del Passeggio,* a very fine painting, which was considered to be an original when in the collections of Queen Christina of Sweden and the Duc d'Orléans, but was later dismissed from the body of Raphael's own work (given for example to his assistant G. F. Penni) though there have been recent suggestions that Raphael may indeed have painted it. Andrea del Sarto has here what is thought to be a self-portrait, a warm, vital work. By his friend Bacchiacca, one of the first Mannerists, there is *Moses Striking the Rock,* possibly painted for the Company of Jugmakers in Florence for there is a great variety of such objects in the picture.

The earliest Venetian picture is an unfinished work by Cima da Conegliano, *Virgin and Child with St Andrew and St Peter.* There are several great works by Titian, the earliest painted about 1515-20, being *The Three Ages of Man,* a title first used in 1675. The *Venus Anadyomene* (Venus rising from the sea), painted about 1526, appears as a paean to the female body. In a completely different vein is the *Madonna and Child with St John and a Donor,* formerly attributed to Palma Vecchio but since the late 19th century accepted by most authorities as an early

Titian. Finally there are the great canvases of *Diana and Actaeon* (Actaeon while hunting surprises Diana and her followers bathing) and *Diana and Calisto* (Diana discovers the pregnancy of Callisto after her seduction by Jupiter), two of a series of seven mythological compositions painted about 1556-9 for Philip II of Spain. Others in the series included *The Death of Actaeon* recently bought for the National Gallery (London) and the *Perseus and Andromeda* in the Wallace Collection.

Tintoretto is represented here too. The *Deposition of Christ,* painted in the 1560s as an altarpiece for the Venetian church of San Francesco della Vigna, had been cut down from its original size but remains a beautiful, moving work. The *Portrait of a Venetian,* probably an early work, is very fine. The *Venetian Family Presented to the Madonna by St Lawrence and a Bishop Saint* may be a studio work. Veronese is not well represented but there is a large fragment of an altarpiece (another fragment is in the Dulwich Gallery) showing *St Anthony Abbot and a Donor.* There is also a painting of *Mars and Venus* in which one surprising feature, in Scotland, is Venus's conspicuous plaid scarf. From Jacopo Bassano there is *Adoration of the Kings* painted in the early 1540s, and a *Portrait of a Gentleman* which has lately, it would seem quite justly, been attributed to Tintoretto. By Paris Bordone there is *A Venetian Woman at her Toilet,* and by Lorenzo Lotto a very lovely *Virgin and Child with Saints.*

Italian 17th-century painting is most notably represented by *The Adoration of the Shepherds* by Domenichino, formerly at Dulwich, a work in the classical tradition. Another painter of the Baroque period, the very individual Bolognese artist Guercino, is represented by the moving image of *St Peter Penitent* and a *Madonna and Child with the Young St John.* Of the Caravaggesque school there is a *St Christopher* by Orazio Borgianni and *The Tribute Money* by Giovanni Serodine.

Most remarkable among Italian 18th-century paintings here is the superb *Finding of Moses* by G. B. Tiepolo already mentioned, probably the most important work of his in Britain and painted in the late 1730s. It is an leegant decorative composition bearing little relationship to Egypt and a lot to Venice, its composition being derived from a work by Veronese. Also by Tiepolo is *The Meeting of Antony and Cleopatra,* a sketch for a fresco for a Venetian palace. On loan here are Canaletto's *Entrance to the Grand Canal* and a large work by Bernardo Bellotto, *View of the Ponte delle Navi, Verona.* There are also a pair of charming Venetian scenes by Guardi and an altarpiece by G. B. Pittoni, *St Jerome with St Peter of Alcantara.*

French painting in the Gallery commences with a portrait of Madame de Canaples attributed to Jean Clouet, Court Painter to Francis I. Then come the great 17th-century French painters. Certainly a visit to the room in which Poussin's paintings of *The Seven Sacraments* are displayed is an experience which the gallery visitor in Great Britain should try not to miss. These seven paintings of the important Christian sacraments make up the second series painted by Poussin on this subject; they were executed between 1644 and 1648 for Fréart de Chantelou, a high-ranking French civil servant and diarist of Bernini's visit to Paris and work for Louis XIV. (The first series was painted for Cassiano dal Pozzo, Poussin's friend in Rome and a connoisseur of antiquities and contemporary art.) Also in the same room is *Moses Striking Water from the Rock*, which Poussin painted about 1637, and strongly attributed to him too is a full-size copy of Bellini's *Feast of the Gods*—the original is in Washington National Gallery. Recently presented to the Gallery is Poussin's *Mystic Marriage of St Catherine*. Poussin's great contemporary Claude is represented by his largest known landscape, *Landscape with Apollo and the Muses*, painted for Cardinal Pamphili in Rome in 1652. It has been cleaned since it was bought by the Gallery in 1960 and is electrifyingly beautiful.

French 18th-century painting is represented by Watteau, with *Fêtes Venitiennes* and *The Robber of the Sparrows' Nest*—the figure of the bagpiper in the former is probably a self-portrait; by Chardin, with an important picture, *A Vase of Flowers*, his only known flower piece, and *Still Life: The Kitchen Table;* by Boucher, with a portrait of Madame de Pompadour, though very likely this was by a studio assistant; by Greuze's *Boy with Lesson Book* and *Girl with Dead Canary*, both very good examples of the genre in which he excelled; by Jean-Baptiste Pater's *Ladies Bathing*, an elegant work inspired by Titian's *Diana and Actaeon;* and by Nicholas Lancret's *The Toy Windmill*.

There is a limited selection of early 19th-century French works. *Arabs Playing Chess* is a small canvas by Delacroix painted about 1847. By Corot there are a number of small works, among them an early painting with a beautiful rendering of light, *Ville d'Avray—Entrance to the Wood, Portrait of the Artist's Mother*, and *The Goatherd*. From the Barbizon School there are works by Diaz, Daubigny and Troyon; and several works by Monticelli with his characteristic brushwork. *The Wave, Trees in Snow* and *River in a Mountain Gorge* are three minor examples of the work of Courbet; *The Painter* is a small work by Daumier.

Then the Impressionists and Post-Impressionists are reached. The Maitland bequest transformed the Gallery's collection. *Haystacks: Snow Effect,* is one of a series of 18 canvases on this subject which Monet painted in 1891. *Poplars on the Epte* is an example of another subject of which he did a group under different light conditions and incorporating a new kind of perspective—even the square shape of the canvas is a new feature. His obsession with this subject between 1890 and 1892 is witnessed by the fact that he bought the row of poplars lest they should be cut down by a timber merchant before he could finish his paintings. Camille Pissarro's *Marne at Chennevières* is an early work of 1864-5, somewhat influenced by Courbet; it was one of the few paintings not destroyed in Pissarro's studio during the Franco-Prussian War of 1870. There is also a small work, *Mother and Child* by Renoir, and *Mother and Child in a Garden* by Berthe Morisot, sister-in-law of Manet. There is a fine work by Sisley, *Molesey Weir, Hampton Court*, painted during his visit to England in 1874. Most notable perhaps among the excellent group of works by Degas is the portrait of the Florentine writer and art critic Diego Martelli, who was one of the first to collect and defend the Impressionists. The others include *Before the Performance, Group of Dancers, Study of a Girl's Head* and a beautiful pastel, *Woman Drying Herself*, as well as several small bronzes cast from Degas's wax models after his death. The *Mont Sainte-Victoire* by Cézanne, painted in the early 1890s, is one of his wonderful studies of this subject. From Van Gogh comes *Head of a Peasant Woman* painted in Holland in 1885; and *The Orchard in Blossom (Plum Trees)* was one of about 15 paintings of trees in blossom painted in Arles in 1888. The agitated *Olive Trees* was painted at Saint-Remy in 1889, the year before his death. *Martinique Landscape* is one of 12 landscapes painted by Gauguin in 1887 in Martinique; *The Vision of the Sermon (Jacob Wrestling with the Angel)* is an important work by him painted at Pont-Aven, Brittany in the following year, while *Three Tahitians*, painted in 1899, belongs to a group of works that may have developed from the *Faa Iheihe* of 1898 in the Tate Gallery. A small study by Seurat for his large *Baignade* in the National Gallery, London, is of the greatest interest. The same can be said for two works by Bonnard, *Lane at Vernonnet*, where the artist owned a house, painted between 1912 and 1914, and *Landscape*, painted about 1930. By his associate Vuillard are *The Open Window* and *The Chat*.

The selection of Dutch pictures is superb, headed by the work of Rembrandt. The *Woman in Bed* appears as an intimately observed portrait of a woman (it used to be known as *Hendrickje Stoffels*) but it may, in fact, have Biblical connotations and represent Sarah on her wedding night watching as her husband Tobias puts the devil to flight (Tobit 8: 1-4). Another Biblical scene is the small panel of *Hannah and Samuel*, which may be partly the work of a pupil. Then there are two portraits: *Young Woman with Flowers in her Hair*, signed and dated 1634, and the *Self-Portrait, aged 51*, a most compelling image. *Portrait of a Jew* is probably from the hand of a pupil. From Frans Hals there are three portraits: two of a Dutch lady and gentlemen painted as a pair, dated about 1643-5, and a third called *Verdonck*, painted about 1627 and evidently of a man reduced to penury. *The Banks of a River* by Jacob Ruisdael is an important early work of 1649-50, and here too is a smaller canvas, *Ruins beside a River. Christ in the House of Martha and Mary* is the largest known Vermeer, very unlike his other work; it is probably the earliest known, painted about 1654-5. Loaned from the Royal Bank of

Scotland is Pieter de Hooch's *Courtyard with an Arbour.* Other Dutch works include Terborch's *A Singing Practice;* Dou's *Interior with Young Violinist;* two landscapes by Hobbema; Terbruggen's *Beheading of John the Baptist;* Jan Steen's moralizing scenes *The Doctor's Visit* and *A School for Boys and Girls;* Cuyp's *Landscape with a View of the Valkhof, Nijmegen,* Jan Lievens's *Woodland Walk* and *Portrait of a Young Man;* and characteristic works by, among others, Avercamp, Jan Weenix and Jan Davidsz de Heem. From the 19th century come works by Jacob Maris, Jozef Israels, and Anton Mauve.

Hugo van der Goes' exquisitely executed Trinity altarpiece is lent to the Gallery by the Queen. It consists of two votive panels: these may have been organ shutters, or there may have been a centre panel destroyed during the Reformation. On the left wing is James III with St Andrew and Prince James (on the reverse the Holy Trinity of the Broken Body); on the right wing is Margaret of Denmark, Queen of Scotland with St Canute, patron Saint of Denmark (on the reverse Sir Edward Bonkil, First Provost of the Church). The altarpiece was commissioned by Bonkil, whose brother was a naturalized citizen of Bruges, for the Collegiate Church of the Holy Trinity in Edinburgh, probably about 1478-9. Hugo van der Goes later died insane in a monastery. Part of another Early Netherlandish altarpiece is also here, *The Three Legends of St Nicholas* by Gerard David; there are three small panels, the last of which is quite extraordinary—St Nicholas as Bishop of Myra resuscitates three boys salted down as meat in a famine. By Quentin Massys there is a *Portrait of a Notary,* and by Bernard van Orley, Court Painter at Brussels from 1518, a panel from an alterpiece, *Before the Crucifixion,* and a portrait, *A Girl from the Hareton Family.* From the Flemish painter Paul Brill there is a tiny fantastic landscape on copper. The energetic genius of Rubens is exhibited here in a large work, *The Feast of Herod;* the idea of Herodias piercing the Baptist's tongue is taken from St Jerome. There is also an oil sketch for an *Adoration of the Shepherds* and a beautiful study of a head *(St Ambrose).*

By Van Dyck there are two portraits, one of an Italian noble painted in Genoa in the 1620s and the other of a *Young Man;* a group portrait of the Genoese Lomellini family is in bad condition. A religious work, *St Sebastian Bound for Martyrdom,* was painted about 1621-3.

From Spain come a 15th-century altarpiece depicting *St Michael* and El Greco's *St Jerome in Penitence* and *The Saviour of the World,* the latter dated about 1600. An outstanding picture is Velazquez's *Old Woman Cooking Eggs,* dated 1618—a type of kitchen scene very popular among Spanish painters of that period. There is also an *Immaculate Conception with St Joachim and St Anne* by Zurbarán—one of at least eight versions of this theme that he painted.

German painting is sparsely but well represented, firstly by a *Venus and Cupid* by Lucas Cranach the Elder painted about 1530 and secondly by two small richly-coloured paintings on copper by Adam Elsheimer, *The Stoning of St Stephen* and *Il Contento*. The latter, painted about 1607 and formerly in the collection of the connoisseur Richard Payne Knight, presented a puzzle as to its theme until fairly recently. Now it has been decided that the picture springs from the fable that Jupiter sent Mercury down to earth to abduct the god Content, whom the people honoured too much, and to leave instead Discontent in the same guise. Elsheimer merges the idea of Fortune with this by presenting the god as a female figure.

Among English paintings exhibited are several small works by Bonington and three Constables, *On the Stour, Noon (Hampstead Heath)* and the *Vale of Dedham,* the design of the last-named being inspired by Claude's *Hagar and the Angel,* now in the London National Gallery, which Constable copied when it was in Sir George Beaumont's collection. There are two small canvases by Cotman and a good portrait by Hogarth of Sarah Malcolm, who sat for two days for him in Newgate before her execution for the murder of her mistress and two fellow servants. Two fine portraits of Scottish beauties, *The Hon. Mrs Graham* and *Mrs Hamilton Nisbet,* are by Gainsborough, as is *A Rocky Landscape,* painted about 1785, for which there is a preliminary chalk drawing in the Cecil Higgins Gallery, Bedford. Among several portraits by Reynolds there is one of the Ladies Waldegrave painted for their uncle Horace Walpole. In addition there are portraits by Romney and Sir Thomas Lawrence, an illustration of a scene from *Macbeth* by John Martin and a landscape, *Somer Hall, Tonbridge,* painted about 1810-11, by Turner.

The representation of Scottish painters is a major feature of the collection. Among the earliest is George Jamesone, whose portrait of the Countess Marischal is here, and there are several still lives by the Dutch-influenced William Gouw Feguson. The first painter of international repute is Allan Ramsay, who was Court Painter from 1767 until his death in 1784 although there is no certain painting from his brush after 1769. Horace Walpole declared he was born to paint women; his *Portrait of the Artist's Wife* would tend to bear this out but there are also several other fine portraits, among them one of Jean-Jacques Rousseau painted for David Hume in 1766. There is a small Italian landscape by Alexander Runciman, and an ambitious *King Lear in the Storm* by John Runciman. From Sir Henry Raeburn comes a large collection of portraits of Scottish notables, among them a self-portrait and the well-known painting of the *Reverend Robert Walker skating on Duddington Loch.* There are works by the Nasmyths, father and son, the first influential painters of Scottish scenery, and several works by Andrew Geddes, particularly notable being the portrait of his mother. By Sir David Wilkie there are a portrait of his parents, a fine early self-portrait,

and several anecdotal paintings, among them *Josephine and the For-
tune-Teller, The Irish Whiskey Still,* and *The Bride at her Toilet,* of
which, when it was exhibited at the Royal Academy in 1838, Thackeray
wrote: 'The colour of this picture is delicious and the effect faultless: Sir
David does everything for a picture nowadays but the *drawing.* Who
knows? Perhaps it is as well left out.' Other 19th-century Scottish
paintings not to be missed are *Portrait of the Artist's Brother* by Robert
Scott Lauder; several works, including *The Traitor's Gate,* by David
Scott; *Shirrapburn Loch* by William Dyce (there are other very large
works by him owned by the Gallery); several works by William
McTaggart; *The Vegetable Stall* by William Macgregor; and scenes from
A Midsummer Night's Dream by Sir Noel Paton.

Scottish National Gallery of Modern Art, Royal Botanic Garden
Tel.: 031 332 3754
Open weekdays 10-6 or dusk; Sunday 2-6 or dusk

Inverleith House, the home of this collection, built in 1774 and standing
at the highest point of the Royal Botanic Gardens, combines some of the
atmosphere of a large private house with the opportunity to see works of
art in a setting of great beauty with a spectacular view of Edinburgh.
The setting itself is pleasurable; what makes it unique is the fact that the
works of art are all of the 20th century. The Gallery was opened in 1960
as the National Galleries of Scotland Department of 20th-Century Art
though as space here is limited to three not very large storeys, one of
which is often used for temporary exhibitions, it was not intended to be
more than a temporary home. A small number of works were transferred
from the National Gallery of Scotland, including a few from the
Maitland Bequest, and there have been other gifts and loans, but the
collection has been largely built up through purchase since 1959.

Though as yet the Gallery does not fully represent all the modern
movements many important 20th-century artists are to be found here.
There are two works by Matisse—*La Leçon de Peintre* and *Head of a
Woman;* two by Picasso—*Mother and Child* and *The Soles; Woman* and
Still Life by Léger; *La Place du Tertre* by Utrillo; a Rouault, a Juan
Gris, and a recently-acquired Derain. Expressionism is represented by
such works as Kirchner's *Théatre Japonais,* an oil and a watercolour by
Nolde, and Jawlensky's *Head of a Woman.* Also to be found are works
by Magritte, Max Ernst, Kokoschka, Klee, de Stael, André Masson,
Morandi, Dubuffet, Karel Appel, Constant Permeke and others.

Representation of 20th-century British art includes *Long Crendon* by
Wilson Steer; *Corner of St Mark's, Venice* by Sickert; *Portrait of a Nun*
by Gwen John; *Western Hills* by Graham Sutherland; *Landscape of the*

Vernal Equinox by Paul Nash; and works by John Piper, Ben Nicholson, Victor Pasmore, Robert Bevan, John Craxton, Wyndham Lewis, David Jones, Josef Herman and others.

Scottish art is represented by works by S. J. Peploe, J. D. Fergusson, Leslie Hunter; and of a later generation Anne Redpath, John Maxwell, Joan Eardley and Robin Philopson are here. *Seascape Erotic* is by Alan Davie.

The Gallery possesses a good collection of modern sculpture. In the garden surrounding the house are to be found examples of the work of Henry Moore, Epstein, Bourdelle, Reg Butler and Marini, while inside the house is an interesting Giacometti—*La Femme Engorgée,* and other sculptures by Lipschitz, Zadkine, Paolozzi, Bugatti, Barbara Hepworth, Lyn Chadwick, Elizabeth Frink and others.

Scottish National Portrait Gallery, Queen Street
Tel.: 031 556 8921

Open weekdays 10-5; Sunday 2-5

The foundation of this gallery was due to the enthusiasm of J. R. Findlay, a member of the Honourable Board of Manufacturers set up in 1727 to administer the Annuity paid to Scotland in compensation for increased taxation under the Act of Union. In 1882 Findlay offered £10,000 anonymously to the Board if the same amount should be given by the Government for the purpose of founding such a gallery. In 1884 he also offered to provide a building for the gallery and for the National Museum of Antiquities if a site was provided, and this having been arranged the present building was constructed and opened to the public in 1889. From small beginnings the collection has grown to be a visual record of Scottish history and culture.

One of the earliest portraits is that of Mary, Queen of Scots, thought to have been painted by Oudry about 1578. Attributed to Corneille de Lyon, painter to Henry II and Charles IX of France, is a portrait of Mary's mother, Mary of Lorraine, wife of James V of Scotland. There is an interesting portrait of George Seton, one of Mary's supporters, by Frans Pourbus, and one of Margaret, Marchioness of Argyll, attributed to George Jamesone, the first Scottish artist to achieve any distinction. Michael Wright's *Portrait of a Highland Chieftain* is one of the earliest works to show Highland dress. Wright, though born in London, is thought to have been apprenticed to Jamesone. There are portraits of James VI and I; one of his eldest son Henry, Prince of Wales, attributed to Robert Peake; and one of his daughter Elizabeth of Bohemia, attributed to Michiel Mierevelt. Charles I is here portrayed by Daniel Mytens, by whom there are also several portraits of Scottish noblemen.

Superior in attraction is a portrait of Charles II by William Dobson. By the Dutch-born William Wissing, who studied in Lely's studio, there is a portrait of Mary of Modena which certainly reveals Lely's influence. Henrietta Anne, younger daughter of Charles I, is here portrayed by Pierre Mignard, first painter to Louis XIV, and Mary, his elder daughter, later Princess of Orange, by Adriaen Hanneman.

From a historical point of view there is an interesting group of Jacobite portraits, among them a portrait of the Old Pretender by Nicolas de Largillière, who also worked in Lely's studio, and of Prince Charles, the Young Pretender, by Antonio David, but the 18th century, for the most part, is distinguished by the recording of Scotland's cultural history. There are some fine works by Allan Ramsay including a good pastel self-portrait, chalk drawings of himself and his wife and an excellent portrait of the philosopher David Hume. Several portraits of Robert Burns include one by Alexander Nasmyth dated 1787. By Alexander Runciman is a portrait of the poet Robert Ferguson and also a self-portrait and there is a drawing of the architect Sir William Chambers by Francis Cotes.

Various members of the Scottish nobility are portrayed by Kneller, Gavin Hamilton, Romney and Zoffany and of considerable interest is a portrait of Flora MacDonald by Richard Wilson. By Sir Joshua Reynolds there are portraits of Robert Hay Drummond, Archbishop of York, and of another eminent theologian. Sir Walter Scott is commemorated by several works, among them a portrait by Raeburn and an excellent sketch by Andrew Geddes painted about 1818.

There are many portrait busts in the Gallery, among them one of *Robert Burns* by Flaxman, a seated *Thomas Carlyle* by Boehm, *Ramsay MacDonald* by Epstein and *W. E. Henley* by Rodin. An interesting section contains a series of casts from portrait gems by James Tassie.

ENGLEFIELD GREEN
Royal Holloway College, Englefield Green, Surrey
Tel.: 389 4455

The paintings in the impressive picture gallery at Royal Holloway College, one of the colleges of the University of London, derive from the collection of the founder of the College, Thomas Holloway. This remarkable philanthropic businessman made his fortune from the manufacture of pills and ointment. He founded first the Holloway Sanatorium for the treatment of mental illness among the less prosperous middle classes and later was inspired to found this college for women—it is now co-educational—which he hoped might become the nucleus of a university for women. The design of the College is loosely based on that

of the 16th-century French château of Chambord. The College was
opened by Queen Victoria in 1886 three years after the death of the
founder and studies began there in the following year. The pictures, like
those in the collections of several other successful Victorian businessmen,
reflect both the taste of the founder and the type of paintings readily
available for him to purchase. But it is an interesting collection despite
these limitations and there are several excellent paintings and many that
are of high quality.

Among the former are Turner's sea piece of 1832, *Van Tromp Going
About to Please his Masters,* Constable's *A View on the Stour* and John
(Old) Crome's *A Woodland Scene.* One of Gainsborough's early land-
scape masterpieces, *Going to Market Early Morning, Peasants and
Colliers,* is also here; it was painted in the early 1770s. And there are
several good examples of George Morland: *The Cottage Door, The Press
Gang,* and *The Carrier Preparing to Set Out.*

There are two works by Sir John Millais belonging to the late 1870s
when he had become a pillar of established Victorian art, the famous
Princes in the Tower and *Princess Elizabeth in Prison at St James's.* From
W. P. Frith there is a characteristically exact scene of contemporary life,
The Railway Station, and from Luke Fildes a work with explicit social
comment, *Applicants for Admission to a Casual Ward,* dated 1874. It was
Fildes's first success though a reviewer thought that the introduction of
such a state of things into art was 'rather matter for regret'. Frank Holl's
Newgate; Committed for Trial of 1878 is motivated by the same kind of
social feeling. From Daniel Maclise there is an historical work of almost
incredible detail but poor composition, *Peter the Great at Deptford
Dockyard.* Many other Victorian artists are represented: two good works
by Thomas Creswick, *The First Glimpse of the Sea* and *Trentside;
Pilgrims Approaching Jerusalem* and *A Street in Cairo* by David Roberts;
Man Proposes—God Disposes, a painting of extraordinary subject and
treatment by Sir Edwin Landseer; *Piazza dei Signori, Verona* by James
Holland; and *Licensing the Beggars in Spain* by J. B. Burgess.

The pictures in the Gallery can only be seen by appointment nowadays
as the hall is so often in use, but there is an open day every year, usually
in August, which is announced beforehand in the press.

EXETER
Exeter Museum and Art Gallery, Royal Albert Memorial Museum, Queen Street
Tel.: 0392 56724
Open weekdays 10-5.30

The genesis of the Exeter Museum is to be traced to the inspiration of the great museums of London founded in the middle of the 19th century under the initiative of Prince Albert. On Prince Albert's death in 1861, the Member of Parliament for Devon Sir Stafford Northcote proposed the founding of educational institutions such as he had advocated as a memorial to him in the town of Exeter. The suggestion was adopted and by 1870 a building had been constructed containing a School of Art, School of Science, Public Library and Museum. The Museum received a large bequest of paintings in the 1890s and after the First World War the large Veitch bequest enriched the collection. Until the early 1950s there had been no particular policy with regard to the art collection but then the Museum began to concentrate on collecting the works of early Devon painters, among them Francis Towne, John White Abbot, Francis Hayman, James Northcote, Thomas Hudson, Sir Joshua Reynolds. Recently the tendency has been to widen the collection of British art and in this field the collection of watercolours is particularly strong. Interestingly enough the Exeter collection of Victorian oil-paintings (no doubt because of the earlier concentration on Devon painting) is sparse compared with the many other provincial galleries, but its emphasis on other schools of painting makes it the more unusual.

The work by Devon artists in the Gallery reveals what an important source of British art that county has been. One of the earliest artists represented is the portraitist Thomas Hudson. His portrait of Anne, Countess of Dumfries, dated 1763, he declared in a letter was the best thing he ever did. Also here are his portraits of the Earl and Countess of Albemarle. There is a delightful *Self Portrait at the Easel* by Francis Hayman, who was born in Exeter but is thought to have begun his working life as a scene painter at Drury Lane. His representation includes six illustrations for Tobias Smollett's translation of *Don Quixote*, a landscape, and a number of the portrait groups in which he excelled.

A portrait of Captain Charles Proby and one of John Burridge Cholwich by Sir Joshua Reynolds are here as well as a large landscape by him. Thomas Patch was an Exeter-born painter who travelled to Italy early in his career, mostly on foot, and settled in Florence. He became noted for his caricature groups, one of which, probably dated 1763 and containing the figure of David Garrick, is to be found in the Gallery together with port scenes and landscapes. Two other natives of Exeter were Francis Towne and his pupil John White Abbott, who was a surgeon. Many of Towne's landscapes, both oil and watercolour, painted in Devon, Italy, Switzerland and Wales, are to be found at Exeter. White Abbott's works are mostly confined to Devon and Somerset though he did visit the Lake District and Scotland. Richard Cosway, mainly known as a miniaturist, is represented by a large oil portrait of *Master Carew*. James Northcote, famous for his *Life of Reynolds* as well as his own paintings, has here a self-portrait dated 1823 and a picture entitled *Sir Walter Scott Bart. and James Northcote Painting his Portrait.* The unfortunate Romantic painter Benjamin Robert Haydon, whose career was full of frustration and culminated in suicide, was born in Plymouth; one of his best-known works, *Marcus Curtius Plunging into the Gulf,* is at Exeter as well as a *Self-Portrait as the Spirit of the Vine* and two oil sketches. Also from Plymouth was Sir Charles Eastlake, whose life contrasts strongly with that of Haydon, whose pupil at one time he was, as he became President of the Royal Academy and Director of the National Gallery. There are three works by him, among them *Cypresses at L'Arricia.* Other painters represented at Exeter who belonged to its environs include Ozias Humphrey, the marine painter Thomas Luny, Richard Crosse—a deaf mute, James Leakey, Samuel Prout.

The recent tendency of the Gallery has been to broaden the representation of British painting. *A View of Castel Gandolfo,* dated 1791, by Joseph Wright of Derby was bequeathed to the Gallery in 1957 as were also two landscapes by John Linnell. In addition, a Richard Wilson, *Dolbadarn Castle and Llyn Peris,* was acquired as were *Perseus and Andromeda* by William Etty, *Diadomene* by Sir E. J. Poynter and *Pastoral Scene near Cairo: Evening* by Frederick Goodhall. Another late Victorian work of contemporary interest is Lucy Kemp Welch's *Lord Dundonald's Dash on Ladysmith* which contains among Dundonald's entourage a portrait of the young Winston Churchill.

Of 20th-century painting the Camden Town Group is represented by good works by Sickert, including *Le Lit de Cuivre* of about 1905-6, *Girl Combing Her Hair* by Harold Gilman; *Reclining Nude* by Duncan Grant; Spencer Gore's *Panshanger Park,* 1909; and Robert Bevan's *Devonshire Valley,* 1913. More recent works include paintings by William Roberts, Lawrence Gowing, Paul Nash—note particularly his collage, *Don't Forget the Diver,* and a constructivist work, *Perspex Group on Orange 1967* by Mary Martin.

Perhaps the most notable European painting in the Gallery is J. L. David's circular portrait of Napoleon presented by him to his sister the Queen of Naples. There is a German late-15th-century polyptych of *The Passion* and a painting, *The Young Martyr,* by Guido Cagnacci, a 17th-century Neapolitan artist.

GATESHEAD
Shipley Art Gallery, Prince Consort Road South
Tel.: 0632 71495

Open weekdays 10-6; Sunday 3-5

The Shipley Art Gallery was opened in 1917. It was founded as a result of a bequest of a collection of pictures and of £30,000 made by Joseph

Shipley, a well-known solicitor in Gateshead and Newcastle. The great majority of the paintings come from the 19th century and most of these are from the British school.

One of the earliest English artists represented is George Lambert with two characteristic classical landscapes. Then there are a *View near Norwich* by John Crome, a *Canal Scene* by James Stark, and several landscapes ascribed to John Linnell. John Martin, who was born near Hexham, is represented by *The Fire, Edinburgh*, and there is a landscape by his rival Francis Danby, *River with Old Ruins, Somerset*. Other 19th-century painters represented include Paul Falconer Poole, Richard Redgrave, J. B. Pyne, David Wilkie, John Varley, Atkinson Grimshaw and Thomas Sidney Cooper, whose *A Sunny Summer Evening in the Meadows* was painted when he was 98. There are also two works by Sir John Millais, *Meditation* and *A Scene with Rosalind and Celia from 'As You Like It'*.

Among other works of great interest are Paul Van Somer's *Portrait of an Elizabethan;* Joachim Uytewael's *Hilly Landscape: Villagers Offering Goods to Troops; Landscape with Cattle and Figures* by Pieter van Laer; *Winter Scene in the Italian Alps* by Swanevelt; *Adoration of the Shepherds* by Benjamin Cuyp; *The Parting of Abraham and Lot* by Peter Lastman, *The Ascension* by Sir James Thornhill; and an altarpiece of the South German School dated 1510.

Many artists of local repute or of Scottish origin are also shown in the Gallery and the collection extends to watercolours and drawings.

GLASGOW
Glasgow Art Gallery and Museum, Kelvingrove Park
Open weekdays 10-5; Sunday 10-5
and its subsidiary, the Camphill Museum, Queen's Park
open weekdays 11-5; Sunday 2-5
Tel.: 041 632 1350

The Glasgow Art Gallery is rightly regarded as among the first rank in art collections to be found in the provincial cities of the British Isles. The origin of the city's collection goes back as far as the 17th century, when, with the building of a new Tolbooth or Town Hall in 1627, the Council resolved upon decorating it with royal portraits. Portraits of James I and VI, Charles I, and Charles II were purchased in the latter part of the century and this policy continued throughout the next century, outstanding being the pictures executed by Allan Ramsay, who painted George II and George III and also the 3rd Duke of Argyll for the Council. A commendable though ultimately abortive attempt was made to foster a permanent interest in art in the city when Robert Foulis and his brother established in Glasgow an Academy of Art, the first of its kind in Britain, fifteen years before the foundation of the Royal Academy. These two men were printers to the University and the University provided facilities for an annual exhibition of art from 1761 to 1775 and a collection of paintings was thus started. In 1776, however, financial difficulties forced Foulis to cease his activities and it was not until 80 years later that his dream began to have some sort of fulfilment. The new development, and indeed the nucleus of the Glasgow Art Collection as it stands today, was due to Archibald McLellan, coach-builder, town councillor, city magistrate and supporter of the arts. McLellan began collecting paintings at the age of 27 with the future aim of handing them on to his native city. He built a block of buildings in Sauchiehall Street with three exhibition rooms for the display of his paintings, but when he died in 1854 it was discovered that he was heavily in debt and it was with some reluctance that the Glasgow council agreed in 1856 to pay £44,500 for the buildings and the pictures in order to carry out his wishes and to settle the claims against his estate. His collection was housed in the McLellan Galleries for many years until the decision to build a new gallery was made and a public competition was held for the design; this was won by Simpson and Milner Allen of London in 1892. The new gallery was opened in 1902 but in the intervening years the collection received many further gifts and bequests, among them an important group of Italian works bequeathed in 1877 by the widow of the portrait painter John Graham-Gilbert. Since 1926 the Hamilton Trust, formed for the purpose of buying paintings, has made additions to the French and British sections; in 1944 the prestige of the Gallery was further enhanced by the gift of Sir William and Lady Burrell's large collection of paintings and art objects. Only a small part of this collection can be shown in the Art Gallery and the Camphill Museum but the same benefactors have endowed a fund with which a new Burrell Art Gallery and Museum will be built—it is hoped by 1977.

Five galleries in the Kelvingrove building are devoted to Continental painting. In the Italian gallery the outstanding works are undoubtedly *The Adultress brought Before Christ* and the small fragment, *Head of a Man,* by Giorgione. The latter is actually a portion from the right-hand side of the former painting and was identified as such by Bernard Berenson through a copy of the original painting at Bergamo. This fragment was bought by the Gallery in 1971; the principal part of the work came from the McLellan bequest. Giorgione's master Giovanni Bellini is represented by two paintings of the Madonna and Child; one of them, particularly beautiful, is from the Burrell collection and was formerly in the Palazzo Barberini in Rome. A large altarpiece, dated about 1520, *Madonna and Child with Saints,* is by one of Bellini's followers and is also worthy of attention. Another member of the

Bellini-Giorgione circle was Vincenzo Catena, who is represented by the *Madonna and Child with St Catherine and St Mary Magdalene*. There are also two paintings of *The Madonna and Child with Saints* by Paris Bordone, a Venetian painter of a slightly later generation. *The Ordeal of Tuccia*, formerly ascribed to Andrea Schiavone, is now thought to be by Tintoretto. Tuccia, a Vestal Virgin accused of incest, appealed to the goddess Vesta to prove her innocence and had power given to her to carry a sieve of water from the Tiber to the temple. Also noteworthy from 16th-century Venice are the *Descent from the Cross* by Palma Giovane and works by followers of Titian and Palma Vecchio. From 18th-century Venice comes a *View of San Giorgio Maggiore* by Guardi and several works including *St John the Baptist Teaching* by Francesco Zuccarelli, who ended by having a successful career as a decorative painter in England and who was one of the founder-members of the Royal Academy.

There are several fine examples of Florentine art, among them a small *cassone* (marriage chest) panel, *The Judgement of Paris*, by Domenico Veneziano from the Burrell collection. There is a vivid *Annunciation* ascribed to Botticelli and a tondo of *The Madonna and Child with the Infant St John* by Filippino Lippi. A *St John the Baptist* is an interesting example of the softer work of Alessandro Allori, pupil and adopted son of Bronzino; and there are two works, *The Adoration of the Magi* and *Salome with the Head of John the Baptist*, by the 17th-century Florentine Carlo Dolci, a precocious painter who did not fulfil his early promise though these two works are of a very high quality.

Not to be missed is a small *Nativity*, a panel from the predella of an altarpiece now in Bologna Gallery, by the Bolognese artist Francesco Francia; it was probably painted in the last decade of the 15th century. *St Jerome in a Landscape* is an interesting early work by Domenichino. From Ferrara comes Dosso Dossi's *Holy Family with Saints* and two panels of saints by Garofalo, whose death in 1559 ended the fine period of Ferrarese painting. Roman painting is represented by several interesting works mainly from the 17th and 18th centuries. A dramatic *Archangel Michael and the Rebel Angels* is by the Cavaliere d'Arpino who employed the young Caravaggio, and a Caravaggesque *Madonna and Child with Saint Anne* is by Antiveduto Gramatica, who was a considerable portrait and history painter but was dismissed in disgrace from his position as President of the Academy of St Luke for attempting to sell a picture of Raphael's that belonged to the Academy and substituting a copy of his own in its place. There is a typical sweet work by Sassoferrato, *Madonna and Child with St Elizabeth and the Infant St John* and a superb tiny work on copper, *Agony in the Garden* by Francesco Trevisani. Also very fine is *A View of Ariccia* by Paolo Anesi.

The second gallery contains Flemish and Early Netherlandish works, one of the most important being *Virgin and Child by a Fountain,* full of symbolic meaning, by Bernard Van Orley, the great tapestry designer. Among other interesting early works are *Christ Taking Leave of his Mother,* attributed to Pieter Cocke, the *Virgin and Child* by Mabuse (from the Burrell collection) and a painting by Jan van Scorel after Raphael, *The Holy Family under an Oak Tree.* Two other early little works from the Burrell collection are Hans Memling's *The Virgin Annunciate* and *The Flight into Egypt.* Outstanding from every point of view is Rubens's *Nature Adorned by the Graces,* which celebrates the fecundity of Nature—the vegetation was executed by his assistant Jan Brueghel. At one time this was in the collection of Sir James Thornhill. *The Fruit Seller* by Jacob Jordaens was painted about 1650 and was probably a design for one of a series of tapestries on country life. Other interesting paintings are by David Teniers the Younger, Hendrik van Balen and Jan van Bloemen. Also in this gallery are *St Maurice with a Donor,* an impressive work by the Master of Moulins (formerly the painter was thought to be Hugo van der Goes) and several Spanish works, notably Ribera's *St Peter Repentant.*

The Dutch gallery contains Rembrandt's famous *Man in Armour:* this once belonged to Sir Joshua Reynolds, who thought that 'upon the whole the picture is too black'. It is dated 1655 and the figure has been variously identified as, among others, Achilles, Mars, Alexander and Pallas Athene. This and the other Rembrandt, *The Carcase of an Ox,* dated about 1640, came from the Graham-Gilbert bequest. In the Burrell collection, as well as several etchings, there are two oval portraits by Rembrandt—a self-portrait and a *Portrait of Saskia.* The gallery abounds in other fine works, from Albert Cuyp's unusual religious work, *Entry of Christ into Jerusalem,* Hals's *Portrait of a Gentleman* (Burrell Collection), Cornelius Johnson's *Portrait of a Woman,* Jacob Ruisdael's *View of Egmond am Zee* and *Landscape with Ruined Tower,* Honthorst's *St Peter Released from Prison,* Philip Wouwerman's *Hawking* to works by Nicolaes Berchem, Jan Both, Jan van Goyen, Willem Kalf, Caspar Netscher, Rachel Ruysch and Swanevelt. Of considerable interest is the 19th-century Dutch school with works by Jozef Israels, Jacob and Willem Maris, and Anton Mauve was was Van Gogh's teacher for a time. Notable from the German school is a *Portrait of a Woman* by Christoph Amberger; she holds a carnation often used in the 15th and 16th centuries as a symbol of love in pictures of betrothed or married persons. Here too is an *Adoration of the Shepherds* by Rottenhammer.

The Gallery's collection of French 19th-century painting is very large, so much so that all the pictures cannot be shown at the same time, especially with the addition of the Burrell collection, which is particularly rich in French works; some of these are shown at the Camphill Museum. From the 17th century there are two Italian landscapes by

Gaspar Dughet and a small *Peasant Children* ascribed to Antoine Le Nain and from the 18th century a number of works by Chardin, among them *Le Paté* and *Pierrot Voleur*. Delacroix's *Expulsion of Adam and Eve from Paradise* was a study for one of the decorations in the Chambre des Deputés in Paris; also by him is *Le Cheval Blanc* and there are a number of works by Géricault, among them *Polish Trumpeter, The Stallion* and *Prancing Grey Horse*. From the Burrell collection also are some remarkable works by Daumier, numerous drawings and small works like *Don Quixote and Sancho Panza, Boys Bathing, La Parade,* but also two large paintings, *Le Bon Samaritain* and *Le Meunier, son Fils et l'Âne*. Millet's famous image of toilers, *Going to Work,* is here, as is an interesting piece in charcoal and pastel, *The Sheepfold*. Of the 'orthodox' stream of French 19th-century painting there are works by Decamps, Meissonier, Michel, Legros, Couture and Ribot. Outstanding by Corot are *Pastorale—Souvenir d'Italie, The Crayfisher, Cottage at Fontainebleau, Mlle de Foudras,* and the Barbizon School is well represented with three works by Troyon and several works by Daubigny, Diaz and Jacque. Among works by Courbet are a splendid *Portrait of a Woman, L'Aumône d'un Mendiant à Ornans, La Dame au Parasol* and several still lives. The Gallery is indebted to the Burrell collection for several small Manets, among them *Marie Colombier, Au Café* and *Aux Folies Bergères*. Excellent too are some 22 works by Degas, among them *Dancers on a Bench, La Répétition, Portrait of Duranty* (the art critic who championed the Impressionists), *Girl Looking through Opera Glasses* and *Jockeys in the Rain*. There are a couple of Monets—*Vétheuil* and *View of Ventimiglia,* the latter dated 1884; several works by Boudin including the charming *La Plage à Trouville—L'Impératrice Eugénie et sa Suite;* two works by Pissarro, *Tuileries Gardens* and *The Towpath;* and *The Sisters* by Mary Cassatt, the American painter, an Impressionist and friend of Degas. Jongkind, Guillaumin, Harpignies, Forain, Fantin-Latour, Renoir, Sisley and Monticelli are all also here. Gauguin is represented by a work done in Denmark, *Oestervold Park, Copenhagen;* Van Gogh by *Le Moulin de la Galette, Montmartre* and the recently acquired portrait of the Glasgow art dealer, Alexander Reid; Cézanne by the very interesting *Maison de Zola à Medan* and *Near Gardanne*. Later French works include a still life by Braque; *Blackfriars* by Derain; *The Pier at Deauville* by Dufy; *Algiers* by Albert Marquet; *The Flower Seller* by Picasso; *House among Trees* and *Boy Sitting on the Grass* by Seurat; *Village Street* by Utrillo; *River Scene* by Vlaminck; *Mother and Child* by Vuillard; *The Seine at Paris* by Othon Friesz; *The Pink Tablecloth* by Matisse; *Le Quai de Clichy* by Signac; *Edge of the Forest* by Bonnard.

The gallery devoted to 18th-century British painting contains one of Glasgow's earliest acquisitions, Allan Ramsay's *Archibald, 3rd Duke of Argyll,* purchased in 1749. Other portraits by Ramsay include one of

Henrietta Diana, Dowager Countess of Stafford. By Sir Henry Raeburn there is a group of portraits of Scottish notables including an imposing one of *Mr and Mrs Robert N. Campbell* and sympathetic ones of *Mrs William Urquhart* and *Mrs Anne Campbell.* The work of David Martin, Ramsay's pupil, is seen to advantage in his portrait of *Provost Murdoch,* and another interesting portrait is that of Robert Burns, known as the 'Auchendrane' portrait, by Alexander Nasmyth. English portraiture from the 18th century includes *Isabella, Countess of Erroll* and *A Boy in Van Dyck Dress* by Reynolds; *Sir Charles Stuart* by Romney; *William Pitt, 1st Earl of Chatham* by Joseph Highmore; *Elizabeth Prowse* and *Lady Villiers* by Thomas Hudson; *Mrs Anne Lloyd* by Hogarth; *Pitt* by Gainsborough; and a charming portrait of Mrs John Trouwer by Sir Thomas Lawrence. By the German-born Johann Zoffany there is a portrait of Mrs Maintrew, and the appealing *A Family Party—The Minuet.* Noteworthy in this gallery are two still lives by the 17th-century Scottish painter William Gouw Ferguson, who spent most of his life in Holland. Landscapes of interest are Gainsborough's *Woody Landscape near Bath* and John Cleveley's *Shipyard on the Thames;* there are also several ascribed to Richard Wilson.

The 19th-century gallery includes a *Hampstead Heath* by Constable and *Modern Italy—The Pifferari* by Turner. Compare the latter with *The Paps of Jura* by the quasi-Impressionist Scottish artist William McTaggart, who has many works in the gallery. Scotland figures as the subject in many of the works, for example in the paintings of Horatio McCulloch and Samuel Bough, the latter's *Burns's Cottage, Alloway* being very popular. The same can be said of Sir David Wilkie's *Cottar's Saturday Night* which is here with another work, *Cardinals, Priests, and Roman Citizens Washing the Feet of the Poor.* Of 19th-century portraiture outstanding is Whistler's portrait of Thomas Carlyle; it was first exhibited at 48 Pall Mall, Whistler's Exhibition, in 1874 and purchased from Whistler by the Glasgow Corporation in 1891. Whistler recounted that when Carlyle had the first sitting he said, 'And now, man, fire away,' adding when he saw Whistler's surprise, 'If ye're fighting battles or painting pictures, the only thing to do is fire away.' Another eminent Victorian here is *Gladstone* by Millais. Besides these there are several by John Singer Sargent, notably *Mrs George Batten Singing.* There are several small works by David Roberts, John Martin, Noel Paton, John Phillip and Alma-Tadema. Here also are *Christabel* by William Dyce; *Wycliffe on Trial* by Ford Madox Brown; *Danae or The Tower of Brass* by Burne-Jones; and *Regina Cordium: Alice Wilding* by Rossetti.

A small gallery is devoted to the Glasgow School of painters which was founded between 1880 and 1885 to combat what they saw as the sentimental and anecdotal quality of much contemporary painting. Of this group the works of George Henry, e.g. *A Galloway Landscape,* dated

1889, are particularly notable; and here too are Sir David Cameron, Joseph Crawhall, Sir James Guthrie, Edward Hornel etc.

Usually to be found in the gallery assigned to 20th-century painting are Augustus John's portrait of W. B. Yeats; Wyndham Lewis's *Froanna—Portrait of the Artist's Wife;* Sickert's *Dieppe Harbour* and his portrait of Sir Hugh Walpole; and Graham Sutherland's *Landscape with Rocks.* Other artists represented include Matthew Smith, Ben Nicholson, Wilson Steer, Stanley Spencer, Roger Fry, Mark Gertler, Duncan Grant, L. S. Lowry, Paul Nash. There is a group of works by the 'Scottish Colourists', who were much drawn to the Fauves and who all spent some time in France—J. D. Fergusson, S. J. Peploe and Leslie Hunter. From succeeding generations of Scottish artists come works by William Gillies, John Maxwell, Anne Redpath, Joan Eardley and Robin Philipson.

Glasgow Gallery has judged a recent purchase, Salvador Dali's *Christ of St John of the Cross,* to be important enough to be given a setting by itself on the balcony of the East Wing. Scattered around the Gallery are also works of sculpture, among them several Rodins, a Degas nude, Renoir's bronze portrait of Madame Renoir, Carpeaux's *Susanna Surprised,* a Houdon bust, and examples of work by Rysbrack, Flaxman, Chantrey, Epstein, Zadkine and others.

The Hunterian Museum, Glasgow University
Tel.: 041 339 8855
Open Monday to Friday 9-5; Saturday 9-12

The founder of this collection, William Hunter, has his assured place in medical history as a famous obstetrician and as the first great teacher of anatomy in this country; even men like Adam Smith, Edmund Burke and Edward Gibbon went to his anatomy lectures. The collection amassed in his lifetime embraced an extensive range of subjects and specimens; among the latter were anatomical, pathological, zoological and geological examples. In addition he possessed a very fine library of printed books and manuscripts, a remarkable collection of coins and medals, and a group of paintings, some of the highest quality. Hunt's request in 1765 that this museum should form part of a medical school for the teaching of anatomy inaugurated at his own expense was defeated by the lack of interest and inaction of the government of the time. Hunter therefore determined to leave his collection to his old university, the University of Glasgow. When he died in 1783 the Museum, much enlarged in the intervening years, was consigned to the care of his nephew and heir Matthew Baillie, and in 1807 Baillie passed it on to Glasgow University.

Since the acquisition of the Hunter collection the University has received a number of other important gifts of paintings. Most remarkable perhaps is a large collection of about 40 paintings and over 200 drawings and watercolours by Whistler which was presented by his sister-in-law Miss R. Birnie Philip in 1936 in conjunction with a number of the artist's personal possessions such as letters, manuscripts, tools, etc. Other collections received by the University include a group of etchings and engravings from Professor W. R. Scott and a group of several thousand prints collected by Dr J. A. McCallum. A collection of drawings and designs by Charles Rennie Mackintosh has also been acquired and in 1963 the Smillie collection of 29 pictures was presented by Miss Ina S. Smillie.

Perhaps most remarkable among the original Hunter gift of pictures are three beautiful works by Chardin: *The Cellar Boy, Lady Taking Tea* and *The Scullery Maid,* all signed and dated 1738 and in their muted serenity typical of his world. Another considerable French picture is the 17th-century work, *A Woman Selling Fruit,* variously attributed to Mathieu or Louis Le Nain.

Italian paintings include: *Birth of St John the Baptist* by Scarsellino, a painter and miniaturist of the Ferrarese School; *Portrait of a Man,* attributed to the Mannerist painter, Salviati; *St Catherine of Alexandria* by Domenichino; a strange little landscape, *Tobias and the Angel* by Grimaldi, called Il Bolognese; *A Boy Singing,* attributed to Bernini; *Laomedon Refusing Payment to Poseidon and Apollo* by Salvator Rosa; *Death of Actaeon* by Zuccarelli, who spent 17 years in England; and *Martha Reproving Mary for Vanity,* the same subject as a lost picture by Caravaggio of which there is a copy at Christ Church, Oxford.

Of English painting Hunter's collection contained four works by Kneller, among them a portrait of Sir Isaac Newton and another of Dr John Arbuthnot, friend of Swift and Pope, to whom this painting once belonged. There is a portrait of Hunter himself by Allan Ramsay, dating from the late 1750s, and also a portrait by Reynolds of Lady Maynard, who was a patient of Hunter's. Three paintings by George Stubbs of game animals, *The Moose, The Nylghau,* and the *Pygmy Antelope,* were specially commissioned for natural history researches.

There are some good examples of 17th-century Dutch and Flemish painting, among them a Rembrandt sketch for the *Entombment of Christ* in Munich, *Hunting the Stag* by Wouwerman, *Panorama* by Philips Koninck, *Dead Game and Fruit* by Frans Snyders, *Landscape with Peasants* by Jan Weenix, *Landscape with Hawking Party,* attributed to Ruben's assistant Lucas van Uden, and a *Landscape with Mercury and Herse* by Swanevelt. Many more minor 17th-century Dutch and Flemish works originate from the Smillie collection, among them: *Portrait of a Woman with a Fan* by Nicolaes Maes; *Landscape with the Castle at Cleve* by de Moucheron; *The First Meeting of Theagenes and Chariclea* by Jan de Bray; and a still life by the Anglo-Dutch painter Edwaert Colyer.

The invaluable collection of Whistler's works here includes a fine self-portrait, a portrait of Miss Birnie Philip, *Harmony in Grey and Silver—Le Petit Souris, Harmony in Fawn and Purple—Miss Millie Finch, Grey and Silver—The Thames, Study of a French Girl,* and many others, including sketches and drawings.

Stirling Maxwell Collection, Pollok House, Pollok Park
Tel.: 041 632 0274
Open weekdays 10-5; Sunday 2-5

Pollok House and the Stirling Maxwell Collection were given to the City of Glasgow in 1967 by Mrs Anne Maxwell Macdonald, daughter of the late Sir John Stirling Maxwell, and her family. The central block of the house was designed by William Adam and completed by his son John in 1752. Additions to the house were designed in the Adam tradition and carried out between 1890 and 1908. The Maxwell family have been associated with Pollok for hundreds of years but the park which surrounds the house was the creation of Sir John Stirling Maxwell. The collection of paintings within the house reflects the taste and discrimination of Sir William Stirling Maxwell, the 9th Baronet, who collected most of them between 1852 and 1859. His interest in Spanish painting means that at Pollok House, next to the Bowes Museum, is to be found the most representative collection of Spanish painting in Britain. He also wrote an important book, *Annals of the Artists of Spain.*

As the paintings are arranged in the various rooms of the house it will perhaps be best to treat them room by room. The entrance hall contains portraits of the Maxwell family by painters of the Scottish school; the lower entrance hall also contains a *St Jerome,* copy of a painting by Ribera, by Francisco Herrara, son of the Master of Velazquez.

Among others in the Morning Room are to be found: a portrait of Queen Elizabeth I attributed to Federico Zuccaro, founder of the Academy of St Luke in Rome; a version of a portrait of Pope Clement VII, painted in 1526 by Sebastiano del Piombo; *St John and the Lamb* by Alonso de Tobar, a follower of Murillo and also an official of the Inquisition; a portrait of Archduke Rudolf of Austria by Alonso Sanchez Coello, Court Painter to Philip II; *Portrait of a Royal Infant* by Claudio Coello, appointed Royal Painter in 1683; and *Charles II, King of Spain* by Juan Carreno de Miranda, who was introduced to the Court by Velazquez and became Court Painter in 1671.

In the library corridor is an oval portrait in oils on copper of Lady Stirling Maxwell by William Etty. The library itself holds the cream of the collection, two works by El Greco, *Portrait of a Man,* painted 1590,

6   *The Holburne, Bath*

7   *The Lady Lever Art Gallery, Port Sunlight, Cheshire*

8   *The Bowes Museum, Barnard Castle, Co. Durham*

9   *The Welsh National Museum, Cardiff, Wales*

and *Lady in a Fur Wrap*, painted 1577-9. She was probably El Greco's mistress and mother of his son. Both these paintings were bought from the collection of King Louis Philippe in 1853.

The Print Room contains a collection of watercolours, drawings and prints including a set of etchings by Goya, *Los Proverbios,* and several portraits including a small oval of Mrs Masham attributed to Sir Godfrey Kneller.

There is a fine collection in the Music Room: a *Madonna* by Murillo; a *Pietà* by Luca Signorelli, predella panel for an altarpiece in the Church of S. Agostino, Siena; two small works by Goya, *Boys Playing at Seesaw* and *Boys Playing at Soldiers;* an *Allegory of Repentance* by Antonio de Pereda, a 17th-century Spanish painter renowned for his paintings on the theme of vanity; a painting by a Dutch artist called *Christ and the Pope,* very interesting historically for the anti-Catholic sentiments it displays; *The Adoration of the Blessed Sacrament* by Francisco de Herrera; a small mellow landscape by the Italianate Dutchman Jan Both; a small landscape by Guardi; *Christ Carrying the Cross,* a copy of a Titian by Juan Fernandez Navarrete, a deaf mute who in 1568 was appointed Court Painter to Philip II; a very dramatic *Pietà* by Luis de Morales, because of his popular devotional art known as El Divina; a large *Adam and Eve* by Alonso Cano, a 17th-century painter and architect who designed the facade of Granada Cathedral; two landscapes by Jakob Hackaert, a German painter whose biography was written by Goethe; and several Spanish miniature paintings.

In the Drawing-Room are a number of portraits, among them the poet *James Thomson* by Hogarth; *Mrs Salisbury* by the Swedish-born Michael Dahl; *George Villiers, 1st Duke of Buckingham* by Cornelius Johnson; *Richard Cumberland* by Romney; *Lady Arabella Stuart* by Isaac Oliver. Here too is Hogarth's impression of *St Peter's Chapel in the Tower of London.*

The dining-room corridor contains further Spanish works. By Juan de Valdes Leal there is an emotion-charged *Madonna and Child* contrasting with a large bright *Madonna and Child and St John* by Murillo. A Manneristic *Adoration of the Magi* by Luis Tristán, probably a pupil of El Greco, is one of seven versions of this painting (another is in the Fitzwilliam Museum). From the school of Velazquez comes a small *Head of a Man.* The Cedar Room contains portraits of Spanish royalty by unknown painters, the dining-room some minor Dutch works and the Business Room further Spanish paintings including *St Ildefonso receiving the Chasuble* by Jerónimo Cosida. St Ildefonso, who wrote a book defending the perpetual virginity of Mary, beheld a vision of her in his Cathedral of Toledo when she bestowed upon him a chasuble made of heavenly material. Also in this room is *The Satyr and the Peasant* by Jacob Jordaens.

Another corridor contains a portrait of *Caroline, Queen of Naples* by Baron Gérard, a very successful early-19th-century French painter; *Christ in the House of Martha and Mary* by Jan Steen; a landscape by Gaspar Dughet; portraits of Philip II of Spain and Anne of Austria by Alonso Coello; and a depiction of *St Julian of Cuenca,* the patron saint of basket weavers, by Eugenio Caxes. Most notable here are five works by William Blake. Two associated works in tempera are *Adam Naming the Beasts* and *Eve Naming the Birds,* the former inscribed with the date 1810. *Christ's Entry into Jerusalem* is in oil on copper, dated 1800, and *The Entombment* is another small work in tempera. A long narrow composition dated 1808 depicts *Chaucer's Pilgrims on their way to Canterbury.*

On the staircase is a portrait, *Girl with Dove,* by the German exponent of neo-classicism Anton Raphael Mengs. Other works here include a landscape by Nicolaes Berchem; *The Guitarist and the Listener* by Godfried Schalcken who, as here, always liked to depict candlelight in his pictures; a portrait of Maria Theresa of Austria by the French 17th-century artist Pierre Mignard; a self-portrait by Vicente Carducho, Court Painter to Philip III; and another Blake, a watercolour, *A Vision of the Last Judgement,* 1806. Numerous other portraits are to be seen on the stairs and in other rooms, including one purporting to be a portrait of Velazquez by his pupil Juan de Alfaro.

near GUILDFORD
The Watts Gallery, Compton
Tel.: 048 634 235
Open weekdays 2-6; October-March 2-4; Wed. and Sat. also open 11-1. Closed Thurs.

This gallery, beautifully situated in the country two miles south of Guildford, is devoted to the work of George Frederick Watts. It was built in 1903, the year before Watts's death, and after his death was enlarged and endowed by his widow, herself an artist. Watts, born in 1817, exhibited a precocious talent, instances of which are to be seen in the Gallery, for example a self-portrait aged 17 and an early portrait of his father. In 1843 he won a first prize in the competition for the decoration of the new Houses of Parliament and after this he spent several years in Italy. Upon his return he pursued a career in which allegorical painting and portraiture both played an important part. Initially however he returned in a pessimistic, depressed mood which found expression in works like *Found Drowned* and *The Irish Famine,* both of which are in the Gallery.

As a portraitist his merits were very considerable; the National Portrait Gallery possesses a large collection of his portraits of eminent Victorians, among them *Lord Tennyson, Matthew Arnold, William Morris* and *Cardinal Manning,* but the Watts Gallery also owns several fine examples, among them *Countess Somers;* the artist *Philip Hermogenes Calderon;* and an unfinished one of Garibaldi. There is an interesting portrait of *Ellen Terry as Ophelia*—Watts married her in 1864 when she was only 17 but they parted the following year. *The Genius of Greek Poetry, Paolo and Francesca,* and *The Denunciation of Cain* are examples of his work in middle life when he also began the series of allegorical works which he continued until his death. Among these should be mentioned *The Slumber of the Ages, Love and Death, Love Steering the Boat of Humanity* and *The Sower of the Systems.*

Watts was also a sculptor and among his works here are *Medusa* of about 1844; *Clytie,* about 1868; a study for the massive *Physical Energy* in Kensington Gardens; and another for the huge monument to Tennyson at Lincoln.

HUDDERSFIELD
Huddersfield Art Gallery, Princess Alexandra Walk
Tel.: 0484 21356
Open weekdays 10-5.30 (Friday 10-7.30)

The major part of the collection in this gallery is made up of works by 20th-century British artists. Among the paintings are: *View of Ramsgate* by Sickert; *The Terrace Gardens* by Spencer Gore; *Tea in the Bedsitter* by Harold Gilman; *The Garden at Cookham Rise* by Stanley Spencer; *Milton East Knoyle* by Lucien Pissarro; *Women in a Clothing Factory* by Charles Ginner; *The Empty Champagne Bottle* by Duncan Grant; *Still Life—Flowers* by Matthew Smith; *Berkshire Landscape* by Keith Vaughan; *Ay Chrisostomos* by David Bomberg; and a portrait of Paul McCartney by John Bratby. There are also works by Robert Bevan, Christopher Wood, William Crozier, John Nash, John Minton, Augustus John, Ivon Hitchens, Frances Hodgkins, John Piper, Robert Medley, Joan Eardley, Carel Weight, Julian Trevelyan, Graham Sutherland, Ceri Richards, Anne Redpath, L. S. Lowry, Alan Davie and others. There is a fine group of watercolours by Wilson Steer and the sculpture here includes a bronze bust of Einstein by Epstein, *Falling Warrior* by Henry Moore, and *Mother and Child* by Frank Dobson.

HULL
Ferens Art Gallery, Queen Victoria Square
Tel.: 0482 35711
Open weekdays 10-5.30; Sunday 2.30-4.30

This gallery possesses a remarkable collection of paintings, some of them bequests, some of them bought for the Gallery, occasionally with government assistance or aid from other institutions. This has resulted in the Gallery owning a small cross-section of interesting works by major and lesser masters.

Italian painting is represented firstly by a small panel depicting a saint from the predella of an altarpiece by the late-15th-century artist Bartolommeo di Giovanni. Even more interesting is a large painting of the *Annunciation* by the 17th-century Vicenza artist Francesco Maffei, of whose work there is little to be seen in England. This cannot be said of the other Italian artists here: Canaletto, who is represented by a charming view on the Grand Canal; and Francesco Guardi, whose decorative painting, *Sophonisba Offering her Life to the Saracen King in Exchange for Christian Captives,* is here. This was one of a series painted in collaboration with his brother Gianantonio to decorate a Venetian palace; the subject was taken from Tasso's *Gerusalemme Liberata.*

Joachim Beuckelaer, the painter of *The Fish Market,* a good painting to find in Hull, was from Antwerp and is thought to have been the first artist to depict fish stalls. Also from Antwerp was Denys Calvaert, whose painting of the legendary Danae is here. He, however, went to Italy and became an important member of the early Bolognese school. Nicolas Regnier was another Flemish painter who went to Italy and finished up in Venice. His *Saint Sebastian Succoured by the Holy Women* reveals a Caravaggesque influence.

From the Dutch School comes *Vertumnus and Pomona* by the Utrecht artist Jan van Bylert. *The Expulsion of Hagar* is by Barent Fabritius, who was influenced by Rembrandt and was the younger brother of the gifted Carel; and *'Het Valkhof' Castle at Nijmegen* is by the 17th-century Amsterdam artist Jacob van der Croos. The *Portrait of a Girl* by Frans Hals in its appealing directness contrasts with the greater formality of Bartholomeus Van der Helst's *Portrait of a Girl aged 19,* dated 1643. A *Portrait of a Man* is by Adrian Hanneman, a Dutchman who lived in England from 1623 to 1637 and was much influenced by Van Dyck's English portraits. This is somewhat revealed in this work, dated 1658, which is thought to be possibly a portrait of the poet Andrew Marvell, who at one time was M.P. for Hull.

Of the greatest interest is an *Annunciation* by the 17th-century French painter Philippe de Champaigne. Of equal importance is the lone Spanish work by Ribera, who left Spain to settle in Naples; it is probably one of a series of paintings of ragged philosophers.

English painting is well represented in the Gallery. There is a *Portrait of a Musician* by William Dobson and a charming portrayal of the young Anne Isabella Milbanke, later Lady Byron, by John Hoppner. Hoppner, generally a mediocre artist, received so much favour from George III it was rumoured that he was the King's son. Outstanding in its harmony of colour and mood is *Coast Scene in Picardy* by Richard Bonington. As befits the gallery of a port there are many sea pieces here too, among them works by Willem van de Velde the Younger, Charles Brooking, Isaac Sailmaker. In addition there are a number of paintings of whaling fleets by local artists. Not to be missed are a number of fine paintings of Hull and the Humber by the Hull artist, John Ward, and there is a striking atmospheric depiction of *Princes Dock, Hull* by Atkinson Grimshaw.

There are a number of sculptures in the Ferens Gallery, among them a bust of Lorenzo Bellini, a physician, by the Florentine artist Giovanni Foggini, and works by Epstein, Henry Moore *(Woman and Child in Ladderback Chair* and *Draped Torso),* Barbara Hepworth and Edoardo Paolozzi.

IPSWICH
Ipswich Museums and Art Galleries, High Street
Tel.: 0473 53246

Open weekdays 10-5 (dusk in winter); Sunday 2.30-4.30

The first Ipswich Art Gallery was built in 1880 as an adjunct of the new Corporation Museum and to serve as an exhibition gallery for the local Fine Arts Club. In 1894 the Christchurch Park Estate was purchased by the Corporation and the large house Christchurch was presented to the town by the banker Felix T. Cobbold, later M.P. for Ipswich from 1906 to 1909, and used as premises for a museum. With the continued growth of the collection of pictures a further gallery was built by the Corporation in 1931, the 'Wolsey' gallery, financed partly by a pageant commemorating the 400th year of Cardinal Wolsey's death. Felix Cobbold also bequeathed money for the purchase of pictures and objects which assisted in the enhancement of the collection. As well as the paintings to be found in these galleries there are a number of 17th-century portraits in Ipswich Town Hall and a series of naval battle paintings by the 18th-century marine painter Dominic Serres.

The earliest works in the Ipswich collection are two 15th-century panels dealing with *The Entombment of Christ* by an unknown East Anglian artist. Then comes an interesting portrait of William Carey, dated 1526; he was a descendant of the Beaufort family and married the elder sister of Anne Boleyn. Several portraits are attributed to Cornelius Johnson and a portrait of Sir Peyton Ventris is by John Riley. As befits a gallery situated in Suffolk there is substantial representation of the works of Gainsborough and Constable. Portraits by the former include the early *Tom Peartree;* portraits of Samuel Kilderbee, John Sparrowe, George Dashwood, and the Reverend Richard Canning from the middle or late 1750s; a portrait of William Wollaston of Finborough Hall, at one time M.P. for Ipswich from about 1760; *'Miss Edgar' in Blue* from about the same date; and of Mrs Kilderbee, and of the Duchess of Montague from the 1760s. Other works by Gainsborough include *A Pool in the Woods*, and *View near the Coast*.

Paintings by Constable include the important *The Millstream*, a portrait of his father Golding Constable, and another of his brother Abram. Besides several small landscapes there are two delightful small pictures, *Golding Constable's Flower Garden* and *Golding Constable's Kitchen Garden*, datable to 1815 and evidently painted from the back of the first floor of his father's house. Another painting of interest is a self-portrait by Johnny Dunthorne, Constable's pupil and assistant.

A work from later in the 19th century is Sir John Gilbert's *Cardinal Wolsey Arriving at Leicester Abbey*, dated 1876-7. Wolsey, a native of Ipswich, died at Leicester Abbey and was buried in the same grave as Richard III. A very different painting of about a decade later is Wilson Steer's *Knucklebones, Walberswick*, and among other works by him here are *The Bend of the River Ludlow*, 1906, and *The Black Bow*.

The paintings of local artists are a notable feature of the Ipswich collection. Among those who should be mentioned are George Vincent, a pupil of John Crome's—his *Travelling Tinker* is here; James Stark, also a pupil of Crome; Henry Bright, who studied under John Sell Cotman; Thomas Churchyard; Frederick George Cotman, a nephew of J. S. Cotman; Ernest Crofts; and John Moore. Of modern work there are paintings and prints by Carel Weight, Roger Hilton, William Scott, Michael Ayrton, Terry Frost, Bridget Riley, Josef Albers and Vasarely.

KETTERING
Kettering Art Gallery, Sheep Street
Tel.: 0536 2315
Open weekdays 10-8

The art collection in Kettering had its first tentative beginnings in 1905 but gained vital impetus in 1913 when Sir Alfred East, a successful Royal Academician who was born in the town, presented his collection of his own paintings and watercolours. The collection remained of an almost wholly local nature until 1953, when the Council put into effect a systematic policy of purchasing, upon advice, works by modern artists. These works are being added to every year.

Among the older oil-paintings in the Gallery are: *The Way to the Farm* by James Stark; *Portrait* by John Linnell; *Town by a River* by William Mulready; *The Day's Bag* by William Collins. From the 20th century come *Old London Bridge* by Walter Greaves; *Peaches and Green Bottle* by Mark Gertler; *The Violinist* by Stanley Spencer; *Roses* by Vanessa Bell; *Landscape* by Robert Bevan; *Abstract* by Wyndham Lewis; *Fotheringhay Church* by John Piper; *The Camera Man* by Edward Ardizzone; *Stable Yard* by Edward Bawden; *Bomb Damage, Poplar* by John Minton; *Winter Sea* by Joan Eardley; *Landscape* by Ivon Hitchens; *The Serpent Goes Tick-Tock* by Alan Davie.

KILMARNOCK
Kilmarnock Museum, Dick Institute, Elmbank Avenue
Tel.: 0563 26401

Open weekdays October to April 10-5; May to September 10-8 (Wed. and Sat. 10-5)

This gallery owns a considerable collection of works by Scottish artists, among them Sir Henry Raeburn with two portraits of Mr and Mrs Menzies, Sir David Cameron, Sir James Guthrie, Edward Hornel and Robert Colquhoun. Of European painting there is a *Nativity* attributed to Benjamin Cuyp; a small *Harvesting Scene* by Corot; and a *Treescape* by his pupil Stanislas Lépine. 19th-century English painting includes three views of Hampstead Heath by Constable; *The Gathering Storm* by John Linnell; and from the latter half of the century come *Audience with Agrippa* by Alma-Tadema; *Greek Girls Playing Ball* by Lord Leighton; *Daydreams* by Millais; and *The Monopolist* by William Mulready. From a later period come three works by Brangwyn.

KIRKCALDY
Kirkcaldy Museum and Art Gallery, War Memorial Grounds
Tel.: 0592 2732

Open weekdays 11-5; Sunday 2-5

Kirkcaldy Art Gallery was opened in 1925 as a war memorial gift from John Nairn. From that time a number of pictures have been donated or bequeathed to the Gallery; others have been purchased. In 1964 the John W. Blyth collection, featuring prominently Sickert and the Camden Town Group and the Scottish artists S. J. Peploe and William McTaggart, was purchased with the aid of a number of grants.

Scottish painting, of which the main body of work in the Gallery consists, begins with a portrait of Sir James Stevenson Barnes by Sir Henry Raeburn. Then come a couple of sketches by Wilkie; a large painting by Andrew Geddes, *The Education of Pan;* and *The Triumph of Love* by David Scott. The considerable group of works by McTaggart mostly depict land and seascapes; by George Henry there are two works,

Spring Time and *Lady with a Goldfish,* and other artists of that period, among them Sir David Cameron, Sir James Guthrie, William McGregor and Edward Hornel are all well represented. Paintings by Leslie Hunter and S. J. Peploe, of the group known as the Scottish Colourists, are also extensively displayed.

Of English painting there is *The Garden of Eden* by John Martin. Then come several works by Sickert among them *What Shall We Do for the Rent?, Lobster on Tray,* and *Marche aux Loques, Dieppe.* There is a small work by Wilson Steer, *Farm at Long Crenden;* three paintings by Harold Gilman including *The Thames at Battersea;* four from Spencer Gore including *The Duck Pond* and *The Gravel Pit.* Other English painters here include J. W. Waterhouse with *Dolce Far Niente;* Duncan Grant with two still lives; L. S. Lowry with *An Old Street;* and Frank Brangwyn and Sir William Nicholson. There are a few French pictures, among them a Boudin and a Fantin-Latour; and there are several 19th-century Dutch works by Jacob and Matthew Maris.

LEAMINGTON SPA
Leamington Spa Art Gallery and Museum, Avenue Road
Tel.: 0926 25873
Open weekdays 10.45-12.45; 2.30-5; Thurs. 6-8; Sunday 2.30-5; closed Wednesday afternoons

This collection was founded by Alderman Holt, who also aided in the foundation of the Gallery itself. The collection was augmented by gifts from the Field family and has also benefited from the assistance of the Contemporary Art Society, the Victoria and Albert Museum and other organizations. Among the earliest works to be seen are several late 16th- and 17th-century Dutch works: *The Prodigal Son* by the Utrecht Mannerist painter Abraham Bloemart; *The Landing of the Pilgrims* by Adam Willaerts; *Night Scene,* ascribed to Aert van der Neer; *Princes of the House of Orange* by David Vinckeboons; *Boy with Spear,* ascribed to Nicolaes Maes; *The Halt at the Ruin,* attributed to Nicolaes Berchem; *Self-Portrait by Candlelight* by Godfried Schalcken; and *Wood Scene and River,* attributed to Jacob Ruisdael.

Richard Wilson's *Faustulus Discovering Romulus and Remus* was formerly in the collection of the Duke of Westminster. A painting of *St Peter's Denial* is attributed to Philippe de Champaigne. There is a large group of works by an early 19th-century local artist, Thomas Baker 'of Leamington' or 'landscape Baker', which provide a clear impression of his talent. Also from the 19th century come *A Girl with a Bird on her Shoulder* by Augustus Egg; *The Red Hat* by Sir George Clausen; *Winter's White Silence* by Lucy Kemp Welch; and several seascapes by

Henry Moore. Works of this century include *Pulpit and Candelabra* by Roger Fry; *Venetian Window* by Vanessa Bell; *Portrait of an Old Lady* by Duncan Grant; *Cookham Rise* by Stanley Spencer; *The Mission Room* by L. S. Lowry; *Conversation Piece* by Henry Tonks; *Fish* by Leonard Appelbee; *The Green Walk* by Ivon Hitchens; six etchings by Sickert and a gouache, *Study for Organic Form, 1961,* by Graham Sutherland.

LEEDS
Leeds City Art Gallery and Temple Newsam House
Tel.: 0532 31301
City Art Gallery: Open weekdays 10.30-6.30; Sunday 2.30-5
Temple Newsam House: Open daily 10.30-6.15 (or dusk); Wed. (May-Sept) 10.30-8.30

The Leeds permanent art collection is housed in both of these places and pictures are on occasion transferred from one to the other. The Art Gallery was built in 1888 at a cost of £10,000 from the Queen's Jubilee Fund, by means of which the earliest paintings to be bought for the collection were also acquired. A small number of paintings were already owned by the city; the City Council also provided certain sums for purchases and various gifts were made to the Gallery, most of the acquisitions being by 19th-century British artists. The important Charles Turner Lockwood bequest of 1891 did, however, include works by artists of European origin. The foundation of the Leeds Art Collections Fund in 1913 led to the purchase of a number of important English watercolours and works by living artists. Since that date there have been numerous other bequests, some of them of paintings and watercolours, others of money for the purchase of works of art, and since 1936 there has been an annual grant which has led to an extensive collection of 20th-century British painting. In 1925 a new extension to the Gallery was opened to house the collection bequeathed in 1918 by Sam Wilson; in 1922 Lord Halifax sold the Jacobean Temple Newsam House, situated about 5 miles from the centre of the city, to the Leeds Corporation and in 1948 he presented a part of the Ingram family collection which had been acquired over the last 300 years.

The Italian paintings at Leeds are mainly by 18th-century artists but from earlier periods come *The Temptation of St Jerome* by Vasari, probably painted about 1546; *St John the Baptist* by Guido Reni, reminiscent of his painting of the same subject at Dulwich; *St James the Greater* by the late Roman Baroque artist Carlo Maratta; and *Still Life* by Giuseppe Recco, a 17th-century Neapolitan who specialized in the fish pieces of which this is an example. From the 18th century come two works, personifications of Europe and Africa by the Neapolitan Francesco Solimena, who lived to the age of 90; a series of landscape and battle pieces intended as decorative scenes by Marco Ricci; and *The Triumph of David* by Luca Giordano. By Paolo de Matteis, a pupil of Giordano, is a sketch for the *Choice of Hercules,* a large painting he executed for the 3rd Earl of Shaftesbury to illustrate visually the Earl's essay on that theme. Other works include: *S. Giorgio Maggiore* by Guardi; *Portrait of Sir Thomas Gascoigne* by Pompeo Batoni (this superb portrait is generally on show at Lotherton Hall, a country house near Aberford presented to the city of Leeds in 1968 by Sir Alvary and Lady Gascoigne); *Baptism of Christ* by Francesco Trevisani; *Hector and Andromache* by Pellegrini; two views of Roman ruins by Panini; *View on the Tiber* and *Architectural Fantasy* by another painter of views, Antonio Jolli; *Imaginary Ruins* by the Neapolitan landscapist Leonardo Coccorante; *Laban Seeking his Idols* by Antonio Bellucci; and *Christ and the Adultress* by the late-18th-century Bolognese decorative artist Gaetano Gandolfi.

French paintings are chiefly from the 19th and 20th centuries though there are several battle scenes by the 17th-century Jacques Courtois, called Il Borgognone, and a portrait by P. H. Subleyras of Horatio, Baron Walpole. *A Frightened Horse* is attributed to Géricault, and there are two small landscapes by Corot, two works by Daubigny, and a number of small scenes by Diaz. From Courbet comes *Les Demoiselles de Village,* dated 1851, from Monticelli *The Banquet,* and from Boudin two characteristic sea pieces. There are several works by Fantin-Latour, among them *Madame Léon Maître,* dated 1884. Other paintings include *River Scene* and *Les Champs* by Alfred Sisley; *Moonlight on a Lake* by Harpignies; *Les Bords de la Seine au Printemps* by Stanislas Lépine; *Barges on the Thames,* datable about 1906, by André Derain; *Wells Farm Railway Bridge, Acton, 1907* by Lucien Pissarro; *Honfleur* by Othon Friesz; *Mother and Child* by Bonnard; *Mademoiselle Natanson* by Vuillard; *Le Port de Marseilles* by Albert Marquet; and two works by Francis Picabia, *St Tropez,* dated 1904, and *Notre Dame in the Morning Sun,* 1906.

There are a small number of works by 17th-century Dutch artists: *A Storm off Scheveningen* by Jacob Ruisdael; *Adoration of the Shepherds* by Matthias Stomer; *A Moonlight Scene* by Aert van der Neer; and further pictures by Rachel Ruysch, Jan Weenix and Ludolf Bakhuysen. Flemish painting includes *Portrait of a Man* by Frans Pourbus; *Portrait of Elizabeth, Daughter of James I* by Paul van Somer; two tiny landscapes painted on copper by Paul Brill; and *Strolling Players* by Adriaen Brouwer.

One Spanish painting, *St Sebastian,* attributed fairly firmly to Ribera, distinguishes the collection.

There is ample representation of British portraiture here. Many by anonymous artists, mostly from the 17th century, were presented by Lord Halifax. Others more notable are a portrait of Thomas Howard, Earl of Arundel, by Daniel Mytens; a version of a portrait of Oliver Cromwell by Robert Walker; *A Young Man with Red Hair* by Lely; full-length portraits of William and Mary by Sir Godfrey Kneller; *Portrait of a Lady* by Joseph Highmore; and a portrait of the 5th Viscount Irwin and his wife by Jonathan Richardson. The Irishman Nathaniel Hone is represented by a *Portrait of a Man* and the Scotsman Allan Ramsay by a *Portrait of a Girl.* By Reynolds there are three works: a small portrait of Viscount Duncannon; a portrait of Lady Amelia Hume; and another of Lady Hertford, at one time a close friend of the Prince Regent. By Joseph Wright is a portrait of Samuel Oldknow, and by Sir Thomas Lawrence one of Sir John Beckett. There is also an important group of Ingram family portraits by the German-born Philip Mercier, who lived in York for a few years about 1740.

But there are other kinds of British painting besides portraiture. Of interest are *Coast Scene* by George Morland; a painting of the Irish House of Commons by Francis Wheatley; and several small works including *The Vale of Dedham,* dated 5th September, 1814, by John Constable. The Norwich School of painters is represented by *Scene on the River Yare* by John Sell Cotman; *Wherries on the Yare* and *St Benet's Abbey* by John Crome; and *Landscape* by James Stark. The Yorkshireman Julius Caesar Ibbetson is widely represented by a number of picturesque works, among them *Ullswater* and *Phaeton in a Thunderstorm.* Two works are attributed to Richard Wilson, and there are several animal studies by George Stubbs, and a tiny Turner landscape, done in Devonshire in 1812. A large history painting, *Mary Queen of Scots when an Infant Shown to the French Ambassador by her Mother Mary of Guise,* dated 1842, is characteristic of Benjamin Haydon's work. Among paintings of the Victorian era are three works by Thomas Sidney Cooper; a collection of paintings by Atkinson Grimshaw, including two of Leeds; several by Ruskin's one-time protégé J. W. Inchbold; *The Return of Persephone* by Lord Leighton; *Noah's Sacrifice* by Daniel Maclise; a small version of *The Shadow of Death* by Holman Hunt; a collection of allegorical works by Millais; *The Lady of Shalott* by J. W. Waterhouse; *Artemis* by G. F. Watts; *Harmony in White and Blue* by Whistler; *The Bridesmaid* by Tissot.

Coming to a later generation there is a comprehensive selection of the works of Sickert and Wilson Steer. The thirteen paintings of the former extend from *The Laundry Shop* of 1885 and *Interior of the New Bedford, Camden Town* and *St Jacques, Dieppe* of the 1890s to *The Open Window* and *Juliet and the Nurse* of the 1930s. Among paintings by Wilson Steer are *Golden Evening,* 1914, *The Needles in the Mist,* 1919, *Nude on a Blue Sofa,* 1930, and *Framlingham Castle,* 1933. A number of large decorative works by Sir Frank Brangwyn derive from the collection of Sam Wilson, and there are also many paintings by Sir George Clausen. Among works by members of the Camden Town Group and other artists of that period are *In Sickert's House, Portrait of Spencer Gore,* and *Interior* by Harold Gilman; *Interior with Nude* and *The Balcony, Mornington Crescent* by Spencer Gore; *Royal Ordnance Stores* and *Leeds Canal* by Charles Ginner; *Ferring Grange* and *A Beach Scene* by Charles Condor; *Still Life* by Duncan Grant; *Miss Morris* by Vanessa Bell; *Still Life with Self-Portrait* and *The Pond at Garsington* by Mark Gertler. There is a large portrait of *Dorelia* by Augustus John and a *Portrait of Chloe Bough-ton-Leigh* by Gwen John. From Wyndham Lewis comes *Praxitella;* from William Roberts, *The Dance Club* and *The Family.* Two natives of Yorkshire, Matthew Smith and Edward Wadsworth are much in evidence; from the former come *The Little Seamstress* and *Flowers in a Blue Vase* among others; from the latter *Slump, Requiescat,* and *Dahlia.* Stanley Spencer is represented by a number of works including *The Sisters, Separating Fighting Swans,* and *Christ Entering Jerusalem.* Among the more recent works in the Gallery are *Painting (1950)* by Francis Bacon, *In the Face of the Witch (1955)* by Alan Davie, *Still Life with Guitar* by Ben Nicholson, *The Deposition* by Ceri Richards, *Blue Still Life* by William Scott, *Landscape at Pyles Copse* by Philip Sutton, and *Three Reds* by John Walker. Other 20th-century painters to be found here include Ivon Hitchens, L. S. Lowry, Jack Yeats, Christopher Wood, Carel Weight, John Nash, Paul Nash, Ethel Walker, John Piper, Victor Pasmore, C. R. W. Nevinson, Jacob Kramer, Frank Auerbach, Robyn Denny, Paul Huxley, Mark Lancaster.

The collection of sculpture at Leeds is also of considerable importance, among the works being the 'Hope' Venus by Antonio Canova; *The Wrestler, 1912* by Gaudier-Brzeska; *Reclining Woman 1929* and *Reclining Figure/Bridge Prop 1963* by Henry Moore; *Configuration—Phira* by Barbara Hepworth; and a large mobile, *Chicago Black,* by Alexander Calder.

LEICESTER
Leicester Art Gallery, New Walk
Tel.: 0533 26832-4
Open Monday-Friday 10-5 (April to Sept. 10-6, May to August 10-7); Saturday 10-7; Sunday 2-5

The nucleus of a collection of pictures in Leicester was formed in 1880 by public subscription but it was not until 1885 that the Gallery was opened in the museum buildings, at the same time being granted financial support from the rates. At first mainly 19th-century paintings were acquired but in 1934 a firmer art-collecting policy was established and since that period, although the representation of English painting through the last few hundred years has been a primary concern, there has also been a decided interest in the work of certain foreign schools. Particularly remarkable has been the acquisition of a group of works by German Expressionist painters which has had the result that Leicester is the only town in Great Britain to have a substantial representation of this school.

Among the earliest paintings here are some 16th- and 17th-century portraits by unknown artists of the English school. Painted about 1655 by that ubiquitous artist Sir Peter Lely is a portrait of Sir Thomas Lee, for many years Member of Parliament for Aylesbury. There is a group portrait of Mrs Michell and her children by Thomas Hudson and a rather pleasing profile portrait of Mrs Catharine Swindell by Joseph Wright of Derby. Also by him is a landscape, *High Tor, Matlock*, which was done over a portrait. *Landscape with Bathers* is by Richard Wilson, probably executed between 1770 and 1775. Other versions of this are in the Tate and in Leeds Art Gallery. Also by Wilson is *Head of a Capuchin*, done in Rome in 1752. Painted in 1780 is *The Valley of the Teign, Devonshire* by the West Country artist Francis Towne.

There are many landscapes here by Sir George Beaumont, painter, collector, and friend of Wordsworth, Coleridge, Benjamin Haydon, David Wilkie and Constable. Most famous among them is *Peel Castle in a Storm*, which inspired one of Wordsworth's poems with its familiar stanza:

> *Ah! THEN, if mine had been the Painter's hand,*
> *To express what then I saw; and add the gleam,*
> *The light that never was, on sea or land,*
> *The consecration, and the Poet's dream;*

Other paintings by Beaumont depict scenes in the Lake District or views near his famous house in Leicestershire, Coleorton, which was designed by George Dance. By Constable himself are one of his many views of Hampstead Heath and an interesting, though unfinished *Portrait of a Gentleman*. Here also are *River Scene with Ferry* by Philip de Loutherbourg, a small oil by Bonington, *The Old Jetty, Boulogne* and a painting of *Kilgerran Castle* by Turner dated 1804.

Many 19th-century painters are here. Particularly notable are *The Meeting of Jacob and Rachel* by William Dyce; *Sabrina and her Nymphs* by William Etty; the large circular *Perseus, on Pegasus, Hastening to the Rescue of Andromeda* by Lord Leighton, painted about 1896 and the last picture he worked on before his death. Also not to be overlooked are John Phillip's *The Balcony*, painted in Seville in 1857, *Jerusalem from the Valley of Jehoshaphat* by David Roberts; *A Scene from 'Two Gentlemen of Verona'* by Augustus Egg; a smaller version of *The Railway Station* by W. P. Frith (the original is in Royal Holloway College Gallery); and *Orlando Pursuing the Fata Morgana* by G. F. Watts, who presented it to the Leicester Gallery in 1889.

Of late 19th- and early 20th-century work there is a portrait sketch of Viscount Allenby by J. S. Sargent and from Whistler a small *Nocturne in Blue and Gold* bearing the butterfly device which he frequently used as a signature. Sickert is represented by a view of Dover and a humorous piece, *The Bart and the Bums,* painted about 1930. There are interesting works by Roger Fry and Vanessa Bell and among several works by Duncan Grant is a portrait of Lady Ottoline Morrell, one of the leading figures of the Bloomsbury group. Other notable paintings include *At the Hippodrome* by William Roberts, one of the Vorticist group; *The Fruit Sorters* by Mark Gertler, painted in 1914; *Reclining Nude* by Matthew Smith; *Portrait of Admiral Fisher* by Augustus John; *Nostalgic Landscape* by Paul Nash; the bizarre *Adoration of Old Men* by Stanley Spencer; and there are equally interesting contributions from Robert Bevan, C. R. W, Nevinson, David Bomberg, Graham Sutherland, Dame Ethel Walker, John Piper, Ivon Hitchens, Francis Bacon, Arthur Boyd and Josef Herman.

Recent purchases include an early Italian predella panel, *St John the Baptist Going up into the Wilderness* by Lorenzo Monaco; a *Youthful Bacchus* attributed to Annibale Carracci; and a small grisaille *Assumption of the Virgin* by the 18th-century Venetian Giambattista Pittoni. Here also are *Portrait of an Unknown Gentleman* by Nicolaes Maes; *The Death of Sophonisba* attributed to Nicolas Regnier, a 17th-century Flemish painter influenced by Caravaggio; *A River Scene* by Salomon Ruisdael. 19th-century French works include *En Hiver, Moret-sur-Loing* by Sisley; the excellent *La Rentrée du Troupeau* by Degas; and *La Route Napoléon* by the former racing cyclist Maurice Vlaminck, painted about 1913 when he was very much influenced by Cézanne.

Included among the oil-paintings of the German Expressionists here is *Girl with Black Hair* by Franz Marc, who helped to found the 'Blue Rider' group and who was killed at Verdun in 1916. Also associated with the Blue Rider group was the American Lyonel Feininger, who is represented by *Behind the Church;* and here too is *Coast Scene with Boats* by Max Pechstein, who was connected with the advanced Expressionist group known as *Die Brücke* (The Bridge). Further examples of Expressionist work are to be found in the medium of watercolour. Here are *Southern Landscape* by Erich Heckel, one of the founder-members of *Die Brücke, The Mask* by Emil Nolde, also a member of that group, *The Bridge at Erfurt* by Pechstein, and numerous drawings, watercolours, etchings and woodcuts by Karl Schmidt-Rottluff, another founder-member of *Die Brücke* and an important German Expressionist.

Sculpture in the Gallery includes a small bronze, *Jolly Pegleg* by Ernst Barlach, an Expressionist sculptor. Also here can be found a small study for a *Funeral Monument* by Gaudier-Brzeska, a member of the Vorticist group, a *Head* by Barbara Hepworth, and *Weeping Woman* by Epstein —the model for this work was formerly Whistler's model. The Gallery is also rich in watercolours by English artists such as John Sell Cotman, David Cox, Edward Dayes.

LINCOLN
The Usher Gallery, Lindum Road
Tel.: 0522 27980
Open weekdays 10-5.30; Sunday 2.30-5

This gallery, opened in 1927, is beautifully situated not far from Lincoln Cathedral and was donated by James Ward Usher, jeweller, art lover, and former Sheriff of Lincoln. It was built in the Palladian style by Sir Reginald Blomfield. An additional wing was built in 1959 through the bequest of Miss Ella Curtois and since then there has been the income from the Heslam Trust to be used for the purchase of works of art. Part of the Usher bequest consisted of a collection of jewelled watches, European and Chinese porcelain, and portrait miniatures which are displayed in the Usher Room. There is also a room devoted to a collection of objects (including the manuscript of *In Memoriam*) connected with Lord Tennyson, who was a native of Lincolnshire.

The most famous artist connected with Lincoln was Peter de Wint, who lived there for a large part of his life and married the sister of his painter friend William Hilton, a native of the city who is also represented in the Gallery. The Gallery contains the most important collection of works by de Wint, here being a number of oils, not commonly thought of as his medium, among them several large landscapes and numerous views of Lincoln. There is a small picture of the burning of the old Houses of Parliament of which Turner painted a much more famous work. De Wint's watercolours consist of studies of parts of Lincoln, country scenes, scenes in Wales, Norfolk, etc.

In addition to de Wint's work there are a number of other notable paintings in the Gallery, among them two panels (parts of a triptych) by Gaudenzio Ferrari of *St Mary Magdalene* and *St Catherine of Alexandria*. He was a Lombard painter strongly influenced by Leonardo da Vinci. There is also a large altarpiece, Venetian in origin, of about 1530, of the *Madonna and Child with Saints*. There are a number of watercolours, mostly of Lincolnshire, by other artists; among them two by Turner, *Stamford, Lincs.*, and *Lincoln Cathedral from the Holmes,*

Brayford. Others are by Thomas Girtin and the architect Augustus Pugin. Twentieth-century artists represented here include Vanessa Bell, L. S. Lowry, John Piper and John Bratby.

LIVERPOOL
Sudley Gallery, Mossley Hill Road, Aigburth, Liverpool 18
Tel.: 051 207 1371
Open weekdays 10-5; Sunday 2-5

The large house, Sudley, in which an interesting collection of pictures is housed is to be found in Mossley Hill, a suburb of Liverpool. Built about 1823-4 the house is faced with the red sandstone ubiquitous in the district but the architect is unknown. It was built for a Liverpool corn merchant but in 1883 it was purchased by George Holt, founder of a large shipping line, to be used as his residence and to house the considerable collection of paintings he had built up. In 1944 the house and the paintings were bequeathed to the City of Liverpool by Miss Emma Holt, George Holt's daughter. The collection, like those of a number of other Victorian businessmen, in the main reflects the fairly conservative taste of one man but included are a number of very important paintings, most of which Holt acquired after he had come to live at Sudley.

Undoubtedly the finest example of 18th-century painting in the Gallery is Gainsborough's portrait of *Elizabeth, Viscountess Folkestone,* which is a superb study of an old lady, probably done in 1776 when she was about 65. A portrait of her sister Harriet Marsham, also by Gainsborough, is in the Barber Institute. By Sir Joshua Reynolds there are two fine female portraits, one of *Mrs James Modyford Heywood* dated about 1755, and the other of *Mrs George Gostling* of 1782. A portrait by Romney of the young *Mrs Sargent* is dated 1776 and another picture of a young lady by Sir Thomas Lawrence is probably of Mrs Beauclerk. By Sir Henry Raeburn there is an attractive picture of an unidentified sitter called *Girl Sketching.*

Schloss Rosenau, seat of Queen Victoria's husband Prince Albert of Coburg, provides the subject for a painting by Turner which he exhibited in 1841 after having visited the scene in September 1840 several months after Queen Victoria's marriage. This picture was viciously attacked when first shown, *The Times* calling it 'a picture that resembles nothing in nature but eggs and spinach'; a defence of the work had to await Ruskin's publication of *Modern Painters* in 1843 where he completes an extended panegyric of the painting with the sentence, 'It is in this power of saying everything and yet saying nothing too plainly that the perfection of art here as in all other cases consists.' Another work by Turner, *The Wreck Buoy,* is authoritatively thought to be an early work

10 *Pollok House, Glasgow*

11 *The Dulwich College Picture Gallery, London*

12 *Ashmolean Museum, Oxford*

13 *Walker Art Gallery, Liverpool*

painted about 1809 and subsequently repainted for the Academy of 1849 because of his dissatisfaction with it. Ruskin described it as 'the last oil which he painted before his noble hand forgot its cunning'. *Margate Harbour* is another Turner, painted about 1840, and *Emigrants Embarking at Margate* is thought to be of about the same date.

Fishing Boats in a Calm is a superb work by Richard Parkes Bonington and *Calais Pier* is the work of David Cox. There are landscape scenes by John Linnell, Thomas Sidney Cooper and Thomas Creswick, those of the latter painter including *Landscape, Morning (Crossing the Stream)* and *Hartlepool,* as well as several set in Ireland. The celebrated 19th-century animal painter Sir Edwin Landseer is represented by a number of paintings, among them *Taking the Deer: The Duke of Atholl with Foresters* and *Dog with Slipper.* Other landscape painters here include J. R. Herbert, Copley Fielding, Clarkson Stanfield; in addition there are several works by French artists notably *La Vache à L'Abreuvoir* by Corot, *Paysage d'Auvergne* by Auguste Bonheur and *Le Retour du Moulin* by Rosa Bonheur.

A genre painting manifesting the influence of some 17th-century Dutch art is *The Jew's Harp* by Sir David Wilkie—'argumentative, unclassical, prudent, poor and simple, but kindled by a steady flame of genius', as Haydon described him in the days when this work was painted. Another scene of contemporary life is William Mulready's *A Dog of Two Minds,* and from William Collins, the father of the novelist Wilkie Collins, comes a mixed genre and landscape subject, *Poor Travellers at the Door of a Capuchin Convent near Naples.* W. P. Frith's *Dr Primrose in the Churchyard* is a preparatory sketch for a work derived from Goldsmith's *The Deserted Village;* Goldsmith figures again in Edward Ward's *Dr Johnson Perusing the Manuscript of 'The Vicar of Wakefield' as the Last Resource for Rescuing Goldsmith from the Hands of the Bailiffs.* (Boswell relates that Johnson obtained £60 from the booksellers for the manuscript.)

There is a group of works by the Pre-Raphaelites and some of their associates in the Gallery. *The Finding of the Saviour in the Temple,* dated 1862, is a study for the larger picture in Birmingham Art Gallery by Holman Hunt. *Ferdinand Lured by Ariel,* was a preparatory sketch by Millais for a painting of 1849-50, and by him also is *Landscape, Hampstead* and an imaginary portrait of Swift's Vanessa. From Rossetti there is a fragment, *The Two Mothers,* cut from a larger work, *Hist, said Kate the Queen* which he abandoned about 1852. Burne-Jones is represented by a watercolour, *An Angel Playing the Flageolet,* and there are a number of paintings by a late follower of the Pre-Raphaelites, John Melhuish Strudwick: *Circe and Scylla, Love's Palace, Oh, Swallow, Swallow,* and *St Cecilia,* the latter painted for Mr Holt as a companion to the Rossetti work. *The Garden of Gethsemane* is a small work by

William Dyce; *Gypsy Sisters of Seville* is by John Phillip; *A Sunny Corner; Weaving the Wreath; Study at a Reading Desk* are all by Lord Leighton, the model in the latter being the child actress Connie Gilchrist who later became a star at the Gaiety Theatre. Other artists represented include Alma-Tadema, Frederick Goodall, and Henry Stacey Marks.

Walker Art Gallery, William Brown Street

Tel.: 051 207 1371
Open weekdays 10-5; Sunday 2-5

The building of the Walker Art Gallery is owed to the munificence of Alderman Andrew Barclay Walker, a prosperous local brewer who was later knighted. Walker became Mayor of Liverpool in 1873 and celebrated his tenure of this office by offering to build an art gallery for the city at his own expense. The Gallery, at that time primarily designed for the holding of the annual autumn exhibition, was duly built and opened to the public in 1877. Annual exhibitions had been a feature of Liverpool life for many years, going back even further than the foundation of the Liverpool Academy of Arts in 1810. From that date they became a regular occasion until 1867 and with the opening of the Walker Gallery the autumn exhibition resumed its importance for both local and national artists and as a social event in Liverpool life. Though the housing of the annual exhibition was the main purpose of the Gallery it was not long before the nucleus of a permanent collection began to be formed through bequests and through the purchase by the Corporation of works from the exhibitions. Acquisitions were however wholly conventional, limited to the anecdotal-type paintings of the latter part of the last century, and the Gallery eschewed completely the newer work which was being done under the influence of French Impressionism. Narrow though this was at the time, with a revived interest in Victorian painting some of the early works purchased are of considerable interest to today's visitor.

Foreign pictures were gradually added to the collection. In 1895 there was a bequest of mostly early Italian works from Alderman P. H. Rathbone. But the Gallery ultimately benefited most from its acquisition of William Roscoe's collection of early Italian and Flemish painting. This widely cultivated man, son of an innkeeper and market gardener, developed a profound interest in the history of art during the last decades of the 18th century, publishing a widely-acclaimed book, *The History of Lorenzo de' Medici*, in 1796. He began collecting 'primitive' works in the very early years of the 19th century long before the much-vaunted activity of Prince Albert in this direction. In 1818-19 Roscoe suffered financial losses, was declared bankrupt, and was obliged to sell his collection. A considerable number of these early Italian works came into the possession of the Liverpool Royal Institution, which for some years made purchases and sustained a collection itself. In 1893, and again in 1915 and 1942 large sections of the Institution's collection were placed in the Walker Art Gallery but it was not until 1948 that it all passed into the hands of the Liverpool Corporation. A bequest from Lord Wavertree in 1932 and an annual grant from the City Council a little earlier enabled the Gallery to begin the purchase of pictures which would provide a representative history of British painting. More recently the policy has also been to augment the collection of foreign painting with the purchase of both modern paintings and those from previous centuries.

One of the earliest English paintings in the Gallery is a portrait of Henry VIII, derived from Holbein's picture in Whitehall Palace, by a follower of Holbein. There is a portrait of Sir Edward Cecil by Paul van Somer, a Flemish painter who successfully worked in England from 1616 onwards, and a portrait of Queen Elizabeth after Nicholas Hilliard. The line of British portraiture continues with a *Portrait of a Lady* by Cornelius Johnson; *The Earl of Northumberland* by Sir Peter Lely, one of many paintings he executed for this nobleman; *A Portrait of his Son* by Jonathan Richardson; *The Duchess of Chandos* by Joseph Highmore; *Elizabeth Cotman,* dated 1740, and *Emily, Countess of Kildare,* dated 1765, by Allan Ramsay; *Ann Stirling* by Sir Henry Raeburn; *Sir Robert Clayton,* probably painted about 1769 by Gainsborough; *The Family of Sir William Young* by Zoffany; and a very pleasing portrait of *Miss Elizabeth Ingram* by Reynolds.

There is an interesting example of the work of William Dobson, Van Dyck's successor as Court Painter, *The Executioner with the Head of John the Baptist,* and certainly impressive is a large canvas by Hogarth, *David Garrick as Richard III. The Card Party* is by Gavin Hamilton, who specialized in this sort of piece, and there are several paintings by Joseph Wright of Derby, who despite his nomenclature spent quite a time in Liverpool. Two of his pictures are landscapes set in Italy, *The Convent at Cosimato* and *Easter Monday at Rome,* the latter a view of the Castel Sant'Angelo full of light effects with fireworks; another is on a romantic theme, *The Old Man and Death,* the subject derived from one of *Aesop's Fables;* and the fourth, *The Lady in Comus,* was originally in the collection of Josiah Wedgwood. There are also some fine examples of the work of George Stubbs: *James Stanley* (a recently acquired early portrait); *Three Brood Mares at Grass; The Lincolnshire Ox; A Green Monkey; Horse Frightened by a Lion;* and *Molly Longlegs and Her Jockey.* The American painter Benjamin West is represented by a version of one of his famous works, *The Death of Nelson.* There are two paintings by Richard Wilson set in Wales—*Valley of the Mawddach* and *Snowdon from Llyn Nantlle.* From John Constable comes *Seashore with Fishermen,* painted about 1816, and of Turner's works there are *Linlithgow Palace,* which was exhibited in his studio in 1812, *Rosenau* and *Margate Harbour.*

There are numerous other 19th-century paintings. Among them are *Flying the Kite—A Windy Day,* 1851, by David Cox; *The Last Man* and an *Italian Landscape* by John Martin; *Bathsheba at the Bath* by David Wilkie; *Dog with Slipper* and several portraits, among them one of Sir Walter Scott, by Landseer; *A Shooting Party* and *A Mastiff* by Richard Ansdell; *Bethlehem* by Edward Lear; *A New Light in the Harem* by Frederick Goodall; *Ruth and Naomi* by P. H. Calderon; *The Night before Naseby* by Augustus Egg; *The Death of Nelson* by Daniel Maclise; *The Last Load Home* by John Linnell; and the famous *When Did You Last See Your Father?* by W. F. Yeames. Most interesting perhaps are the paintings of the Pre-Raphaelites and their associates, and the work of the painters of the latter part of the century. Millais's first fully Pre-Raphaelite work, *Lorenzo and Isabella,* painted in 1849, is here; a much later and inferior painting by him, *The Martyr of the Solway,* is also here. From Holman Hunt comes a study for *The Eve of St Agnes* which is in the Guildhall Gallery, and *The Triumph of the Innocents* of 1883-4. Hunt here visualized the Holy Family being accompanied on the Flight into Egypt by the murdered children and the rather extraordinary bubbles to be seen in the picture signified 'magnified globes which image the thoughts rife in that age in the minds of pious Jews'. From Rossetti comes *Dante's Dream at the Time of the Death of Beatrice,* dated 1871, a large replica of the watercolour in the Tate Gallery; Jane Morris was the model for Beatrice. From Ruskin's protégé John Brett comes *The Stonebreaker,* exhibited at the Royal Academy in 1858; Ruskin wrote of it ' . . . it is a marvellous picture and may be examined inch by inch with delight.' Some of Brett's later seascapes are also in the Gallery. Of interest also are the works of W. L. Windus, a Liverpool painter influenced by the Pre-Raphaelites. Among them are *Bishop Shaxton Interviewing Anne Askew in Prison; Cranmer Endeavouring to Obtain a Confession of Guilt from Catherine Howard;* a self-portrait; and *Burd Helen,* a painting given qualified praise by Ruskin. Also to be seen are *The Coat of Many Colours* by Ford Madox Brown, and *Judith and Holofernes* by J. R. Herbert. By Burne-Jones there is a large exotic watercolour, *Sponsa de Libano,* and a study for *Sleeping Knights.* From G. F. Watts are four works depicting the *Four Horsemen of the Apocalypse,* two paintings of *Eve,* and studies for the well-known painting of *Hope* and for *Found Drowned.* Very much in evidence are the painters of classical themes: E. J. Poynter with *Psyche in the Temple of Love* and *Faithful unto Death;* J. W. Waterhouse with *Echo and Narcissus;* and Albert Moore with his colourful paintings filled with languid girls, *Seashells* and *A Summer Night;* Lord Leighton is represented by *An*

Elegy, shown at the Royal Academy in 1889. Another work which achieved great popularity was Henry Holiday's *Dante and Beatrice.*

In a very different vein are W. R. Sickert's paintings: a fine *Interior of the Old Bedford Theatre* (this music hall was burned down in 1889), *Bathers at Dieppe,* and *Fancy Dress.* From Wilson Steer comes *The Wye at Chepstow* and other members of the Camden Town Group are also represented: Harold Gilman by *Interior with Flowers* and *Mrs Mounter;* Spencer Gore by *The Garden at Garth House. Under the Hammer* by Robert Bevan should also be noted. Other British works include Augustus John's *Two Jamaican Girls;* J. D. Innes's *Ranunculus; Mount St Hilarion* by David Bomberg; Stanley Spencer's *Saturday Afternoon* and *Villas at Cookham;* Matthew Smith's *The Black Hat;* Victor Pasmore's *Still Life with Skull;* Paul Nash's *Landscape of the Moon's Last Phase,* 1944; Ivon Hitchens's *The Great Mill, Fordingbridge;* and Lucian Freud's *Paddington Interior.*

As has already been indicated Italian painting in the Gallery is of the greatest interest. Here, for example, is an exquisite painting of a very rarely treated subject, *Christ Discovered in the Temple by his Parents* by the Sienese painter Simone Martini. It his last dated work (1342) and the only one known from the period when he worked in Avignon. From Siena too, from the studio of Vecchietta, comes another beautiful work, *St Bernardino Preaching.* Also outstanding are two fragments of fresco by Spinello Aretino, from the Church of the Carmine in Florence, one of *Salome,* the other of the *Infant St John Presented to Zacharias.* Other Florentine paintings here are *Virgin and Child with Saints* by Neri di Bicci, painted about 1460, and the *Martyrdom of St Sebastian* by Bartolommeo di Giovanni. A very fine work is an illustration of the birth of John the Baptist from a book illumined for an order of hermits at Florence by an artist, also a monk, identified as Don Silvestro dei Gherarducci. There are many other panels by minor Florentine masters or deriving from the workshops of painters such as Lorenzo di Credi or Filippino Lippi, about which there is little certainty of attribution but much pleasure to be gained in the viewing of them. Later developments in Florentine painting are to be seen in the work of several Mannerist painters: *Portrait of a Young Man with a Helmet* by Rosso Fiorentino; *The Preaching of John The Baptist* by Balducci; and *Saints Peter, Paul, and Jerome* by a follower of Vasari. From Umbria there is a *Birth of St John the Baptist* from the studio of Verrocchio, attributed to the young Perugino; and a *Virgin and Child* by Signorelli. From Ferrara comes another great work, a *Pietà,* part of a predella panel by Ercole de' Roberti. The black-clad Virgin, the background detail, and the stark figure of Christ combine to make this a very impressive painting. Also from Ferrara, from the studio of Garofalo, come *The Virgin and Child* and *The Circumcision.* The earliest Venetian painting appears to be a

Portrait of a Young Man from the studio of Giovanni Bellini. Two works, a *Virgin and Child* and a *Virgin and Child with Saints Mary Magdalen, Nicholas and Francis,* are by Vincenzo Catena, for a time the partner of Giorgione. *The Finding of Moses* is from the workshop of Veronese, *The Dead Christ* from a follower of Palma Giovane; a robust *Country Scene* is by Jacopo Bassano, and *The Court of Heaven* is attributed to Domenico Tintoretto.

Italian 17th-century painting is represented by a typically romantic work by Salvator Rosa, *Landscape with Hermit,* and by several other Neapolitan painters. *The Nativity, The Adoration of the Magi, The Marriage at Cana,* and *Christ in the House of Simon* are all by Mattia Preti; *The Rape of Europa* is by Bernardo Cavallino; a later work, *The Birth of the Baptist,* is by Francesco Solimena; and another *Adoration of the Magi* is by Luca Giordano. Of the 18th-century Roman school is *Ruins of Rome* by Pannini. From 18th-century Venice are two allegorical figures in grisaille, *Merit* and *Abundance* by Francesco Guardi or his brother Gianantonio. Among the Italian group of paintings which belonged to William Roscoe and which hold considerable interest for the visitor are 39 portraits of famous men painted by artists of the North Italian school about 1600. Here among others are Cosimo and Lorenzo de' Medici, Isabella d'Este, Henry VIII, Erasmus, Leonardo Bruni, and Marsilio Ficino.

Of Netherlandish painting perhaps the most important example is the triptych *The Descent from the Cross,* a copy of a lost work by Robert Campin, who is now generally accepted to have been the Master of Flemalle. This is no place to go into the picture's art-historical problems; enough to say that it is certainly a fine work possibly from the hand of the young Rogier van der Weyden and painted during the first half of the 15th century. Other interesting works are an *Entombment* by the Master of the Virgo inter Virgines; *Martyrdom of St Lawrence* from the Master of the Groot Adoration, a painter from Antwerp; *Portrait of a Young Man* by Jan Mostaert; and *Massacre of the Innocents* by a follower of Bernard van Orley. Later Flemish painting is magnificently represented by a beautiful Rubens, *The Virgin and Child with St Elizabeth and John the Baptist,* painted in the early 1630s and formerly in the collection of the Dukes of Devonshire. There is also a portrait of the Infanta Isabella-Clara Eugenia, the Regent of the Netherlands, from the studio of Van Dyck, a variation on an original portrait by Rubens.

In the collection of Dutch painting is a self-portrait by Rembrandt, *Portrait of the Artist as a Young Man,* thought to have been executed about 1629. This, like the portrait of the artist's mother at Windsor, was in Charles I's collection and was thus one of the first paintings by Rembrandt to come to England. There are some good pictures by some of Rembrandt's pupils and followers: *The Angel Appearing to Hagar* by

Ferdinand Bol; *The Betrothal* by Gerrit Willem Horst; *Portrait of a Bearded Man* by Carel Fabritius, painted 1650-2; *Portrait of an Oriental,* attributed to Govaert Flinck; *Portrait of a Woman as Magdalen* by Paulus Bor. Of Dutch landscape painting there are among others a typically fine *River Scene with Ferry Boat* by Salamon Ruisdael, a *River Scene* by Jan van Goyen, and a *Hawking Party* by Philips Wouwerman. Another interesting Dutch work, artist unknown, is *The Butcher's Shop,* a subject frequently treated by Dutch painters, the most notable example being the Rembrandt in the Louvre.

Probably the earliest example of German painting in the Gallery is a triptych by the Master of the Aachen altarpiece of which the central panel of the *Crucifixion* is on loan from the National Gallery. The two wings are of *Pilate Washing his Hands* and *Lamentation over the Dead Christ. Mercenary Love,* inscribed with a monogram and the date 1527, is by Hans Baldung Grien who from 1502 to 1506 worked in the studio of Dürer. *The Nymph of the Fountain* is by Lucas Cranach the Elder, and there is a portrait of Margaret Rauschen, probably by one of his followers. Leaping forward 250 years there is a self-portrait painted in Florence in 1774 by the neo-classical artist Anton Rafael Mengs who spent most of his working life in Rome. Later still comes *Cottage Interior* by Max Liebermann, the principal Impressionist painter in Germany.

From the French school comes a much deteriorated *Lamentation over the Dead Christ* of about 1500. Then there is a charming *Portrait of a Lady with a Parakeet* of about 1520-30. She is thought to be Marguerite de Valois, sister of Francis I, and the painting to derive from the workshop of Clouet. A *Landscape with Arcadian Shepherds,* very much in the manner of Nicholas Poussin, is probably by one of his Roman followers. *Landscape with Pyramus and Thisbe* is by Gaspar Dughet. To the 18th-century painter Jean-Honoré Fragonard belongs a fine *Head of an Old Man,* and there is a *Landscape with Figures* by de Loutherbourg, who later in his career lived in England. *The Ruins of Holyrood Chapel* is by Louis Daguerre, who gave his name to a form of photography. *Napoleon Crossing the Alps* is by Paul Delaroche, who hero-worshipped Napoleon and painted this subject many times. His pupil Adolphe Monticelli has here a group of five paintings, among them *Ladies in a Garden* and *Scene from Bocaccio. Christ Tempted by Satan* is a rare example in this country of the work of Ary Scheffer. From Courbet comes a lovely seascape, *Marée Basse à Trouville,* and *Landscape, Ville d'Avray* is by Corot, Painted about 1860. *The Murder* is interesting as an example of the early work of Cézanne. From Monet comes one of his winter scenes, *Break-up of the Ice on the Seine, near Bennecourt,* probably painted in 1893; and there is a small Seurat, *Maisons Blanches, Ville d'Avray,* painted about 1882 before his great pointilliste works. Among other paintings are *Woman Ironing* by Degas; *Madame Hessel au Sofa* by Vuillard; a striking portrait, *L'Italienne,* by André Derain; *Les Rochers Roses* by Maurice Denis; *Le Pont* by Matisse; and *Environs de Rouen* by Vlaminck.

Spanish painting is sparsely represented; *The Virgin and Child in Glory,* dated 1673, is characteristic of Murillo, and there is *St Francis in Ecstasy* by Gutierrez, a late-17th-century artist.

LONDON
Bethnal Green Museum, Cambridge Heath Road, London E2 9PA
Tel.: 01-980 2415
Open weekdays 10-6; Sunday 2.30-6

This museum is a branch of the Victoria and Albert Museum and its association with the parent body is indeed close as its very structure was once part of the temporary buildings erected in 1856 for the South Kensington Museum, the predecessor of the Victoria and Albert. The building, transferred to its present site in the East End of London and opened in 1872, is now the most important surviving example of the type of iron and glass architecture used by Joseph Paxton when he built the Crystal Palace. This structure was designed by Major-General Scott, the designer of the Albert Hall, and when moved was encased in brick with a glass and slate roof. The mosaic frieze on the exterior was designed by F. W. Moody. The Museum is particularly remarkable for its collection of dolls and dolls' houses and is also rich in collections of costume, textiles, furniture, silver and pottery. But also here is a very important collection of sculpture by Auguste Rodin, much of which was given by him to the Victoria and Albert Museum in 1914, while other works have been lent by the Tate Gallery. A number of the works arose out of Rodin's project *The Gates of Hell* for the Museum of Decorative Arts in Paris.

Some of the works are of bronze, others of marble, and there are one or two plaster casts. Most notable are Rodin's first major statue, *The Age of Bronze* of 1875, *The Prodigal Son* (1885-7), *St John the Baptist,* and *Cybele.* There are two busts of the Duchesse de Choiseul, two of Camille Claudel, the sculptress whom Rodin loved, and two heads of Balzac, preparatory studies for a commemorative statue. A marble of *Cupid and Psyche* was among those given to the Victoria and Albert too, and a plaster cast of the *Metamorphoses of Ovid* was given by Rodin to the poet W. E. Henley who championed him. Interesting also are two lithograph portraits of Rodin by Renoir and William Rothenstein.

Other sculptors are also represented in the Museum, among them being Jean-Baptiste Carpeaux; Jules Balou with several versions of

Charity, a *Seated Lady*, and *A Peasant Woman Nursing a Baby;* Anton-Louis Barye; the Belgian Sculptor Constantin Meunier; and Canova,
who is represented by a bust of Napoleon.

Courtauld Institute Galleries, Woburn Square, London W.C.1.

Tel.: 01-580 1015
Open weekdays 10-5; Sunday 2-5

In this gallery is to be found one of the most enjoyable collections in the
British Isles. It is situated, as befits its position as the gallery of the
University of London, in Bloomsbury very close to Senate House and
other University buildings and within a short distance of the British
Museum. The Gallery is housed on the top floor of a building which it
shares with the Warburg Institute. The atmosphere greeting the visitor,
contributed to by the furniture and carpets collected and donated by
Viscount Lee of Fareham, is exceedingly pleasing and conducive to a
leisurely examination of works of art of the highest quality and ranging
through vastly different periods.

The foundation of the collection is owed to the generosity of Samuel
Courtauld, the textile manufacturer, who, with the advice and
collaboration of Viscount Lee, founded the Courtauld Institute of Art in
1931 and shortly after gave his house in Portman Square, built by Robert
Adam, to be the home of the Institute. Both Courtauld and Viscount Lee
gave the bulk of their collections to the University of London and since
1958 when the Courtauld Institute Galleries in Woburn Square were
opened the collection has been accessible to public view. Courtauld gave
a large part of his collection, consisting mainly of Impressionist works
gathered together during the 1920s, to a trust for the University in
1931—more paintings were also acquired at his death in 1947. In 1933
the University was further enriched by a bequest of paintings and other
works of art from Roger Fry and in 1952 by a gift of Old Master
drawings collected by Sir Robert Witt. 1966 saw the bequest of the
collection of early Italian paintings formed by Thomas Gambier Parry
during the middle of the 19th century and in 1967 the Gallery acquired
important examples of English landscape watercolours from the William
Spooner bequest.

In the first room of the Gallery, divided as it is into three sections, the
Lee collection and the Gambier Parry collection of 14th- and 15th-
century paintings are to be found. Among the first group of these can be
seen an exquisite panel of *The Crucified Christ with Donors* attributed to
Simone Martini and an interesting triptych of 1360-75, the *Estouteville
Triptych*, which appears to be English. The centre panel bears a coat of
arms probably belonging to a Norman family settled in England. Among

other paintings in this section are *Madonna and Child* by Barnaba da Mòdena; the central panel of a triptych by Paolo Veneziano, an early Venetian primitive painter; *The Birth of St Augustine* by Antonio Vivarini, who came from a family of 15th-century Venetian painters; *Noli Me Tangere* from the school of Giotto; *Madonna and Child Enthroned* by Guariento; *St Catherine of Bologna* by the Master of the Baroncelli Portraits; and a 13th-century *Coronation of the Virgin,* the earliest known Italian representation of the subject, by Guido da Siena, the somewhat nebulous founder of the Sienese school.

In the second section of Room 1 is a large display of ivories and majolica from the Gambier Parry collection. On the walls are 14th- and 15th-century paintings from the same collection, all of the greatest interest and most in a fine state of preservation and representing the Florentine, Sienese, Lucchese and Rimini schools. Particularly noteworthy are two very fine paintings of the Annunciation from 15th-century Florence, one of them being by Francesco Pesellino. Among the paintings in the third section of the room, also from the Gambier Parry collection, are three predella panels of *The Dead Christ with Saints* from the circle of Fra Angelico; and two further predella panels, *The Visitation* and *The Adoration of the Kings* from an altarpiece by Lorenzo Monaco, probably painted about 1405. At one time attributed to Masaccio but now thought to be by an unnamed Tuscan painter are three panels telling the little-known story of St Quiricus and St Julitta, a child and his mother martyred by the Romans for their conversion to Christianity.

Room 2 is devoted to further examples of the Gambier-Parry collection of glass, ivories, brass, majolica and enamels, together with a number of marble reliefs, one of the *Madonna and Child with Angels* by Mino da Fiesole, and two others in the style of Andrea del Verrocchio and Rossellino respectively. On the walls are a polyptych and a panel of *St Peter* attributed to the early 14th-century Florentine artist Bernardo Daddi, a follower of Giotto. Of great beauty is a *St Julian* by a Sienese artist of about 1340. Another important painting in the room is a large panel from an altarpiece of the *Coronation of the Virgin* by Lorenzo Monaco, one of the painters of the style known as International Gothic. Two other small panels should also not be missed; the first, *God the Father in the Attitude of Benediction,* is usually attributed to Cosimo Rosselli, a Florentine painter of the second half of the 15th century; and the second, a *Madonna and Child* which, it has been proposed, may be an early work of Andrea del Verrocchio, later to be the master of Leonardo. Also here is *The Creation* by Albertinelli, for a time an associate of Andrea del Sarto, and this is flanked by *The Holy Family* by Bartolommeo Montagna, a painter from Vicenza. Lastly there is a *Holy Family with Saint John and St Elizabeth* by the Ferrarese painter called

Garofalo. It appears that at one time this work belonged to Charles I, whose cipher is to be found on the back.

Rooms 3 and 4 contain the collections donated by Lord Lee. There is an excellent example of the work of Rubens, *The Descent from the Cross*, a preliminary study—but a highly finished one which repays careful examination—for the central panel of an altarpiece which Rubens executed for Antwerp Cathedral in 1612. From the studio of Velazquez comes a small *Philip IV on Horseback* related to the much larger one in the Prado. A representation of *Charity* by the French 17th-century painter Jacques Blanchard hangs near a very fine small painting by Veronese of *The Baptism of Christ* which may have been a study for an altarpiece. A focus of attention in Room 3 is a painting by Botticelli of the *Holy Trinity with St John the Baptist and Mary Magdalen and Tobias and the Angel*. It is surmised that this was possibly an altarpiece, painted 1490-4 for a convent for penitent courtesans. Van Dyck's *Christ on the Cross* also hangs here and Giovanni Bellini's *Assassination of St Peter Martyr* is a smaller version of a similar painting in the National Gallery. There is a fascinating anthropomorphic detail in the picture where the axed trees are depicted as bleeding just like the human victims. A large panel by Leonardo's follower Bernardino Luini, *The Madonna and Child with St John the Baptist, St Antoninus and a Female Donor* is the most important example of this painter's work in England. Three portraits, one of an unidentified sitter, the second *Portrait of a Man* attributed to Joos van Cleve, the third of an old man and a younger man by William Dobson, are perhaps surpassed in interest by an extraordinary allegorical portrait by Hans Eworth of the merchant adventurer Sir John Luttrell. One outstanding work in the room is a *Madonna of Humility* by Andrea del Sarto. This was at Petworth from the 17th century onwards; recent cleaning has revealed its authenticity, which was previously doubted because of extensive overpainting. Among other paintings in the room are *The Woman Taken in Adultery* by L'Ortolano; *Lamentation over the Dead Christ* by Marco Palmezzano; a fragment from an altarpiece by Cima da Conegliano; *Moses and the Burning Bush*, attributed to Giorgione but most unlikely to be his work; and an *Adam and Eve*, dated 1526, by Lucas Cranach the Elder with the winged dragon signature he used on so many of his paintings.

Room 4 contains a large group of portraits from the Lee collection, most of them 18th-century although there is a 17th-century portrait by Sir Peter Lely of Sir Thomas Thynne, heir to Longleat, and one dating from 1536 of an unknown lady by a painter much influenced by Holbein. The portrait George Romney painted of the short-lived Georgiana, Lady Greville hangs beside Goya's portrait of the liberal minister Don Francisco de Saavedra. Other portraits include *A Young Woman* by Jacques van Oost the Elder; *Dr Daniel Lysons* by Tilly Kettle; *Mrs Malcolm* by

Sir Henry Raeburn; a *Portrait of a Soldier* by Allan Ramsay; *Queen Charlotte* by Sir William Beechey; *Charles Tudway* by Gainsborough; and his excellent *Portrait of the Artist's Wife* from the Courtauld collection.

Now the visitor reaches the rooms for which the Courtauld Galleries are most widely known. These rooms provide remarkable examples of Impressionist and particularly Post-Impressionist art. In Room 5 an outstanding work by Daumier, entirely characteristic of his style, is *Don Quixote and Sancho Panza,* one of the earliest works to be acquired by Samuel Courtauld. Three works by Degas are here, an oil, *Two Dancers on the Stage,* and two pastels, *Woman Drying Herself* and *Woman at a Window.* One of the best-known pictures in the collection also has a theatrical theme—*La Loge* by Renoir, exhibited in the first Impressionist Exhibition in Paris in April 1874. Two famous paintings by Manet are also in this room, *Le Déjeuner sur l'Herbe*—a smaller version of the large painting in the Louvre which was an outstanding exhibit at the Salon des Refusés of 1863 and *A Bar at the Folies-Bergère,* Manet's last important work, dated 1882. The core of the Impressionist school is represented in this room by Monet's *Autumn at Argenteuil* of 1873 and his *Vase of Flowers* painted in 1882, Camille Pissarro's superb *Quays at Rouen* of 1883, and Alfred Sisley's *Snow at Louveciennes* and *Boats on the Seine.*

The art of Cézanne is here represented most remarkably by several landscapes: the first, *The Étang des Soeurs, at Osny,* painted in 1877 while Cézanne was with Pissarro at Pontoise; then the *Trees at the Jas de Bouffan*—Cézanne's home—painted in 1885-7; thirdly *Montagne Sainte Victoire,* one of Cézanne's favourite themes and painted 1886-8; and finally *The Lake of Annecy,* painted in the summer of 1896. Other works by Cézanne here are *The Card Players,* one of several versions of this subject, *Man Smoking a Pipe, Pot of Flowers and Pears,* and *Still Life with a Plaster Cast,* painted 1895.

Room 6 contains four works by Georges Seurat: *A Young Woman Holding a Powder-Puff*—the young woman was Seurat's mistress; *The Bridge at Courbevoie; Gravelines;* and a study for *'Le Chahut'.* These were all painted between 1886 and 1890. Here too is *St Tropez* by Seurat's follower Paul Signac. Pissarro and Monet are here again, the former with *Penge Station,* painted when he was a refugee in London in 1871 after the Franco-Prussian War, the latter with the almost too beautiful *Antibes* of 1888. There are two more works by Renoir, a portrait of the famous dealer and friend of the Impressionists Ambroise Vollard done in 1908, and the powerful *Woman Tying her Shoe,* painted in 1918, the year before his death. Van Gogh is also represented by two works painted in 1889 the year before his death, a *Self-Portrait with Bandaged Ear* and *Peach Trees in Blossom.* Two interesting paintings from Gauguin's Tahiti period, painted within a very short time of each other in 1897, are also in this room; they are called *Te Reroia* (Day-dreaming) and *Nevermore*. 'Not the raven of Edgar Allen Poe,' wrote Gauguin, 'but the bird of the devil that is keeping watch ... ' This painting was once in the collection of the composer Frederick Delius. A marble bust of his wife by Gauguin, done in 1877, is also here as well as a painting of *Haystacks* executed at Pont-Aven in 1889. Other paintings in this room include two canvases by Toulouse-Lautrec, *The Tête-à-tête Supper* and *Jane Avril in the Entrance of the Moulin Rouge*, 1892, a lovely nude by Modigliani, a street scene by Utrillo and small works by Boudin, Rousseau, Dufy, Bonnard and Vuillard.

Room 7, sometimes used together with Room 8 for special exhibitions of drawings and watercolours belonging to the Collection which are not normally on show, usually houses the Fry collection. Here are several paintings by Bonnard, a number of gouaches by Rouault, and paintings by Derain, Othon Friesz, Sickert, Duncan Grant, Vanessa Bell, together with several by Roger Fry himself.

Dulwich College Picture Gallery, College Road, London S.E.21
Tel.: 01-693 5254
Open weekdays (except Mon.) 10-8; Sept. 1-Oct. 15 and March 16-April 30,
10-5; Oct. 16-March 15, 10-4; Sunday Summer only 2-6; Sunday, April and
Sept. 2-5

The Dulwich Gallery, situated in a south-eastern suburb of London, houses one of the finest collections in Great Britain. The building itself is of considerable interest, having been designed by the eminent architect Sir John Soane. Opened in 1814, it reveals his characteristic inventiveness; though, unfortunately, it was badly damaged during the last war it has been rebuilt with close observation of Soane's original details.

The collection itself has a long and colourful history. It originated with the pictures, of historic interest rather than artistic merit, bequeathed by the Elizabethan actor Edward Alleyn in 1626 (his portrait is one of those meeting you as you enter the Gallery) to be part of the educational foundation which he initiated at Dulwich and out of which sprang Dulwich College. Alleyn's collection was added to by another actor, William Cartwright, but was raised to an entirely different artistic level by the bequest of Sir Francis Bourgeois, son of a Swiss watchmaker and at one time landscape painter to George III, in 1811. The Bourgeois Collection came from a quite unusual source. A dealer of great repute, Noel Joseph Desenfans, had been commissioned to buy paintings for King Stanislaus of Poland but on the latter's abdication Desenfans was left with the paintings he had acquired on his hands. He attempted to persuade the British Government to purchase them as a starting point for a National Gallery and in 1799 drew up a plan with this end in view which, however, was disregarded by the government of the day. Some were sold and the rest Desenfans bequeathed to his friend Sir Francis Bourgeois, who in turn bequeathed them to Dulwich College. Madame Desenfans gave £6,000 to add to Bourgeois' bequest of £2,000 for the purpose of building a gallery. The collection was further enriched by gifts from Charles Fairfax Murray and a bequest of Gainsborough portraits by the Linley family in 1835.

Dulwich Gallery has been the source of much delight to various literary figures. Browning in a letter to Elizabeth Barrett called it 'the gallery I so love and am so grateful to, having been used to going there when a child far under the age allowed by the regulations'. Ruskin was a continual visitor, walking there from his parental home in Denmark Hill and often referring to the paintings there in his writings. Hazlitt devoted an enthusiastic essay to its praise in the *New Monthly Magazine* in 1823.

There are twelve rooms in the Gallery; the contents are occasionally changed around so they will be described by school rather than room by room. Of the Dutch school there are three Rembrandts: *A Girl at a Window* is particularly beautiful; *Portrait of Jacob de Gheyn III* is an interesting example of his middle period; *Portrait of his Son Titus,* is also attributed to him. There are two good examples of the work of Jacob Ruisdael, *A Waterfall* and *Landscape with Windmills;* and a group of fine paintings by Albert Cuyp: *Evening Ride near a River; Cattle and Figures near a River; Cattle near the Maas* being particularly remarkable. A number of landscape pictures with peasants and ruins by Nicolaes Berchem and Jan Both represent 17th-century Italianate Dutch painting; and there are several works by Bartolomeus Breenbergh—especially notable is *Mountain Valley with Ruins.* Not to be missed is Aert de Gelder's *Jacob's Dream;* he was a pupil of Rembrandt and during the 19th century this work was thought to be by his master and was highly praised as such by many, among them Hazlitt and Browning. Later cleaning revealed Aert de Gelder's signature but it remains nevertheless an outstanding work. Another pupil of Rembrandt, Gerard Dou, is represented by a charming panel, *A Lady Playing on the Virginals,* and Gerrit Horst's *Isaac Blessing Jacob* also betrays Rembrandt's influence. Mention must be made of two Italian mountain landscapes, and a larger picture of *The Arch of Constantine* by Swanevelt, who became a decorative painter in Paris. Philips Wouwerman, Adam Pynacker, Karel Dujardin, Adriaen van Ostade and Jan Wynants are also well represented in the Gallery.

Outstanding among the works of the Flemish school on display here are those of Rubens and Van Dyck. The Rubens paintings are particularly interesting, a number of them being oil sketches which allow insights into his manner of working. There is a sketch of *St Amandus and St Walburgus* and another of *St Catherine and St Eligius,* both intended for the wings of an altarpiece. There is another interesting sketch of *The Flight of St Barbara,* a modello for a ceiling panel in the Antwerp church of St Charles Borromeo which Rubens decorated but which was destroyed by fire in 1728. There is an oil sketch of Hélène Fourment, Rubens's second wife, sitting by a pool (it has been called *Hagar in the Wilderness)* and a portrait of *Catherine Manners, Duchess of Buckingham.* Finished paintings include *Venus, Mars and Cupid,* an example of his late style, and *Landscape with a Shepherd and Flock*—not perhaps one of Rubens's best landscapes: Ruskin speaks of its 'bold absurdity' and 'violent licence'. A variety of Van Dyck's work is to be seen. There is a portrait of William Russell, 1st Duke of Bedford, and a more formal one of Emanuel Philibert. An extraordinary portrait, painted in whites and grays, is that of *Lady Venetia Digby on her Deathbed.* This was commissioned by her husband Sir Kenelm Digby, who was shattered by his much-loved (and much discussed—it was said that she had been a courtesan) wife's premature death. Two Biblical paintings by Van Dyck are also here: *The Madonna and the Infant Saviour* and a large, dramatic *Samson and Delilah,* painted early in his career. Among other Flemish paintings are *Interior of an Alehouse* by Adriaen Brouwer, which Hazlitt said 'almost gives one a sick headache', and a group of works by David Teniers the Elder. Many of the latter's paintings are genre and landscape pieces but there are also one or two religious works such as *Mary Magdalen in a Cave.* His son David Teniers the Younger is also well represented.

The paintings of Nicholas Poussin are one of the important attractions of the Gallery. Here are his early work, *The Triumph of David;* an unusual *Assumption of the Virgin* in which can be seen one of his earliest attempts at landscape painting; *The Nurture of Jupiter,* dated 1637; *The Lamenting Venus and Mercury in a Wood; Rinaldo and Armida,* the subject derived from Tasso's *Gerusalemme Liberata; The Flight into Egypt; Landscape with a Roman Road.* Claude is represented by only one picture but this is a masterpiece of his later style and in a well-preserved condition, *Jacob with Laban and his Daughters.* There is a surprising monochromatic work by Sebastien Bourdon, *A Brawl in a Guardroom,* and of great interest are two works by Charles Lebrun, the powerful administrator of the arts under Louis XIV, *The Massacre of the Innocents* and *Horatius Cocles Defending Rome.* From the 18th century comes Watteau's exquisite *Le Bal Champêtre* of which Constable wrote in a letter to his biographer, '[it] seems as if painted in honey; so mellow, so tender, so soft, and so delicious . . .' In addition there are two works by Nicholas Lancret, *Fête Champêtre* and *A Troop Encampment,* and several land and seascapes by Claude Joseph Vernet.

The German school is represented by but one splendid work—a small picture on copper of *Susannah and the Elders* by Adam Elsheimer.

Early Italian painting was hardly valued when the collection at Dulwich was formed and there is little of that period here. Of considerable interest however are a splendid *Portrait of a Young Man* by Piero di Cosimo and two very small panels depicting *St Francis of Assisi* and *St Anthony of Padua* by Raphael. These came from the predella of the Sant'Antonio altarpiece painted by Raphael about 1504-5 for a convent in Perugia but sold by the nuns in 1577; the main panel is now in the Metropolitan Museum in New York. Of 16th-century work most notable is a large canvas of *St Jerome Blessing a Venetian Gentleman* by Veronese, a fragment of a very large altarpiece, another section of which is in the National Gallery of Scotland. To Annibale Carracci are ascribed three small paintings: *The Entombment of Christ; Magdalene in Contemplation; Virgin, Infant Christ and St John.* There are also three small works by his brother Lodovico Carracci, and *The Death of St Francis* by his cousin Agostino. A striking canvas of *The Woman Taken in Adultery* is by Guercino, another great Bolognese painter and a pupil of the Carracci; influenced by them also was Guido Reni, whose fine large painting of *St John the Baptist Preaching in the Wilderness* is also to be seen. Not to be overlooked are *St Catherine of Siena* by Carlo Dolci; *A Roman Emperor Rewarding his Soldiers* by Pietro da Cortona; and *Soldiers Gambling* by Salvator Rosa. From 18th-century Venice come *Diana, Diana and Apollo,* and *A Decorative Design* by Giovanni Battista Tiepolo, and *Joseph Receiving Pharoah's Ring* by his son Giandomenico. *The Doge's Palace, Venice* is an example of the work of Canaletto but particularly to be noted by him is *Old Walton Bridge,* painted during the time he was in London.

The Spanish painting at Dulwich is chiefly remarkable for the Murillos, of which there are four excellent examples, *Flower Girl, Two Peasant Boys and a Negro Boy, La Madonna del Rosario,* and *Two Peasant Boys.* Hazlitt surmised the latter to be one of the ten best paintings in the world and Disraeli wrote of them to a friend, 'Run, my dear fellow and for the first time in your life know what a great artist is—Murillo, Murillo, Murillo!' A very good copy of Velazquez's portrait of Philip IV (the Fraga Portrait), which is in the Frick Collection in New York, is also in the Gallery.

English painting, particularly portraiture, is extensively exhibited. There is a portrait of Sir Harry Vane by William Dobson whom John Aubrey called 'the most excellent painter that England yet hath bred', and two portraits by the Swedish-born Michael Dahl. By John Greenhill, a pupil of Sir Peter Lely, there are several portraits of the Cartwright family, and by Isaac Fuller there is a little *Head of a Girl,* one of the few portraits firmly attributable to him. Cornelius Johnson is represented by three charming portraits and by Sir Peter Lely there is a portrait of a youth, possibly identifiable as Abraham Cowley, and a painting, *Nymphs at a Fountain,* which verges on the lascivious. Further portraits are by Thomas Hudson, Joseph Highmore and Sir Godfrey Kneller but the most remarkable come from the hands of Gainsborough and Reynolds. By the former there is an expressive portrait of the Linley sisters and an equally beautiful one of Mrs Moodey and her children; in addition there are other portraits of the Linley family, a portrait of the painter de Loutherbourg, and a delightful picture called simply *A Lady and a Gentleman.* Other members of the Linley family are portrayed by Sir Thomas Lawrence. The most outstanding canvas by Sir Joshua Reynolds is that of *Mrs Siddons as The Tragic Muse,* a replica he did in 1789 of the original portrait now in America. There is also a self-portrait, a picture of *The Infant Samuel,* and *A Mother and her Sick Child.* From Hogarth come two works, *Portrait of a Man* and *A Fishing Party.* From Richard Wilson come a landscape, *Tivoli Cascatelle and 'Villa of Maecenas',* and a portrait of Lord Egremont. There are also two land-scapes by de Loutherbourg.

The Foundling Hospital Pictures, 40 Brunswick Square, London W.C.1

Tel.: 01-278 1911

Open Mondays and Fridays 10-12 and 2-4 except Bank Holidays

The Foundling Hospital, or as it is now called, the Thomas Coram Foundation for Children, is situated in a corner of Bloomsbury rapidly being rebuilt. The original hospital built in the middle of the 18th century was pulled down in 1920 and the present building erected as the headquarters of the Thomas Coram Foundation. Certain features of the old building such as the Court Room were dismantled and rebuilt within the new structure. Thomas Coram, born about 1668, was a sailor in his youth who went to America and there achieved some success as a shipwright. He returned to this country and devoted his life to public service, especially the welfare of foundlings. After prolonged struggles on his part the Foundling Hospital was given a Royal Charter in 1739. Extraordinarily enough this institution devoted to the 'Maintenance and Education of Exposed and Deserted Young Children' became for a time a prominent centre of art. This was due to the initiative of Hogarth, a friend and admirer of Coram and a Governor of the Hospital from the outset, who conceived that the Hospital could provide a place for artists to put their work on view other than in their own studios. Hogarth gave some of his own paintings to the Hospital and his example induced other artists to do likewise; several also became Governors of the Hospital.

Among the finest treasures of the Thomas Coram Foundation is

Hogarth's portrait of Thomas Coram, dated 1740, which he is said to have declared gave him more pleasure in painting than any other. It is indeed a fine portrait and provides a landmark in the history of British portraiture. In the Court Room, which is now arranged as it was originally, hang Hogarth's *Moses Brought before Pharoah's Daughter,* Joseph Highmore's *Hagar and Ishmael,* Francis Hayman's *Finding of Moses in the Bulrushes* and Wills's *Little Children Brought to Christ.* Between these are eight tondos of views of various hospitals, among them a View of St George's Hospital and a view of the Foundling Hospital both painted by Richard Wilson before his visit to Italy.

There is another Hogarth here given by the artist, the famous, lively *March of the Guards to Finchley* of 1746 which depicts the English guards, in various states of disorder, marching to defend London from the possible attack of the Young Pretender. *The Charterhouse from the Terrace* is a pleasing landscape by Gainsborough, painted when he was only 21. There are several portraits of note: Joshua Reynolds's portrait of William Legge, Earl of Dartmouth; Thomas Hudson's portrait of Theodore Jacobsen, architect of the Hospital; Allan Ramsay's portrait of Dr Richard Mead; and Sir John Millais's portrait of the surgeon Luther Holden. Other paintings which should be mentioned include the marine painter Charles Brooking's *Flagship before the Wind under Easy Sail with Other Vessels;* George Lambert's *Landscape with Figures;* Benjamin West's *Christ Presenting a Little Child;* John Singleton Copley's sketch for his huge painting *The Seige of Gibraltar* (the painting is in the Guildhall); Andrea Casali's *Adoration of the Magi* and a cartoon of the *Massacre of the Innocents* which is in very bad condition but is probably by Giulio Romano. On the beautiful oak staircase which derives from the original building is *Elijah Raising the Son of Zarephath,* formerly attributed to Lanfranco but more probably by an unknown North Italian artist. The sculpture in the building includes a terracotta bust of Handel by Roubiliac and a marble relief, *Charity,* by John Michael Rysbrack, who was also a Governor of the Hospital.

Guildhall Art Gallery, Cheapside, London E.C.2

Tel.: 01-606 3030

Open weekdays 10-5

The origins of the Guildhall collection go back to the years after the Great Fire of London in 1666 when twenty-two of the chief judges were set the task of settling disputes and commercial claims arising as a consequence of the fire and, in appreciation of their work, their life-size portraits were painted by John Michael Wright and hung in the Guildhall. Other pictures including royal portraits and scenes commemorating historical events were added to the collection but it was not until 1886 that an actual Guildhall Art Gallery was established, to be maintained by the Corporation of the City of London. Unhappily the Gallery was destroyed during the Second World War together with a number of its important possessions. Recent rebuilding of the Guildhall and its precincts will however enlarge the Gallery's capacity to show more of its permanent collection in addition to the temporary exhibitions which it sponsors.

One of the earliest works in the Gallery is a portrait of Sir Thomas Exmowe, Lord Mayor of London in 1517, by a member of the school of Holbein. Sir Peter Lely's group portrait of Sir Edward Hales and his family, painted about 1655, is also of importance. A portrait of Sir Charles Pratt, later Lord Camden, was commissioned from Sir Joshua Reynolds by the Corporation of the City of London after his fair conduct of the trial of John Wilkes, and a portrait of Thomas Tomkins, writing master, painted in 1792 and probably Reynolds's last work, is also among the Gallery's possessions. By Allan Ramsay is an impressive portrait of George III, to whom he was Painter-in-Ordinary, and also one of Queen Charlotte. The actor John Philip Kemble is commemorated in a dramatic representation of him as Coriolanus by Sir Thomas Lawrence. From Alderman John Boydell, Lord Mayor of London in 1790 and founder of the Shakespeare Gallery, came a large gift of paintings to the City's collection in 1793, among them John Hoppner's portrait of Viscount Duncan of Camperdown, Sir William Beeching's portrait of Nelson, and *Charles, Marquis Cornwallis* by John Singleton Copley.

Outstanding among the landscapes possessed by the Gallery is Constable's large study, *Fording the River—Showery Weather with Salisbury Cathedral in the Background.* Other works are John Linnell's *Timber Wagon,* Patrick Nasmyth's *Meeting of the Avon and the Severn, Gillingham on the Medway* by W. J. Müller, *Echoes of a Far-off Storm* by John Brett, and the more exotic *Early Morning in the Wilderness of Shur* by Frederick Goodall.

Narrative pictures, most of them from the 19th century, are another group to be found in the Gallery. An earlier work, another gift of Alderman Boydell, is *The Murder of Rizzio* by John Opie; *Early Morning Scene from 'The Winter's Tale'* is by Augustus Egg, dated 1845, and from Holman Hunt comes *The Flight of Madeline and Porphyro during Drunkenness Attending the Revelry,* from Keats's *Eve of St Agnes,* dated 1848. William Dyce's *George Herbert at Bemerton,* first exhibited in 1861, was considered by a critic 'a marvellous triumph of manipulative success and skill'. Other paintings include *The Wounded Cavalier* by W. S. Burton; *The Banquet Scene in 'Macbeth'* by Daniel Maclise; *The Pyrrhic Dance* by Alma-Tadema, his first exhibit at the Royal Academy in 1869, where it was well-received although Ruskin later wrote of it that 'the general effect was exactly like a microscopic view of a small detachment of black beetles in search of a dead rat.' *Israel in Egypt* by Sir Edward Poynter is a huge exposition of the first chapter in Exodus, first exhibited in 1867; *A Chat round the Bayero,* 1866, is a scene set in Spain by John Phillip; and *Ariadne in Naxos* was spoken of by G. F. Watts as 'perhaps the most complete picture I have painted'. *Too Early* and *The Last Evening* are two polished works by James Tissot, a French artist who settled in London for some years after the Franco-Prussian War. A religious work, J. R. Herbert's *Our Saviour Subject to his Parents at Nazareth,* exhibited at the Royal Academy in 1847, seems like a precursor of Millais's later controversial *Christ in the Carpenter's Shop* in the Tate. From Millais himself come *The Woodman's Daughter,* 1851, and a portrait of his daughter Effie, *My Second Sermon.* Another 19th-century portrait of childhood is Landseer's *The First Leap; Lord Alexander Russell on the Highland Pony Emerald.* Also here is Lord Leighton's *The Music Lesson,* exhibited in 1877; the model for the pupil was Connie Gilchrist who danced at the Gaiety Theatre and was also a model for Whistler.

The Guildhall is also rich in ceremonial pictures and graphic works commemorating some aspect of the historic civic life of the City of London. Another gift of Boydell is a painting representing the swearing in of Alderman Nathaniel Newnham as Lord Mayor in 1782. *The Procession of the Lord Mayor on Lord Mayor's Day in 1789* with the figures painted by Francis Wheatley, is the subject of another work. Later pictures include *Lord Mayor's Day, 1836* by David Roberts; *Queen Victoria's Visit to the Guildhall in the Year of her Coronation, 1837; Coronation Luncheon of George VI and Queen Elizabeth* by Frank Salisbury; and the *Coronation of Queen Elizabeth II* by Terence Cuneo.

Hampton Court Palace

Tel.: 01-977 8441
Open daily May-Sept. 9.30-6 (Sunday 11-6); March, April and October 9.30-5 (Sunday 2-5); Nov.-Feb. 9.30-4 (Sunday 2-4)

This great palace on the banks of the Thames was built by Thomas Wolsey, the powerful Cardinal and Lord Chancellor of England under Henry VIII until his disastrous fall from grace in 1529. Wolsey built this residence in a style and with a magnificence befitting any royal palace and indeed in a desperate attempt to win back Henry's favour he presented this treasure to the King. Henry proceeded to enlarge Hampton Court and make it an even more luxurious residence for his series of wives. Succeeding monarchs held court there: Edward VI, Mary Tudor, Elizabeth, James I, Charles I and Charles II. But the great rebuilding of the palace took place under William and Mary when the original building was nearly 200 years old. The new constructions were designed by Sir Christopher Wren. Since the death of George II in 1760 the palace has never been used by a reigning monarch and under Queen Victoria the State Rooms were opened to the public and 'grace and favour' residences, formed out of the many other rooms in the palace, were granted to the widows or children of distinguished servants of the Crown.

There are two sets of State Rooms in the Palace which contain the paintings available to public view—those of the King and those of the Queen deriving from the period of Wren's rebuilding when William and Mary were joint rulers of England. Some of the paintings here come from the oldest parts of the royal collection, several of them having originally belonged to Henry VIII and Charles I. The King's staircase, leading to the King's apartments, was painted by Antonio Verrio, an Italian artist who came to England at the request of Charles II and who executed a considerable number of wall and ceiling paintings in various great houses, including those at Hampton Court for William and Mary.

In the First Presence Chamber hangs a huge equestrian portrait of William III landing at Margate after signing the Peace of Ryswick in 1697, painted by Sir Godfrey Kneller. Also his work is the series of full-length portraits of Hampton Court beauties which he executed for Queen Mary.

The Second Presence Chamber contains a number of extremely fine works: *Portrait of a Man,* usually called *Jacopo Sannazaro,* by Titian; *Esther and Ahasuerus* by Tintoretto; *Shepherd with a Pipe* by Giorgione, originally bought by Charles I and later in the collection of Queen Anne; *St William* by Dosso Dossi; *Virgin and Child with Donors* by Paris Bordone; *Adoration of the Shepherds* by Jacopo Bassano; *A Man with a Cuirass* by Savoldo; *The Expulsion of Heresy* by Palma Giovane; *The Concert,* at various times attributed to Giorgione and to Lorenzo Lotto though now the weight of opinion tends to ascribe it to Giovanni Bellini in his old age; and the fascinating *Lady in Green* by an artist of the North Italian school. Over the chimney-piece is a large portrait of Christian IV of Denmark, brother of Anne, wife of James I, by Karel van Mander. Above the doors are landscapes by the Frenchman Jacques Rousseau, who was in England towards the end of the 17th century.

The Audience Chamber contains a number of works by Tintoretto: the masterly *Apollo and the Nine Muses; A Knight of Malta; Portrait of a Dominican;* and *Portrait of a Man.* Here too are a superb portrait of Andrea Odono by Lorenzo Lotto and *Portrait of a Man* by the Mannerist painter Parmigianino. From Veronese comes *The Marriage of St Catherine;* and other works include *The Judgement of Midas* by Schiavone; *Virgin and Child with Donors* by Savoldo; *Portrait of a Man* by Dosso Dossi; and a portrait of Elizabeth of Bohemia, sister of Charles I (The Winter Queen) by Honthorst.

The King's Drawing-Room also contains a number of fine Italian paintings. There are two works by Correggio, the worn but beautiful *St Catherine*, and *Virgin and Child*, both of which belonged to Charles I, and a *Virgin and Child* by Andrea del Sarto. Here also are *Lucretia*, probably dated about 1530, by Titian, another portrait, *Head of an Old Man* by Lotto, and a striking *Portrait of a Venetian Senator* by Tintoretto. *Judith with the Head of Holofernes* is by Cristofano Allori; there are several paintings by Bassano, *Jacob's Journey*, *The Good Samaritan*, and a self-portrait; a *St Catharine* by Domenichino; and a portrait of Isabella of Austria attributed to Frans Pourbus is framed by an overmantel carved by Grinling Gibbons. The ceiling of William III's state bedroom was painted by Verrio—the subject *Endymion Asleep in the Arms of Morpheus*. Among the paintings in this room is a painting of *David* by the Roman artist Domenico Feti, who has a considerable number of works in the Palace. The ceiling of the Dressing-Room was also by Verrio, who here depicted *Mars in the Lap of Venus*. On the walls are a contemporary portrait of Henry VIII attributed to Joos van Cleve, and another portrait also attributed to him of Queen Eleanor of France, wife of Francis I. There is a very important work by Holbein, *Noli me Tangere*, one of his few religious paintings; also of great interest is Mabuse's *Adam and Eve*. Both these paintings and another one by Mabuse, *The Children of Christian II of Denmark*, were in the collection of Henry VIII. Two portraits of Erasmus are copies of works done by Holbein and Massys respectively.

In the King's writing closet is a magnificent portrait of Isabella d'Este by Giulio Romano, Raphael's principal assistant from about 1515 onwards and one of the originators of Mannerism. This painting was among a collection presented to Charles II by the Dutch States General. Other examples of the Mannerist style are also here: a striking *Portrait of a Boy* by Parmigianino and an equally compelling picture of *The Gardener to the Duke of Florence* by Franciabigio. Pierino del Vaga, like Giulio Romano one of Raphael's followers, is also represented by two parts of an altarpiece painted for the Roman church S. Maria sopra Minerva depicting *The Repentant Thief* and *The Unrepentant Thief*. There is a *Holy Family* by Andrea del Sarto and another fascinating work attributed to Pedro Berruguete or, more probably, to Justus of Ghent, the subject being *Federigo Montefeltro, Duke of Urbino, with his son, Guidobaldo, Listening to an Oration*.

The next room, Queen Mary's Closet, was once hung with needlework done by her and her ladies but now contains an interesting collection of German and Flemish paintings. There is a good copy of Pieter Brueghel the Elder's *Massacre of the Innocents* (the original is in Vienna) which has

the extraordinary feature that the murdered children have been changed
into animals. This apparently was an alteration executed in the 17th
century which it seems cannot now be rectified. There are also two
paintings by Lucas Cranach—the *Judgement of Paris*, and *Adam and Eve;
Wedding of Psyche* by the Mannerist artist Abraham Bloemaert; *Niobe's
Children* by Rottenhammer; and a *Still Life with Dead Birds* by Van
Aelst.

In the Queen's Bedroom are to be found *Diana* by the French
17th-century painter Simon Vouet; *An Allegory of Truth and Time* by
Annibale Carracci; *A Concert* by Bernardo Strozzi; and a charming
Sleeping Cupid by the Neapolitan painter Caracciolo, known as Battis-
tello. The Queen's Audience Chamber contains a copy of Velazquez's
Don Balthasar Carlos; a formal full-length portrait of Anne of Denmark
by Paul van Somer; and perhaps most interestingly a portrait of the
dwarf court jester Sir Jeffery Hudson by Daniel Mytens.

The Public Dining-Room is decorated with four large works with
episodes from the life of Christ by the 18th-century Venetian artists
Sebastiano and Marco Ricci, uncle and nephew, whose works were
bought by George III from the collection of Joseph Smith, the British
consul in Venice. Another painting·here is *Augustus and the Sibyl* by the
17th-century Baroque artist Pietro da Cortona, who spent a large part of
his working life in Rome.

The Prince of Wales Presence Chamber is hung with a splendid
collection of Italian primitives purchased mostly by the Prince Consort
during the middle years of the last century. Most remarkable perhaps is
a triptych by Duccio with panels of *The Crucifixion, The Annunciation,
The Stigmatization of St Francis,* and the *Virgin and Christ Enthroned,*
but also of the greatest interest are Gentile da Fabriano's *Virgin and
Child,* the centre panel of the Quaratesi altarpiece, and side panels of
which are in the Uffizi; and Fra Angelico's little panel of *St Peter
Martyr.* There is a beautiful *Marriage of the Virgin* by the 14th-century
Florentine artist Bernardo Daddi; a *Madonna and Child with Saints* by
Orcagna; *Madonna and Child* by Sano di Pietro; an altarpiece from the
school of Jacopo di Cione; small panels by Cima da Conegliano, and *The
Death of Simon Magus* by Benozzo Gozzoli. Not to be overlooked is
Portrait of a Man by Giovanni Bellini.

Alone in the Prince of Wales Dining-Room at the time of writing is
Mantegna's *Vase Bearers,* a most remarkable painting which is one of a
set of nine in tempera executed by Mantegna for a room in the castle of
the Gonzagas at Mantua. They depict the various stages in the triumphal
march of a Roman Emperor. These paintings are among the most
splendid illustrations of Italian Renaissance art in Great Britain and were
bought from the Duke of Mantua by Charles I. They will be on view as
a whole when the Lower Orangery reconstruction is completed.

In the next room is to be found a *Holy Family* by Annibale Carracci often called *The Silence* because of the gesture of the Virgin which seems designed to prevent St John from waking the infant Christ. *The Labyrinth of Love* is attributed to Tintoretto and there is a series of half-figures of saints together with *The Sacrifice of Elijah* by Domenico Feti; these also were bought by Charles I. Van Dyck's portrait of his mistress Margaret Lemon was also possibly acquired by Charles from the studio of the artist after his death. Daniel Mytens, who was superseded by Van Dyck in the royal favour, has here a self-portrait and a portrait of the Duke of Buckingham. A painting of *St Jerome* is by Georges de la Tour and other paintings include a small landscape by Paul Brill, a *River Scene* by Salamon Ruisdael, *Death and Judgement* by Martin van Heemskerck, and a portrait of Elizabeth, Countess of Ogle by Sir Peter Lely.

In the Cartoon Gallery, designed by Wren to display the seven Raphael designs for tapestries for Pope Leo X which Charles I had acquired in 1632 and which are now in the Victoria and Albert Museum, hang seven tapestries copied from the original cartoons and given to the Crown in 1905. Here also hang three historical paintings illustrating events from the reign of Henry VIII: *The Meeting of Henry with the Emperor Maximilian; The Embarkation of Henry at Dover; The Meeting of Henry and Francis I at the Field of the Cloth of Gold.*

The Communication Gallery which links the King's and the Queen's State Apartments contains Sir Peter Lely's famous series of 'Windsor Beauties'—portraits of the fairest ladies adorning Charles II's Court. Pepys called them 'good, but not like'. Further rooms contain a series of paintings by Luca Giordano on the story of Cupid and Psyche; portraits by Frans Pourbus of Henry IV of France and Marie de' Medici; *Adoration of the Shepherds* by Joos van Cleve; *The Children of the King of Bohemia* by Honthorst, *The Continence of Scipio* by Sebastiano Ricci; *Sibyl* by Guercino, *Cleopatra* by Guido Reni; *St John of the Lamb* by Baglione, one of the minor followers of Caravaggio; and a *Sibyl* by Orazio Gentileschi, who was a much more significant follower. In addition there is a portrait of Cardinal Richelieu by Philippe de Champaigne; a portrait of Caroline of Ansbach by Joseph Highmore; and a beautiful *Cupid and Psyche*, probably painted about 1639-40 and one of the last paintings done by Van Dyck for Charles I.

The Iveagh Bequest, Kenwood, Hampstead, London N.W.3

Open daily 10-5 (November-January 10-4; April-September 10-7)

The collection of paintings at Kenwood is remarkable not only for its high quality but also for its setting in a house of great distinction situated in a park of considerable charm and beauty, adjacent to Hampstead Heath. The collection is part of one formed by the 1st Earl of Iveagh who, at his death in 1927, gave it to the nation together with the house and park which he had only acquired in 1925. A house was originally built on the site in Jacobean times but it was reconstructed at the beginning of the 18th century. After passing through several hands, in 1754 it finally came into the possession of the 1st Earl of Mansfield, who employed Robert Adam to remodel it. Much of the present appearance and attraction of the house is due to Robert Adam, for example the magnificent library, the south front with its Orangery, and the portico on the north front, but in later years additions were also made by the architect George Saunders. The painted panels in the Library are by Antonio Zucchi, an associate of Adam's and the husband of Angelica Kauffmann, by whom there are several paintings in the house.

Many of the fine paintings here are English in origin. As those by Van Dyck belong to his English period perhaps they should also be mentioned with the English school. From him come a portrait of Henrietta of Lorraine with a negro page; a portrait of Jane Goodwin, wife of the 4th Lord Wharton (lent by the present Lord Wharton); and a superb half-length portrait of James Stuart, Duke of Richmond and Lennox. Equally superb but in a very different manner is the exquisite *Mary, Countess Howe* by Gainsborough. Other portraits by him are the staider *Lady Brisco* and a portrait of Miss Brummell, the sister of 'Beau' Brummell, as a child; attributed to him is a *Man in the Livery of the Prince of Wales.* Gainsborough's dramatic capabilities are to be seen in *Two Shepherd Boys with Dogs Fighting,* and there is also a landscape, *Going to Market,* painted about 1770. Several excellent portraits by Sir Joshua Reynolds include that of Lady Chambers, wife of the architect Sir William Chambers, painted in Paris in 1752; *Kitty Fisher as Cleopatra Dissolving the Pearl*—this lady was a famous courtesan; *Mrs Tollemache as Miranda; Mrs Musters as Hebe; Lady Louisa Manners; Lady Mary Leslie;* and several depictions of children such as that of William Brummell and his brother, George Bryan (later known as 'Beau' Brummell); *Master Philip Yorke;* and *The Angerstein Children,* probably painted 1782-3, (they were children of J. J. Angerstein, whose collection, purchased by the nation in 1824, formed the basis of the National Gallery collection). In a different vein is Reynold's *Venus Chiding Cupid,* a subject which he attempted upon more than one occasion. Other charming pictures of children in the collection are Sir Thomas Lawrence's well-known *Miss Murray,* and Sir Henry Raeburn's *Portrait of Sir George Sinclair as a Boy.* George Romney, who lived in Hampstead, is represented by his famous portrait of *Lady Hamilton at the Spinning-Wheel;* a portrait of her at prayer; a painting of *Mrs Musters;*

another of *Mrs Crouch; Anne, Countess of Albemarle and her Son;* and an attractive picture of *Miss Martindale.*

Though portraiture is outstanding there are some good examples of other kinds of English painting. *Old London Bridge* by Claude de Jongh, painted in 1630, is surely among the first English landscapes. There is an important sea piece by Turner, first exhibited in 1802, *Fishermen upon a Lee Shore in Squally Weather;* and in the Orangery, lent by Earl Fitz-william, is to be found *Whistlejacket,* a magnificent large study of a rearing horse by George Stubbs. Also here are a landscape by George Morland and *The Yarmouth Water Frolic* by John Crome, probably finished by his son.

Though so far the English aspect of the Kenwood collection has been stressed it is perhaps among the fewer Dutch pictures that the greatest masterpieces are to be found. Here is a remarkable self-portrait by Rembrandt, painted about 1663, and a splendid example of his later work. It was cleaned 20 years or so ago and the removal of discolouring varnish revealed its high quality. In the same room as this is a portrait of Pieter van den Broecke, *'The Man with the Cane',* by Frans Hals, and here also is *The Guitar Player* by Vermeer, a painting of the utmost charm and subtlety which does not appear to have suffered from its temporary theft in 1974. Among other Dutch painters represented are Albert Cuyp with a characteristically beautiful *View of Dordrecht;* Ferdinand Bol, to whom is attributed a fine *Portrait of an Unknown Woman,* until 1951 thought to be by Rembrandt; Jan Weenix, Jan Wynants, Willem van der Velde, Jan van der Cappelle, Isack van Ostade. And from the Flemish painter Frans Snyders comes a painting of *Figures with Fruit and Game.*

There are several French pictures at Kenwood including two *Fêtes Champêtres* by Pater and several pastoral scenes by Boucher. From the Swiss painter Angelica Kauffmann come several works, among them *Rinaldo and Armida.* A limited number of Italian paintings are also to be seen: two beautiful studies of churches on the Grand Canal, Venice by Guardi; two views by Bellotto, lent anonymously; and two studies by Panini of the Piazza del Popolo and St Peter's in Rome, also lent anonymously.

Leighton House Art Gallery, 12 Holland Park Road, London W.14

Tel.: 01-602 3316

Open weekdays 11-5

The district of Holland Park Road and the adjoining Melbury Road in which this gallery is to be found was one in which many Victorian artists made their homes; indeed, by some the area was known as the Leighton Settlement. Lord Leighton, the great High Victorian painter and the first artist to be elevated to the peerage, built this house in collaboration with the architect George Aitchison in 1866 and lived in it for 30 years. The house, now set aside for the exhibition of Victorian art lent by the Victoria and Albert Museum and the Tate, has an outstanding Arab Hall decorated with tilework from Rhodes, Cairo, Damascus and other places. Many of the works here are by Lord Leighton himself and include paintings, numerous studies, and illustrations to various books such as the Bible, the poems of Elizabeth Barrett Browning, and George Eliot's *Romola*. His major paintings here, *Orpheus and Eurydice*, *The Bath of Psyche*, and *Clytemnestra*, illustrate his strongly classical vein.

Alma-Tadema, another High Victorian classicist, was actually a Dutchman who studied in Belgium and who did not settle in England until the 1870s. Here are two works by him, *Priestess of Apollo* and *A Favourite Custom*. Represented also is Sir E. J. Poynter, like Leighton President of the Royal Academy and also Director of the National Gallery at the same time for ten years; here is one of his most famous and probably most successful works, *A Visit to Aesculapius*. A number of works by Burne-Jones are also to be seen: a study for *King Cophetua and the Beggar Maid* (the picture is in the Tate); the *Morning of the Resurrection* and several gouaches. There are also several drawings by Ford Madox Brown and Millais as well as a study for *The Execution of Mary, Queen of Scots* by the former and a portrait of Robert Rankin, dated 1889, by the latter. Other paintings include *Brynhylde* by G. F. Watts; *Summer Sundown* by William McTaggart; *The Siesta* by J. F. Lewis; *Berenice, Queen of Egypt* by Frederick Sandys; *Love Locked Out* by Anna Lea Merritt; and two works by Whistler, a portrait of Miss A. M. Alexander, a study in greys and black, and *Hearts are Trumps*, painted in 1872.

London Museum, Kensington Palace, The Broad Walk, Kensington Gardens, London W.8

Tel.: 01-937 9816

Open weekdays 10-6; Sunday 2-6. November to January closes at 4; October and February closes at 5.

The idea of a London Museum was proposed in a memorandum to King George V in 1910 by the 2nd Viscount Esher, who had long cherished such a dream. The dream was realised and the museum was opened to the public in 1912, becoming a National Museum in July 1913. Pictures were acquired for their historical and topographical association with London rather than their intrinsic merit, which means that the selection is of varying quality though on the whole of the greatest interest. The Museum does, of course, contain many other objects which illustrate the varying aspects of London's history and life.

The earliest picture here is probably a portrait of Henry, Prince of Wales, son of James I, by Robert Peake the Elder. The earliest known view of London from a distance is a *Prospect of London and the Thames from Above Greenwich*, painted between 1620 and 1630 by an unknown artist. Two works of great fascination are by Abraham Hondius: *The Frozen Thames*, a record of the great freeze of 1676—the picture is dated 1677 but the ice began to break on 3 January 1677; and *Frost Fair on the Thames*, 1683-4 (compare John Evelyn's *Diary*, where he writes that by New Year's Day 'streets of boothes were set up on the Thames . . . all sorts of trades and shops . . . even to a Printing Press where the People and Ladys took a fansy to have their names Printed and the day and yeare set downe, when printed on the Thames.') Another London drama was the Great Fire which is depicted in a painting of about 1666, and there is also a view of *The Pool of London* before the fire by Cornelius Bol. Another early view is of *Chiswick from the River*, painted between 1675 and 1680 by Jacob Knyff.

There are several views of Covent Garden Piazza and Market, mostly done in the 18th century, and some drawings of Ranelagh Gardens by Thomas Rowlandson. A rare interior by Canaletto is of *Henry VII's Chapel, Westminster Abbey*. Also of interest is a painting of *The London River Front from Westminster to the Adelphi* 1771-2—a view of the project of Robert and John Adam by William Marlow. Thomas Luny's *Westminster Bridge* and *The Burning of the Houses of Parliament, October 16th, 1834*, and David Roberts's *The Palace of Westminster from the River after the Fire of 1834*, provide records of that historic occasion. John Piper's *Christ Church, Newgate Street after its Destruction in 1940* is a record of another catastrophe.

Among other glimpses afforded of parts of London are John Linnell's *Collins's Farm, North End, Hampstead* (both Linnell and Charles Dickens lived here for a time); Sir John Lavery's *St John's Church, Hampstead;* George Joy's *The Bayswater Omnibus;* John Ritchie's *A Summer's Day in Hyde Park;* Robert Bevan's *A Street Scene in Belsize Park;* C. R. W. Nevinson's *Cleopatra's Needle and Hungerford Bridge from the Savoy, City from South End of Waterloo Bridge*, and *Amongst the Nerves of the World*.

The Museum also owns a number of portraits of actors in various parts, among them a painting of Sir Henry Irving and a scene by Francis Hayman of *David Garrick and Hannah Pritchard in 'The Suspicious Husband'*, painted about 1747.

The National Gallery, Trafalgar Square, London W.C.2
Tel.: 01-930 7618

Open weekdays 10-6; Sundays 2-6

The idea of a National Gallery was beginning to receive a certain amount of support in England at the beginning of the 19th century but it was largely through the offer of Sir George Beaumont to give his collection to the nation if suitable accommodation could be found for it, and following this a similar offer from the Reverend W. Holwell Carr, that the whole matter came under more urgent consideration. When it was learnt that in 1824 the splendid collection of the city broker John Julius Angerstein was to be sold Lord Liverpool's government persuaded the House of Commons to vote a large sum for the purchase of these pictures and in April 1824 38 paintings from the Angerstein collection were bought for £57,000. On 24 May of the same year this nucleus of a National Gallery was opened at 100 Pall Mall, a house leased by Angerstein. Trustees and a Keeper were appointed and in 1826 the Beaumont collection was added, to be followed by that of Holwell Carr in 1831. By 1834 new accommodation had to be found for the growing collection (several important purchases had also been made in the intervening years) and it was temporarily housed at 105 Pall Mall, though by 1831 plans were already accepted for a new building to be constructed on the site of the Royal Mews on the north side of what was later to become Trafalgar Square. This building, designed in classical style by William Wilkins, was opened to the public in 1838; the National Gallery was housed in the West Wing, while the East Wing was given over to the Royal Academy. This arrangement remained until the Royal Academy moved to Burlington House in 1869. The Gallery's possessions expanded rapidly by virtue of further bequests and through purchases—the acquisitions made by Sir Charles Eastlake, the Gallery's first Director, are particularly notable—and over the years further galleries have been added to the building to house the growing collection. A further extension, planned to open in 1975, will add to the exhibition space of the main and lower floors.

The collection of the National Gallery is so large and so eclectic that it can only be treated cursorily in a book such as this. An attempt will be made to indicate most of its treasures but those in search of detailed information should consult the very informative guides and catalogues published by the Gallery itself. The earliest paintings originate in Italy. Active around 1262 was Margarito of Arezzo (called Margaritone by Vasari) and by him here is a large altar screen with a Virgin and Child flanked by scenes of the Nativity and from the lives of certain saints. From the great Sienese painter Duccio come three panels from the Maestà altarpiece, *The Transfiguration, The Annunciation,* and *The*

Healing of the Blind Man; a small triptych of the *Virgin and Child;* and a *Virgin and Child with Four Angels.* Examples of 15th-century Sienese painting are *Scenes from the Life of St Francis* by Sassetta; *Scenes from the Life of John the Baptist* by Giovanni di Paolo; and the *Assumption of the Virgin* by Matteo di Giovanni. An early Florentine panel of the *Pentecost* is possibly from the studio of Giotto, and also not to be missed is an altarpiece by Narda di Cione. From Fra Angelico comes *Christ Glorified in the Court of Heaven,* the predella of the high altarpiece of San Domenico near Fiesole which has been called by far the most hagiological picture in the Gallery. Also from early-15th-century Florence are *The Coronation of the Virgin* by Lorenzo Monaco, and even more notably a *Madonna and Child* by Masaccio, the central panel of an altarpiece painted when he was only 25 by this great master of European art. From Masolino who worked with him are two panels, *St John the Baptist and St Jerome,* and *A Pope and St Matthias.* Other Florentine pictures of a slightly later date include an *Annunciation* by Filippo Lippi, an altarpiece by Pesellino, *Virgin and Child Enthroned* by Domenico Veneziano, and from Uccello *The Battle of San Romano* (one of a series probably done for a room in the Palazzo Medici) and *St George and the Dragon.* Botticelli is splendidly represented by a number of works: *Adoration of the Kings; Portrait of a Young Man; Mars and Venus;* a tondo, *Adoration of the Kings;* four scenes from the early life of St Zenobius; and the *Mystic Nativity,* signed in a Greek inscription and the only known signed picture by Botticelli. Influenced by Botticelli, with whom he worked, was Filippino Lippi, by whom there are several paintings, and painters of the late 15th century in Florence represented include Baldovinetti with *Portrait of a Lady in Yellow,* Ghirlandaio, and Antonio Pollaiuolo with *Apollo and Daphne.* The large *Martyrdom of St Sebastian* is also attributed to the Pollaiuolo brothers. By that strange painter Piero di Cosimo are *The Battle between the Centaurs and the Lapiths* and the mysterious *Mythological Subject* which continues to defy interpretation. Great treasures of the Gallery are the paintings by Piero della Francesca, an Umbrian painter who studied for a while in Florence. His *Baptism of Christ* was purchased by Sir Charles Eastlake for £241; also here by him are a panel of *St Michael,* and *The Nativity,* one of his later works. Other Central Italian painters of the 15th century include Signorelli, represented by *Triumph of Chastity, Coriolanus and his Family,* and *Virgin and Child with Saints;* Pintoricchio with *Scenes from the Odyssey;* and Perugino, teacher of Raphael, with an altarpiece, *Madonna and Child with St Michael and St Raphael.* From 15th-century Northern Italy come enchanting works by Pisanello, *The Vision of St Eustace,* and *The Virgin and Child with St George and St Anthony Abbot;* and the great Paduan painter Mantegna is represented by *Madonna and Child with the Magdalen and John the Baptist, The Triumph of Scipio,*

Samson and Delilah, and the powerful, harsh *Agony in the Garden.* Interesting to compare with this picture is the *Agony in the Garden* of Mantegna's Venetian brother-in-law Giovanni Bellini, but there are other great examples of Bellini's work, among them *The Madonna of the Meadow, The Blood of the Redeemer, Virgin and Child, Pietà, Portrait of the Doge Loredano* and, ascribed to his studio, *The Assassination of St Peter Martyr.* Also active during the early years of Bellini was Antonello da Messina, by whom there are a *Portrait of a Man,* dated about 1475, *Christ Crucified,* and *St Jerome in his Study.* From late 15th-century Ferrara come Cosimo Tura's *Madonna and Child Enthroned,* and *Allegorical Figure,* and Francesco Cossa's *St Vincent Ferrer.*

From early-16th-century Florence, the period of the High Renaissance, come some of the greatest masterpieces among the Gallery's possessions. Leonardo da Vinci's cartoon of the *Virgin and Child with St Anne and John the Baptist* is accorded a room to itself. Also by Leonardo is the disturbing *Madonna of the Rocks,* painted for a church in Milan. Like the *Entombment* by Michelangelo, which is also here, it was unfinished. Ascribed to Michelangelo and also unfinished is a *Madonna and Child with St John and Angels.* Among the paintings by Raphael in the Gallery are the *Ansidei Madonna, St Catherine of Alexandria, Vision of a Knight,* and a portrait of Pope Julius II, recently concluded to be an authentic work. Fra Bartolommeo is represented by *Adoration of the Child* and another work, and from Andrea del Sarto come *Madonna and Child with Saints Elizabeth and John* and a *Portrait of a Young Man.* Not to be overlooked is *Joseph in Egypt* by Pontormo, who worked under Andrea del Sarto, while hardly likely to be missed is Bronzino's *Allegory with Venus and Cupid.* Turning to the school of Parma, from Correggio come several works, among them *Mercury Instructing Cupid* and *The Madonna of the Basket;* and from Parmigianino a large altarpiece, *Madonna and Child with John the Baptist and St Jerome,* painted when he was only about 20 years old.

Giovanni Bellini has already been mentioned but painting at the same time in Venice was Carlo Crivelli, to whose religious works a small room is devoted. Here are the splendid *Annunciation,* the *Virgin and Child with St Jerome and St Sebastian,* the *Immaculate Conception,* and the many-panelled *Demidoff Altarpiece,* named after its Russian owner. Among the few extant paintings of Giorgione two are to be found here, an *Adoration of the Magi,* and *Sunset Landscape with Saints George and Anthony Abbot* (sometimes thought to be a legendary scene with Aeneas and Anchises). Giorgione's life was short, while that of his contemporary Titian was long and consistently active. Among his works in the Gallery are the recently cleaned *Bacchus and Ariadne,* one of those painted for a room in the palace of Alfonso d'Este at Ferrara; *Portrait of a Man; Noli Me Tangere; The Vendramin Family; Madonna and Child;* an

Allegory of Prudence; and the late work *The Death of Actaeon* purchased
in 1972. Tintoretto is also here with *The Origin of the Milky Way*
and *St George and the Dragon,* while from Veronese come four allegories,
the *Consecration of St Nicholas* and the remarkable *Family of Darius
before Alexander.* Other 16th-century Venetian artists to be found in the
Gallery include Jacopo Bassano; Lorenzo Lotto—*Family Group* and
Lady as Lucretia are examples of his work; Vincenzo Catena; Palma
Vecchio; but there are also numerous other artists from different parts of
Italy. Among these are Sebastiano del Piombo with his large
Michelangelesque *Raising of Lazarus;* Ambrogio da Predis, a pupil of
Leonardo's, with among others his *Profile Portrait of a Lady;* Bernardino
Luini with *Christ among the Doctors;* and Giovanni Boltraffio, Leonardo's
chief pupil in Milan, with a *Madonna and Child.* Other painters who
should be mentioned include Bramantino, Vincenzo Foppa, Bergognone,
Francesco Francia, Garofalo, Lorenzo Costa and Giovan Battista
Moroni.

A splendid example of Italian painting at the beginning of the 17th
century is Caravaggio's *Supper at Emmaus.* Ascribed to him also is
Salome with the Head of John the Baptist, though the attribution is in
some considerable doubt. From Caravaggio's contemporary Annibale
Carracci come *Domine Quo Vadis?* (Christ appearing to St Peter on the
Appian Way), *The Dead Christ Mourned,* often called *The Three Maries,*
and several others, and there are also works by his brother Agostino and
cousin Ludovico. Domenichino's works include *St George Killing the
Dragon, Landscape with Tobias Laying Hold of the Fish, The Vision of St
Jerome,* and a small room is devoted to a number of frescoes which he
originally executed in the garden pavilion of the Villa Aldobrandini at
Frascati. Guercino is represented by *The Incredulity of St Thomas* and an
early work on copper, *Angels Weeping over the Dead Christ.* Among
Guido Reni's works here are *Lot and his Daughters Leaving Sodom, The
Coronation of the Virgin* (on copper) and the very large *Adoration of the
Shepherds.* An interesting work is *St Andrew and St Thomas* by the
sculptor Bernini, so far the earliest documented example of a painting by
him. Among other 17th-century paintings in the Gallery are *Christ
Driving the Traders from the Temple* by Bernardo Cavallino, *Landscape
with Mercury and the Woodman* by Salvator Rosa, and there are works
by Andrea Sacchi, Sassoferrato, Bernardo Strozzi and others.

Venice is the source of most of the 18th-century paintings. There
are numerous views by Canaletto, particularly notable being *Regatta on
the Grand Canal, The Basin of S. Marco on Ascension Day, The Upper
Reaches of the Grand Canal,* and *The Stonemason's Yard.* Two views
done by Canaletto when he was in England are also here, *Eton College*
and *The Rotunda at Ranelagh.* Complementing Canaletto's vision are the
Impressionistic views by Guardi of Venice, some of them tiny caprices

concentrating on ruined architecture and others like *The Doge's Palace* and the *Punta della Dogana* giving more generalized, airy views of the city. Probably influential upon Guardi was Michiel Marieschi, by whom there are a couple of works, and an intimate view of Venetian interiors is to be found in several pictures by Pietro Longhi. Of great importance are several paintings by Giovanni Battista Tiepolo, among them several decorative panels, *The Vision of St Clement*, and the ceiling painting, *An Allegory with Venus and Time*, and there are also a number of works by his son Giandomenico Tiepolo. Other 18th-century works are by Panini, Pellegrini, G. B. Pittoni and Pompeo Batoni.

The collection of Early Netherlandish painting contains works by the greatest of them all, Jan van Eyck. His famous *Arnolfini Marriage Portrait*, dated 1434, the *Man in the Red Turban*, and the *Portrait of a Man*, inscribed 'Tymotheos Léal Souvenir 1432', are all in the Gallery. Robert Campin, thought to be synonymous with the Master of Flémalle, is represented by a pair of portraits, *A Man* and *A Woman*, and *The Virgin and Child before a Firescreen*. From Rogier van der Weyden, who was probably his pupil, come *Pietà, Magdalen Reading, Portrait of a Lady*, and *St Ivo;* and from Dieric Bouts, who was much influenced by him, are *The Entombment* and a *Portrait of a Man*. Less intense but equally fascinating are the paintings of Hans Memling: the *Donne Triptych*—a *Virgin and Child with Saints and Donors; A Young Man at Prayer;* and *St John the Baptist* and *St Lawrence*, wings of an altarpiece. Other Flemish 15th- and 16th-century painters represented include Gerard David, Jan Gossaert, called Mabuse, Quentin Massys, Bartholomeus Spranger, and Pieter Brueghel the Elder, whose *Adoration of the Kings* is devoid of idealization, reaching out instead to the fantastic and the grotesque. Outstanding among the later Flemish paintings are the works of Rubens and Van Dyck. Among the works of the former here are: *Peace and War*, a canvas he presented to Charles I when sent to England as envoy of Philip IV of Spain in 1629-30; *The Rape of the Sabine Women; St Bavo about to Receive the Monastic Habit at Ghent; The Brazen Serpent; Autumn Landscape with a View of the Château de Steen; Landscape with Shepherd and Flock; The Apotheosis of the Duke of Buckingham; The Judgement of Paris; A Roman Triumph; The Miraculous Draught of Fishes; Portrait of Susanna Lunden*, the sister of Rubens's second wife; *A Lion Hunt; The Birth of Venus*, a painting in grisaille; *The 'Coup de Lance'*—the piercing of Christ's body by St Longinus; *Aurora Abducting Cephalus;* a *Portrait of the 2nd Earl of Arundel; The Watering-Place; A Shepherd with his Flock in a Woody Landscape;* and another *Judgement of Paris*, which came to light in 1966 and has been attributed to a very early period in Rubens's career around 1600. There are also a considerable number of paintings attributed to Rubens's studio. Representative of the work of Van Dyck are *The Emperor Theodosius*

Forbidden by St Ambrosius to Enter Milan Cathedral—a very Rubensian work; *Portrait of Cornelis van der Geest;* the huge *Equestrian Portrait of Charles I,* painted during the 1630s; *Portrait of the 1st Earl of Denbigh,* an unusual picture of this gentleman out hunting with his servant and dressed in pyjamas. Other Flemish painters include Jacob Jordaens with, among others, *The Holy Family and John the Baptist;* David Teniers the Younger with such paintings as *Peasants Playing Bowls outside a Village Inn;* Gonzales Coques; and Jan Brueghel.

Dutch painting comes mainly from the 17th century and embraces the greatest quality and variety. Rembrandt's work is to be seen in all its aspects. Of portraiture there are two self-portraits, one done in flamboyantly rich clothes about the age of 34, and the other, moving in its uncompromising honesty, done in old age. An early portrait of his wife Saskia in Arcadian costume is also here, as are portraits of the two old people Jacob Trip and his wife Margaretha. There is a splendidly baroque Biblical scene, *Belshazzar's Feast,* and on a smaller scale come religious works such as *Christ Presented to the People, The Deposition,* and *The Woman Taken in Adultery.* Not to be overlooked is the small *Man Reading in a Lofty Room* where light and shadow present a particularly telling image. One of Rembrandt's most talented pupils was Carel Fabritius, whose work is illustrated by a *Portrait of a Man in a Fur Cap.* Among the other great Dutchmen here is Frans Hals, whose *Portrait of a Man Holding Gloves* is very fine and whose *Family Group* hangs near it. Dutch landscape painting is well illustrated; there are many works by Jacob Ruisdael, among them *Waterfall in Rocky Landscape, Bleaching Ground, Shore at Egmond-aan-Zee, Ruined Castle Gateway,* and *Pool Surrounded by Trees;* and there are a number of paintings by Salamon Ruisdael also. The beauties of Albert Cuyp's vision are to be found in *Ubbergen Castle,* two distant views of Dordrecht (the 'Large Dort' and the 'Small Dort'), *Landscape with Cattle,* and *Hilly River Landscape.* A landscape of great renown is Meindert Hobbema's *The Avenue, Middleharnis,* and here also by him are *The Ruins of Brederode Castle* and *View of the Herring Packer's Tower, Amsterdam.* Other land and seascapes come from Jan van Goyen, Jan van de Cappelle, Philips Wouwerman, Simon de Vlieger, Willem van der Velde, Hendrick Avercamp, and there are Italianate scenes from Jan Both, Bartolomeus Breenbergh, Nicolaes Berchem, Karel Dujardin. Not to be overlooked are the sweeping landscapes of Philips Koninck. Another source of delight are the paintings of Dutch interiors, foremost among them Vermeer's *Lady Standing at a Virginal* and *Lady Seated at a Virginal,* profound studies of seemingly insignificant moments. Pieter de Hoogh's scenes of courtyards in Delft also conjure up another world as, in their own way, do the scenes of Gabriel Metsu, Gerard ter Borch and Jan Steen. Also of interest are the city scenes of Gerrit Berckheyde, Jan van

der Heyden, and the church interiors of Pieter Sanredam. Another group
of painters, the Dutch Caravaggisti, are also represented by such works
as Gerrit Honthorst's *Christ before the High Priest* and Hendrick
Terbrugghen's *Lute Player.*

Spanish painting also is most richly represented by the 17th-century
artists, above all by Velazquez. Here is his early *St John on the Island of
Patmos* and here too is *The Immaculate Conception of the Virgin,* bought
by the Gallery in 1974. These two pictures were painted in 1618 for the
Convent of the Shod Carmelites in Seville. Another early work is *Christ
in the House of Martha and Mary,* dated 1618. Two portraits of Philip
IV, one full-length, the other a bust, done 25 years later, are examples
of a series which immortalized this king. *Christ after the Flagellation
Contemplated by the Christian Soul* is a sombre work, probably done in
the early 1630s. A totally different later work is the famous nude, *The
Rokeby Venus.* From Zurbarán come two works, *St Margaret* and *St
Francis;* by Murillo are *Christ at the Pool of Bethesda, The Two Trinities,
The Infant John with the Lamb,* and a self-portrait; from Valdes Leal
comes an *Immaculate Conception;* from Ribera a *Lamentation over the
Dead Christ;* from Ribalta, *The Vision of Father Simon;* and from del
Mazo, Velazquez's son-in-law, *Queen Mariana of Spain in Mourning.*
The art of the 16th century is displayed in the work of El Greco. Here
are *Christ Driving the Traders from the Temple, The Adoration of the
Name of Jesus* (once known as the Dream of Philip II), *The Agony in the
Garden.* Goya represents the art of the 18th and early 19th centuries. *The
Picnic* was probably painted in the 1780s; a portrait of Doña Isabel
Cobos de Porcel dates from 1806; *Dr Peral* from 1800; and a portrait of
the Duke of Wellington from 1812-14.

The representation of German painting begins in the 15th century
with the panel of *St Matthew, St Catherine, and John the Evangelist* by
Stephen Lochner, and *The Presentation in the Temple* by the Master of
the Life of the Virgin. From Lucas Cranach come *Cupid Complaining to
Venus* and *Portrait of a Woman; Mystic Pietà, The Trinity,* and *Portrait
of a Man* are by the Strasbourg painter Hans Baldung Grien who was
once employed in the workshop of Dürer. A *Portrait of the Painter's
Father* is doubtfully attributed to Dürer himself. *Landscape with a
Footbridge* by Albrecht Altdorfer is an extraordinary work to come from
that time—a landscape with no subject other than Nature. Masterpieces
of the German school are two works by Holbein; the impressive portrait
of Christina of Denmark, Duchess of Milan, painted at a time when
Henry VIII wished to marry her, and said to have been executed after
only one three-hour sitting; and *The Ambassadors,* two Frenchmen who
at different times represented their country in England, depicted with
objects symbolizing their cultural heritage, dated 1533. Representative of
the early 17th century is Adam Elsheimer. His works here are *St Paul*

on Malta, *Tobias and the Angel*, *Baptism of Christ*, and *St Lawrence Prepared for Martyrdom*. Among the 17th-century French paintings are a number of magnificent works by Claude: *Seaport with the Embarkation of St Ursula*, dated 1641; *Landscape with a Goatherd*; *Landscape with Hagar and the Angel*; *Landscape, Narcissus*; *Seaport with the Embarkation of the Queen of Sheba*, dated 1648; *Landscape, David at the Cave of Adullam*, dated 1658; *Landscape, Cephalus and Procris Reunited by Diana*, 1645; *A Seaport*, 1644; *Landscape, Aeneas at Delos*, 1672. Nicholas Poussin is also well represented, among his works being *Cephalus and Aurora*, of about 1630; *The Adoration of the Golden Calf*; *Landscape with a Snake*, dated about 1648; *The Annunciation*; *Bacchanalian Revel before a Term of Pan*; *View in the Roman Campagna*. Not to be overlooked are *A Woman and Five Children* by Antoine Le Nain, and *The Adoration of the Shepherds*, ascribed to his brother Louis. In a very different vein are Philippe de Champaigne's triple portrait of Cardinal Richelieu, probably painted for the use of the sculptor Francesco Mochi, and a full-length portrait of the Cardinal. Several landscapes come from the hand of Gaspar Dughet, and from the Caravaggesque painter Le Valentin is *The Four Ages of Man*. Though not so rich in French 18th-century painting as the Wallace Collection the Gallery possesses *La Gamme d'Amour* by Watteau; *The Four Times of the Day* and *The Four Ages of Man* by Lancret; two portraits by Nattier; and three works by Chardin, *The Young Schoolmistress*, *The House of Cards*, and *La Fontaine*. Other 18th-century artists include Saint-Aubin, C. J. Vernet, Perroneau, Greuze. Of early 19th-century painters Ingres is represented by several works, notably *Madame Moitessier Seated*, dated 1856, and Delacroix by a portrait of Baron Schwiter and *Ovid among the Scythians*, dated 1859. There are numerous works by Corot, Diaz, Daubigny, Théodore Rousseau; from Courbet comes *Les Demoiselles des Bords de la Seine* and several other works which, being part of the Lane bequest, spend some of their time in Dublin. The same can be said of *La Musique aux Tuileries* by Manet, and by him also are several fragments from *The Execution of Maximilian*, and *La Servante de Bocks*, dated 1878 or 9. Monet is represented by, among others, *Le Bassin aux Nymphéas*, *L'Inondation*, and *Waterlilies*; Renoir by *La Nymphe à la Source*, *Les Parapluies* (which is also shared with Dublin) and several later works; Camille Pissarro by *The Boulevard Montmartre at Night* and others; and Degas by *La La at the Cirque Fernando*, *Young Spartans*, *Combing the Hair*. A superb Seurat, *Une Baignade, Asnières*, is here, and from Cézanne come several landscapes, *La Vieille au Chapelet*, a portrait of his father, a self-portrait, and *Les Grandes Baigneuses*, one of several paintings on this theme. Also here are a flower-piece by Gauguin and several pictures by Van Gogh, among them *Cornfield with Cypresses*, *The Chair and the Pipe*, *Sunflowers*; in 1972 the Gallery acquired a work by

Henri 'Douanier' Rousseau—*Tropical Storm with a Tiger*. Other 19th-century artists include Fantin-Latour, Boudin, Bonvin, Lépine, Harpignies, Monticelli.

One English painting, if it may be termed thus, is to be found displayed with the early Italian works in the Gallery. The *Wilton Diptych*, as it is known, is by an unknown painter who may have been English or French and depicts Richard II presented by his patron saints to the Virgin and Child. On the reverse (it was made to fold like a book) are the King's coat of arms and his personal emblem, the white hart. The next group of English paintings comes from the 18th century and contains many fine portraits by Sir Joshua Reynolds, among them *Captain Robert Orme, Lord Heathfield, Anne, Countess of Albermarle* and *General Tarleton*. There are several delightful Gainsboroughs: *Mr and Mrs Andrews*, painted about 1750; *The Morning Walk* of about 1785-6; *The Watering-Place; The Painter's Daughters*. Hogarth is here too with his celebrated series *Marriage à la Mode* and *The Shrimp Girl;* and there is an accomplished portrait of Queen Charlotte by Sir Thomas Lawrence done when the painter was only 21. To see the full range of British painting it is necessary to visit the Tate Gallery, or for Constable the Victoria and Albert Museum, but there are some magnificent examples of the work of Turner and Constable at the National Gallery. By the former are *Fire at Sea, Snowstorm at Sea, Rain, Steam and Speed, Hero and Leander,* the *Fighting Témeraire, Calais Pier—the English Packet,* and a picture in which Turner directly competed with Claude, *Dido Building Carthage.* From Constable come *The Haywain* of 1821, *Salisbury Cathedral, The Cornfield,* and *The Cenotaph,* which depicts the cenotaph erected to Reynold's memory in 1812 by Sir George Beaumont at Coleorton.

National Maritime Museum, Romney Road, Greenwich, London S.E.10

Tel.: 01-858 4422

Open weekdays Summer 10-6; Sunday 2.30-6. Winter 10-5; Saturday 10-6; Sunday 2.30-6

This museum is located in a magnificent group of buildings in Greenwich Park by the side of the Thames. Nearby are the buildings of the Royal Naval College and the Royal Observatory both designed by Christopher Wren with, in the case of the former, additions by Nicholas Hawksmoor and John Webb. The central building and most remarkable feature of the Maritime Museum is the Queen's House, designed by Inigo Jones in an innovatory Palladian style. The house was begun in 1617 for Anne of Denmark, wife of James I, and completed for

Henrietta Maria, Charles I's Queen, in 1635. Its entrance hall is a perfect cube, 40 feet by 40 feet, and leading off one corner is the beautiful Tulip Staircase designed by Jones. Adjoining the Queen's House and connected with it by colonnades are the two wings of the Museum, originally built in 1807-16 to be part of the Royal Hospital School, for which purpose the Queen's House was also used. In 1934 the National Maritime Museum was formed and these buildings were given over to it. It was finally opened to the public in 1937. The paintings in the Museum form but one part of the collection, which deals with every kind of object connected with maritime activity.

The genesis of the collection goes back as far as Samuel Pepys, who became Secretary of the Admiralty in 1673 and collected the ship models from which the shipwrights constructed their men-of-war. Even before that some of the paintings had been commissioned by the Lord High Admiral, James, Duke of York, with the idea of commemorating the glory of the officers who had fought against the Dutch at the Battle of Lowestoft. These paintings are the twelve famous portraits of the 'Flaggmen' by Sir Peter Lely which are to be found together in the Queen's House. Among them is a portrait of Sir William Penn, father of the founder of Pennsylvania. In the 1670s the two famous Dutch marine artists Willem van de Velde the Elder and his son Willem the Younger were invited to England and given a studio in the Queen's House, where they painted some of the scenes involving British ships which are to be seen there in such profusion today. Other paintings in the Queen's House are portraits of the Tudor monarchs Henry VII, Henry VIII, and Elizabeth, and one of the latter's adversary Philip of Spain. Portraits of the great Elizabethan seamen and adventurers Drake, Essex, Hawkins and Frobisher hang alongside fascinating stylized depictions of Armada battles. Hanging in the Great Hall is a fine full-length portrait by Daniel Mytens of Lord Howard of Nottingham, the commander of the English fleet in the Armada campaign of 1588. The ceiling of this Hall was originally covered with paintings by Orazio Gentileschi but these were later removed to Marlborough House. On the first floor are to be found several interesting works: a portrait of Inigo Jones by Hogarth, after Van Dyck; engravings by the great etcher Jacques Callot of the ill-fated expeditions of 1627 and 1628 to relieve La Rochelle; a portrait of Henrietta Maria by Van Dyck; portraits of Samuel Pepys and John Sheffield, Duke of Buckingham by Kneller. There is an imposing portrait of the Dutch Admiral Michiel de Ruyter by Ferdinand Bol and many of the rooms contain marine paintings by 17th-century Dutchmen. Besides the van de Veldes there are works by Adam Willaerts, Ludolf Bakhuyzen, Simon de Vlieger, Porcellis, Vroom, Dubbels, and others.

The wings of the National Maritime Museum contain numerous portraits of seamen and admirals throughout British history. Notable are

Sir George Rooke by Michael Dahl, and *Admiral Byng* and *Admiral Benbow* by Kneller. The naval portraits by Reynolds are of considerable interest. Here is his full-length painting of Viscount Keppel, with whom he went to Italy in 1750. This portrait secured Reynolds's reputation as a portrait painter with its dramatic reverse pose of the *Apollo Belvedere*. There are three other portraits by Reynolds of Keppel, and also of other sailors, notably *Lieutenant Roberts*. There are also good portraits of *Earl Howe* and *Viscount Duncan* by John Singleton Copley and of *Viscount Hood* by James Northcote. One group of pictures centres round the figure of Nelson. There are two works by Benjamin West, *The Death of Nelson* and *The Apotheosis of Nelson;* and another well-known *Death of Nelson* comes from Arthur William Devis. Lemuel Abbott's fine portrait of Nelson is here and there are pastels of him and Lady Hamilton by J. Schmidt together with one of Romney's famous portrayals of Lady Hamilton, this time as Ariadne. Romney is in sterner form with his portraits of Sir Charles Hardy and William Bentinck among others. Among several depictions of the battle of Trafalgar is Turner's huge picture of the scene, commissioned by George IV and painted in 1823 to be a companion piece to de Loutherbourg's *Battle of June 1st, 1794,* which is also in the Museum. Several paintings of Napoleon include a portrait by Sir Charles Eastlake, but an especially poignant record of the Napoleonic Wars is a painting by Louis Garneray of *Prison Hulls containing French prisoners of war in Portsmouth Harbour.*

Besides the Dutch marine paintings in the Que·.n's House already mentioned there are numerous marine pictures of every description by other, mainly English, artists. Notable are works by Samuel Scott, Charles Brooking, Nicholas Pocock, and Dominic Serres, but there are many others covering events at sea up to the present day. Worth looking for are Francis Wheatley's *The Sailor's Return* and David Wilkie's *Landing at Dover.*

The journeys of Captain Cook provide an interesting series of paintings. There is a portrait of him by Nathaniel Dance, and a *Death of Cook* by Zoffany, but most fascinating are the paintings by William Hodges of the places seen on Cook's second voyage. Hodges, a pupil of Richard Wilson, was the official artist to the expedition and his evocations of Easter Island, Tahiti, and New Zealand are of considerable beauty—he seems to combine the classical style in which he was trained with a form of naturalism compelled by the new places he was seeing. Unfortunately he abandoned the career of artist to become a banker and two years afterwards committed suicide.

Before quitting Greenwich the visitor should not fail to visit the Painted Hall of the Royal Naval College which was decorated by Sir James Thornhill between 1707 and 1727. Its grand illusionism in the tradition of the Italian High Baroque is a sight not to be missed.

National Portrait Gallery, St Martin's Place, Trafalgar Square, London W.C.2

Open Mon.-Fri. 10-5; Saturday 10-6; Sunday 2-6

This gallery, the first in the world in which an effort was made to record the appearances of a country's national figures, was founded in 1856. The 5th Earl of Stanhope, supported by Prince Albert, Lord Palmerston, Thomas Carlyle and Lord Macaulay, was the prime mover in its foundation but it was not until 1896 that it was opened on its present site. During the years since that date the purpose of the Gallery has been to collect and evaluate portraits of figures of importance in some aspect or other of English life. In this its function has not only been to show an impressive array of portraits but also to provide an archive of physiognomies for anyone to consult. In recent years photographs have naturally begun to play an increasing part; also in recent years the arrangement of the portraiture has provided a fascinating journey through English history for the visitor.

The portraits begin in Room I on the top floor of the Gallery with a series of copies of portraits of early kings, but the first king to be vividly portrayed as an individual is Henry VII by Michel Sittow; this painting was commissioned for Margaret of Austria, whom Henry sought as a wife after the death of Elizabeth of York. A striking historical and artistic document is the great cartoon designed by Holbein for a mural in the Whitehall Palace which was destroyed by fire at the end of the 17th century. What is to be seen here is but a fragment of the original cartoon with the massive figure of Henry VIII behind whom stands the much diminished figure of his father. In the painting itself the stance of the King was apparently changed so that he faced the spectator even more dominatingly, as can be seen from the copy now in Liverpool's Walker Art Gallery. There are portraits of several of Henry's wives, and also portraits of his advisers and ministers Thomas Wolsey and Thomas Cromwell; the portrait of the latter is after a lost original by Holbein. Thomas Cranmer, created Archbishop of Canterbury by Henry after the break with Rome, is nearby, painted by Gerlach Flicke; here too is Sir Thomas More, this portrait being the finest copy of the original by Holbein now in the Frick Gallery in New York. An interesting picture shows Henry VIII on his deathbed commending his son, Edward VI, to his counsellors, while the Pope is depicted collapsing in one corner of the picture and the desecration of statues and religious buildings is shown in the other corner. Edward VI is depicted in a portrait by William Scrots remarkable for its trick perspective. There are charming portraits of Lady Jane Grey and Mary I, including one of the latter by Hans Eworth, whose work is also represented by a portrait of the 1st Viscount Montague.

There is a portrait of Mary, Queen of Scots, painted when middle-aged and bereft of all romantic aura and there is, of course, a selection of portraits of Elizabeth I, who was often painted. The full-length 'Cobham' portrait gives perhaps one of the few more realistic glimpses of the monarch; the 'Ditchley' portrait, commissioned by Sir Henry Lee in commemoration of a visit to Ditchley in 1592 and thought to have been painted by the Fleming Marcus Gheeraerts, shows Elizabeth as a gloriously attired image with her foot planted upon the globe. Portraits of her ministers and other great Elizabethans are also to be found. Here are Lord Burghley, his son Robert Cecil, Sir Walter Raleigh, the Earl of Essex, Sir Philip Sidney, Sir Christopher Hatton and Sir Henry Lee, the last-named painted by the Fleming Antonio Mor who also painted Mary I. The 'Chandos' portrait of William Shakespeare is also here; it has the best claim to authenticity of all portraits of him, its provenance being traceable to within a generation of his death. Another painting of great interest is the biographical painting of Sir Henry Unton, a minor English diplomat, whose life is depicted in the one picture in great and fascinating detail.

Few of the portraits already mentioned can be traced with any certainty to a definite artist but with the advent of the 17th century more becomes known of the artists themselves. After the almost hieratic images of Elizabeth the portrait of James I by Daniel Mytens in Room II appears much more human. There is also a portrait of his wife Anne of Denmark, by William Larkin. James I's short-lived eldest son Henry, Prince of Wales, who anticipated his brother Charles in his love of art, is depicted by Robert Peake the Elder; there is also a charming portrait of Charles himself on horseback. Some of the distinguished men of the Jacobean period are here: John Donne portrayed by a follower of Isaac Oliver; Inigo Jones the architect, a portrait after Van Dyck; and Ben Jonson, whose masques were often designed by Inigo Jones. There is a portrait of the royal favourite, the Duke of Buckingham, and also here are leading figures of Charles I's court, the Earl of Strafford, Archbishop Laud, and an oil sketch of the Earl of Arundel by Rubens. Elizabeth of Bohemia and her husband Frederick are also portrayed, either by Gerard Honthorst or one of his followers. And also in Room II is a portrait of Oliver Cromwell by Robert Walker in a pose derived from Van Dyck's portrait of Strafford, which itself echoes a Titian portrait.

In Room III the intellectual giants of the middle and the second half of the 17th century are to be found. There is a portrait of Milton at the age of about 19, and portraits of Andrew Marvell, John Evelyn, Thomas Hobbes, John Locke, Samuel Butler, John Bunyan, Sir Robert Boyle. There is a fine revealing portrait of Sir Isaac Newton by Sir Godfrey Kneller, who is also represented by a portrait of Dryden. Here too is an engraving by Houbraken of William Harvey, who discovered the circulation of the blood.

The next room reveals an array of Charles II's mistresses, among them a portrait of Nell Gwynn from the studio of Lely. There is a portrait of the King himself by Edward Hawker, and members of his government, the Cabal, are also portrayed. Most interesting is a portrait of Samuel Pepys by John Hayls. James II is here portrayed by Kneller and by him also is a portrait of Sir Christopher Wren. The other great architects are not forgotten; there is a portrait of Sir John Vanbrugh and a bust of Nicholas Hawksmoor.

Room V is notable for Kneller's sketch for an allegorical painting of the Duke of Marlborough and his victory over Louis XIV; and for a fine self-portrait by this German-born artist who dominated English art for 30 years. His portraits of the members of the Whig Kit-cat Club, among them Addison, Steele, Congreve and Walpole, fill the next two rooms. The club derived its name from the fact that its meeting place was in the house of Christopher Catt, a pastrycook, who used to make mutton pies called kit-cats which were eaten at the club.

The next room is perhaps the most distinguished for its collection of self-portraits. Here are self-portraits—drawings or paintings—by Hogarth, Stubbs, Zoffany, Angelica Kauffmann, Joseph Wright, Allan Ramsay, James Thornhill, Jonathan Richardson, Reynolds and Gainsborough—the last being particularly outstanding. There are portraits of many literary figures: Reynolds's remarkable portraits of Samuel Johnson and his biographer Boswell; Alexander Pope by Jonathan Richardson; Samuel Richardson by Joseph Highmore; Fanny Burney by her cousin Edward Burney. Very prominent is a plaster bust of Colley Cibber, the poetaster whom Pope loathed, and also here are a bust of Laurence Sterne by Joseph Nollekens and a terracotta bust of Hogarth by Roubiliac.

Soldiers and politicians who made their mark on 18th- and early-19th-century history are next to be found: a portrait of Warren Hastings by Reynolds; a bust of General Wolfe by Joseph Wilton; a bust of William Pitt the Younger by Nollekens. Pitt is the main figure in a large group portrait of him addressing the House of Commons in 1793 and there is also a portrait of him by John Hoppner. A number of portraits by Sir Thomas Lawrence reveal the quality of some of his work: there is an excellent portrait of Lord Castlereagh, another of the 2nd Earl of Liverpool, one of Sir John Moore, the hero of Corunna, and a half-length of George IV. There is a dashing portrait of Nelson by Sir William Beechey and one of Lady Hamilton by Romney. A bust of Canning is by Sir Francis Chantrey. Other faces to appear here include the religious leader John Wesley painted by Nathaniel Hone; Sir Humphrey Davy portrayed by Thomas Phillips; and the architect Sir John Soane by John Jackson.

Reformers figure next in the Gallery's survey of English history. There is a large painting of the reformed House of Commons of 1833 by Hayter, the portrayal of a significant moment in British constitutional history. The faces of many prominent reformers are on the wall: Jeremy Bentham by Henry Pickersgill; the Earl of Shaftesbury by G. F. Watts; a bust of Richard Cobden by Thomas Woolner; Stephen Lushington, a leader of the movement for the abolition of slavery and of capital punishment, by Holman Hunt; John Bright; Elizabeth Fry; and two surprising works, one of John Thelwall, a radical speech-therapist, attributed to William Hazlitt, and another of Joseph Lancaster, an educational reformer, attributed to John Hazlitt, William's brother.

In the next room are some of the Great Victorians: Disraeli, Gladstone, the 2nd Marquess of Salisbury, all painted by Sir John Millais; Sir Charles Dilke and Cardinal Manning painted by G. F. Watts; and a double portrait by Ford Madox Brown of the politician Henry Fawcett and his wife Dame Millicent, the advocate of Woman's Suffrage.

From now on figures in the world of art and letters predominate. The well-known bust of Sir Walter Scott by Chantrey is here as well as a sketch of him by Landseer. Byron, exotically portrayed in Greek costume by Thomas Phillips, hangs near a portrait of Wordsworth by Henry Pickersgill, a portrait of Shelley, and a depiction of Keats after Joseph Severn's miniature. There is a cast of Blake's life-mask and a drawing of him by John Linnell. Confronting the visitor too are likenesses of Charles Lamb (by Hazlitt), Coleridge, Southey—a bust by Chantrey, and Leigh Hunt. There is a self-portrait drawing by Constable, a drawing of Turner, and portraits of Richard Bonington, Flaxman, William Dyce and David Cox. From George Richmond come a number of interesting portrait drawings, firstly of the religious leaders, Cardinal Newman, Pusey and Keble, and even more interestingly, of the novelists Elizabeth Gaskell and Charlotte Brontë, though perhaps a more haunting image of the latter is to be found in the triple portrait of the Brontë sisters done by their brother Branwell, crude and creased though it may be. The only known portrait of Jane Austen is here, and there is one of George Eliot, who abhorred the portrait of Charles Dickens by Daniel Maclise which hangs in the Gallery. Robert and Elizabeth Browning hang together as do four other great poets of the 19th century, Tennyson, Arnold, Swinburne and Rossetti, all painted by G. F. Watts. There is a double portrait of Rossetti's mother and Christina Rossetti by Rossetti himself together with a self-portrait drawing; and there is a very interesting group of portraits done of each other by the original Pre-Raphaelites to send to one of their group, Thomas Woolner, who had emigrated to Australia.

Among other giants of the Victorian age represented are Carlyle, Darwin, John Stuart Mill, Ruskin, William Morris, Huxley, Trollope,

Sir Richard Burton and the freethinker Charles Bradlaugh who was painted by Sickert. These lead on to the great figures of the Edwardian era. Kipling is represented by Philip Burne-Jones, George Meredith by Watts. There is a bust of Conrad by Epstein, and not to be missed are John Singer Sargent's portrait of Henry James and his *Ellen Terry as Lady Macbeth.* Sickert is painted by Wilson Steer and vice versa; Whistler by Walter Greaves and George Moore by Henry Tonks. Other figures of the time, Oscar Wilde, Aubrey Beardsley, Max Beerbohm and Thomas Hardy are also in evidence. Musicians of the 19th and 20th centuries also have their place: there are portraits of Gilbert and Sullivan side by side by Holl and Millais, and also displayed are likenesses of Elgar, Delius, Vaughan Williams and Sir Thomas Beecham.

The Gallery is already rich in representations of figures of the 20th century. There is a portrait of Churchill by Sickert and a striking drawing of T. E. Lawrence by Augustus John. John recorded other faces too, among them W. B. Yeats, Walter de la Mare, Epstein; there is also a bust of John here by the latter. The Bloomsbury group are much in evidence: Lytton Strachey painted by Henry Lamb and by Nina Hamnett; a portrait of Bertrand Russell and a self-portrait by Roger Fry; Gwen Raverat with a portrait of Maynard Keynes; Vanessa Bell with a portrait of Leonard Woolf, and Duncan Grant with a portrait of Vanessa Bell. The portrait of Virginia Woolf by Stephen Tomlin is very good, especially as she appears to have been an unwilling sitter. Other Bloomsbury figures are E. M. Forster, portrayed by Dora Carrington, and Lady Ottoline Morrell by Simon Bussey. From the Vorticist group come a self-portrait by Wyndham Lewis and two dynamic portraits by him of Edith Sitwell. There are self-portraits also by David Bomberg and Gaudier-Brzeska and by William Roberts an interesting group portrait of *The Vorticists at La Tour Eiffel.* Another interesting self-portrait is by Isaac Rosenberg, the poet who was killed in the First World War. Other works which should not be overlooked are the busts of G. B. Shaw, Somerset Maugham and T. S. Eliot by Epstein.

Before leaving the Gallery the visitor should also look at the splendid selection of miniatures on the ground floor by artists such as Nicholas Hilliard and Isaac Oliver among others.

The Royal Academy, Burlington House, Piccadilly, London W.1
Tel.: 01-734 9052

The Royal Academy, founded in 1768 at the instigation of the leading painters, sculptors and architects of the time and placed under the patronage of King George III, has since that date had several homes, among them Somerset House, a wing of the National Gallery building, and its present home, where it has been firmly established for over a hundred years. The constitution of the Royal Academy required that each newly-elected Academician should present to the Academy 'a picture, bas-relief, or other specimen of his abilities' in order that he might be awarded his Diploma and his membership be approved. The Royal Academy thus possesses a considerable number of interesting works and it is proposed to open a gallery shortly within its precincts so that the public may have an opportunity of viewing some of the permanent collection. Outstanding in this collection is Michelangelo's sculptured tondo of the *Virgin and Child and St John*. Other remarkable works are Constable's *Leaping Horse* and a group of his oil sketches, and there are paintings by Reynolds, Lawrence, Richard Wilson, Turner, Raeburn, Millais, Watts, Sickert, Augustus John and many others. The Summer and Winter Exhibitions continue, of course, to be the Academy's main attraction.

Sir John Soane's Museum, 13 Lincoln's Inn Fields, London W.C.2
Tel.: 01-405 2107
Open Tuesday to Saturday 10-5

Sir John Soane's Museum is of unique interest as being the highly individual, almost perverse creation of Soane himself. The architecture of this house, which Soane acquired in 1811 and rebuilt for his own occupation and for the housing of his treasures, is itself an intriguing piece of work, and is perhaps of primary importance in revealing the idiosyncratic nature of this architect's talents. Second in importance perhaps is Soane's collection of antiquities, objets d'art and architectural drawings. The paintings which Soane purchased during his lifetime are not for the most part of the highest quality, but among them are a number of great interest, an interest which is only enhanced when the fact that the collection remains entirely as it was during Soane's life is considered. In 1833 an Act of Parliament was passed 'for the settling and preserving Sir John Soane's Museum, Library and Works of Art, in Lincoln's Inn Fields in the County of Middlesex, for the Benefit of the Public, and for establishing a sufficient Endowment for the due Maintenance of the same'. Trustees were appointed and upon Soane's death in 1837 they took over the administration of the Museum. It is organized in the same manner today, with an additional grant from the Treasury.

As the house is arranged more or less as it was in Soane's day it will be as well to enumerate the pictures as they are to be found. Over the fireplace in the dining-room on the ground floor is a portrait of Soane himself by Sir Thomas Lawrence; also here are two bas-reliefs by John Flaxman and a painting by Reynolds, *Love and Beauty*. The ceiling contains paintings by Henry Howard which were commissioned by

Soane in 1834. In the picture room the paintings are displayed in a unique way devised by Soane himself. He designed the walls with hinged panels which could open to display further pictures inside. Thus the room can contain considerably more pictures and as Soane himself said, 'Another advantage to this arrangement is that the pictures may be seen under different angles of vision.' The most important pictures in the room are Hogarth's two series, *The Rake's Progress* and *The Election*. The former consists of eight pictures: *The Heir; The Levée; The Orgy; The Arrest; The Marriage; The Gaming House; The Prison; The Madhouse. The Election* is in four parts: *An Election Entertainment; Canvassing for Votes; The Polling; Chairing the Member.* These twelve paintings are replete with the satire and social comment for which Hogarth is deservedly famed. Also in this room are *Landscape with Figures* by Zuccarelli; *Scene from 'The Merchant of Venice'* by Francis Danby; *Una Delivering the Red Cross Knight from the Cave of Despair* by Sir Charles Eastlake; *Mr Kemble as Coriolanus* by Sir Francis Bourgeois (the founder of the Dulwich Gallery); and works by Fuseli, Antonio Zucchi, Sir James Thornhill and others. There is a watercolour by Turner *Refectory of Kirkstall Abbey,* bought from the artist by Mrs Soane in 1804, and numerous sketches and drawings by such artists as Watteau, Piranesi, Clérisseau and Soane himself.

Going down to the lower floor a bust by Flaxman of the Corsican General Paoli is to be seen on the stairs and in the lower storey are further models for works by Flaxman and Thomas Banks. In the Dome, the oldest part of the Museum, is a cast of the *Apollo Belvedere,* a bust of Soane by Sir Francis Chantrey and statuettes by Flaxman of Michelangelo and Raphael. The New Picture Room, built in 1889-90 on the site of Soane's old office and original picture room, contains three paintings by Canaletto, *Venetian Scene; Piazza S. Marco, Venice; The Rialto, Venice. Admiral Tromp's Barge,* dated 1831, is by Turner, and there are several more models by Flaxman including *Charity, Hope,* and *Maternal Tenderness.*

Other works in the Museum include a miniature of Napoleon by Isabey; a number of watercolours by Francis Wheatley and William Hamilton; a *Scene on the Thames* by Samuel Scott; an interesting work, *L'Accordée du Village* or *Les Noces,* by Watteau; and other paintings and drawings by Henry Howard, John Jackson, John Downman.

Tate Gallery, Millbank, London S.W.1
Tel.: 01-828 1212
Open weekdays 10-6; Sunday 2-6

The Tate Gallery, opened in 1897, was founded for the purpose of displaying a national collection of British painting. Such a collection is now housed there together with the national collection of modern foreign painting and sculpture. The Gallery was not founded without a tremendous struggle carried on through several decades of the latter half of the 19th century. The concept of a British Gallery was inaugurated by the bequest of the sculptor Sir Francis Chantrey in 1841 of a large sum of money for the purchase of paintings and sculpture executed in Great Britain but specifically not for the purpose of erecting a building to house them. When Turner bequeathed his paintings to the nation on condition that a gallery was built to house them, though the paintings were accepted, the government avoided the question of housing them adequately. Various people such as John Ruskin protested and made suggestions, but nothing was done until in 1890 it became known that Mr Henry Tate, the sugar manufacturer and philanthropist, was prepared to offer his collection to the nation and that he proposed a new national gallery should be built devoted to British art and maintained by means of annual grants from the Treasury. The Treasury procrastinated and offered the Eastern and Western Galleries in the South Kensington Museum for the purpose, a proposal which was widely criticized and which caused Mr Tate to withdraw his offer. But in 1891 he anonymously offered to build a gallery at his own expense if the Government would provide a site at South Kensington large enough to permit future extension of the gallery. This site was, however, coveted for an extension of the Royal College of Science and the protagonists of this cause succeeded in persuading the Government that it should not be used for a new picture gallery. After further proposals miscarried Tate withdrew his offer of both money and pictures in March 1892. By November however his offer was renewed with the proposal by the Government of the site of Jeremy Bentham's 'model' penitentiary at Millbank. The construction of the building began and the Gallery was finally opened in July 1897 by the Prince of Wales. The core of the collection was the group of paintings and sculpture given by Tate himself to which were added works from the National Gallery, the Chantry bequest from the South Kensington Museum, and certain other works. In 1899 the Gallery was extended to more than double the original size by virtue once more of the bounty of Tate (now Sir Henry Tate) and in 1910 additional galleries provided by Sir Joseph Duveen were opened to house the Turner pictures. In 1919 it was recommended that the Tate should become the National Gallery of British Art of all periods and this resulted in a further shift of pictures from the National Gallery. The Gallery was already in possession of a group of foreign paintings, a bequest by Sir Hugh Lane, which a monetary gift by Samuel Courtauld enabled to be much enlarged. Further galleries and a sculpture hall were built through the munificence of Lord Duveen and opened in

1926 and 1937. Plans for the rebuilding of the Tate are again in progress and this will involve a new arrangement of the displays. At the moment the series of galleries to the left of the entrance hall contain the display of British painting from the 16th century onwards and in those to the right is to be found modern painting of all countries right up to the present day. Beyond the large central sculpture gallery are galleries usually given up to special exhibitions. The following is an abbreviated account of what is to be found in the Gallery's permanent collection.

The first British paintings deriving from Elizabethan and Jacobean times include: *Man in a Black Cap* by John Bettes, dated 1545; *Portrait of an Unknown Lady* by Hans Eworth; *Portrait of Lady Anne Pope* by Robert Peake the Elder; *Portrait of an Unknown Man*, probably by Isaac Fuller; and two appealing works by unknown artists, *Young Lady* and *The Cholmondely Sisters*, a rigidly stylized portrait of these two who were 'born the same day, married the same day and brought to bed the same day'. By Marcus Gheeraerts the Younger there is a portrait of Captain Thomas Lee, and *Elizabeth, Lady Tanfield* is by the Antwerp painter Van Somer, who was in London by 1616. Of individual charm are two portraits of *A Lady* and *A Gentleman* by Cornelius Johnson, born in England but of Dutch extraction, and a truly superb work is William Dobson's *Endymion Porter*. The favourite painter of the Royalists, Dobson succeeded Van Dyck as Court Painter. After him as Court Painter to Charles II came Lely, by whom there are several splendid works, among them *Two Ladies of the Lake Family* and *Elizabeth, Countess of Kildare*. Close to paintings by Lely can be seen portraits by his successor Sir Godfrey Kneller, notably *The First Marquis of Tweeddale* and *John Smith*, the engraver. A smaller room is devoted to the paintings of Hogarth and here are displayed the various facets of his talent. Here is his first success, *Scene from 'The Beggar's Opera'* (he did several versions of this, which was probably the first painting of a stage scene in Britain). Nearby are: the highly satirical *Calais Gate: O the Roast Beef of Old England; The Doctor's Visit; The Carpenter's Yard; The Staymaker; The Happy Marriage; The Dance*. Numerous portraits include a *Self-portrait; The Graham Children; Dr Hoadley, Bishop of Winchester; Mr Salter;* and a fascinating array of *The Artist's Six Servants*, a group portrait in which the faces all betray the unmistakeable stamp of Hogarth's vision. The extraordinary *Satan, Sin and Death* and *Sigismonda Mourning over the Heart of Guiscardo* are clear examples of Hogarth's ambition to attempt and excel in other forms of painting.

Other interesting examples of English 18th-century painting include: Joseph Highmore's *Portrait of a Gentleman in a Brown Velvet Coat* and his illustrations to Samuel Richardson's *Pamela;* Francis Hayman's *Wrestling Scene from 'As You Like It';* some contrived landscape pieces by Arthur Devis; and important examples of the work of Gainsborough

14 *Wellington Museum London*

15 *The Fitzwilliam Museum, Cambridge*

16 *Laing Art Gallery and Museum, Newcastle-upon-Tyne*

and Reynolds. From the former come *Mr and Mrs Joshua Kirby Pictured in a Landscape; The Watering-Place; Mrs Graham as a Housemaid; The Market Cart; Landscape: Sunset.* From Reynolds there are three riveting self-portraits in youth and middle age and as a deaf man; a half-length portrait of Viscount Keppel; *The Age of Innocence; Three Ladies Adorning a Term of Hymen*—this was a portrait of three sisters who wished to have 'their portraits together at full length, representing some emblematical or historical subject'. Among the other glories of the 18th century here are several works by George Stubbs: *Horse Attacked by a Lion; A Lion Devouring a Horse,* dated 1769; *Mares and Foals in a Landscape;* and there are a number of landscapes by Richard Wilson: *Hadrian's Villa; Cader Idris;* and *Holt Bridge on the River Dee.* Johann Zoffany and Francis Wheatley, who was possibly his pupil, are both represented, the former by one of his theatrical scenes, *Charles Macklin as Shylock.* Of considerable importance are the works of Joseph Wright of Derby, among them his portrait of Sir Brooke Boothby, which hints at a new attitude to nature (his subject holds a volume of Rousseau) and *An Experiment on a Bird in the Air Pump,* which, besides illustrating his interest in the use of artificial light in a painting, also describes the new attitude of scientific inquiry. *Moonlight with a Lighthouse; Coast of Tuscany* is an example of his landscape work where the depiction of light also plays an important part. Paintings in the grand manner of the latter part of the 18th century include works by the American-born Benjamin West and his countryman John Singleton Copley. By the former should be mentioned *Cleombrotus Ordered into Banishment by Leonidas, King of Sparta;* by the latter *The Death of Major Pierson.* Other foreigners in England who made their names about this time were Henry Fuseli and Philip de Loutherbourg. Fuseli, who began his career as a clergyman, is well represented at the Tate by some of his fantastic works, among them *The Nightmare, The Shepherd's Dream from 'Paradise Lost', Titania and Bottom, Lady Macbeth Seizing the Daggers,* and a personal fantasy, *Percival Delivering Balisame from the Enchantment of Urma.* De Loutherbourg's works, which considerably influenced Turner, are on the grand scale, dealing with what in the Romantic period had become an important aspect of nature—its sublimity. Here among others are *An Avalanche in the Alps, The Battle of Camperdown, The Battle of the Nile, Lake Scene in Cumberland,* and *A Distant Hill Storm.* Of the same period James Barry's *Lear Weeping over the Body of Cordelia* should not be missed; nor should Lawrence's impressive *John Kemble as Hamlet,* painted in 1801. There are also interesting works by Gavin Hamilton, George Romney, John Hamilton Mortimer, Allan Ramsay, George Morland, John Opie and Samuel Scott.

It would be impossible to comprehend fully the art of William Blake without a visit to the Tate, as here is an unrivalled collection of his works—drawings, watercolours (including the large colour prints of 1795) and paintings in the medium of tempera which he invented for himself and which in some cases did not sustain the passage of time. Not all of these can be mentioned but to give an indication of the scope of the collection, here are *Elohim Creating Adam; God Judging Adam; Newton; Nebuchadnezzar; Hecate; Satan in his Original Glory; Satan Smiting Job with Sore Boils; The Ghost of a Flea;* and the illustrations to *Dante.* Also to be seen is a group of works by Blake's foremost disciple Samuel Palmer, among them *The Harvest Moon, The Bright Cloud, Hilly Landscape.*

The collection of Turner's works is incomparable, for with the exception of a few outstanding examples all the oils in his possession at his death, numbering about 300, are now in the Tate. These and 19,000 watercolours and drawings were bequeathed by him to the nation. The bulk of the watercolours are in the British Museum but a selection of them is always on show in the Tate. Where there is such a plenitude of works to be seen it may be invidious to name any, but it may be helpful to name and date just a few to indicate how his career is charted here: *Fishermen at Sea off the Needles,* 1796 (the first oil he exhibited); *Morning amongst Coniston Fells,* 1797; *Destruction of Sodom,* 1805; *Battle of Trafalgar,* 1806-8; *Fall of an Avalanche in the Grisons,* 1810; *Snowstorm: Hannibal Crossing the Alps,* 1812; *Crossing the Brook,* 1815; *Bay of Baiae,* 1823; *Pilate Washing his Hands,* 1830; *Interior at Petworth,* c.1837; *Shade and Darkness—the Evening of the Deluge,* 1843; *Light and Colour—the Morning after the Deluge,* 1843; *Peace—Burial at Sea,* 1842. This last picture records the burial of Sir David Wilkie, who died at sea on his way home from the Near East. A few examples of Turner's late style are *Sunrise with Sea Monsters; Yacht Approaching the Coast; Norham Castle, Sunrise;* and *Heidelberg Castle.*

Constable, the other great landscape painter of the early 19th century, is also well represented, though to see his works in the same comprehensive fashion as Turner's it is necessary to go to the Victoria and Albert Museum. Here are representations of favourite and often painted subjects, to mention but a few: *Dedham Mill; Flatford Mill; Hadleigh Castle; Hampstead Heath with a Rainbow; Chain Pier, Brighton.* Examples of other landscape painters include: *Slate Quarries* by John Crome: *Landscape in Normandy* by Bonington; *The Drop Gate* by J. S. Cotman; *The Woodcutter* by John Linnell; *A Windy Day* by David Cox; *Gordale Scar* by James Ward. The last named is a vast romantic evocation exceeded in scale and conception only by such works as Francis Danby's *The Deluge* and John Martin's *The Great Day of his Wrath* of about 1853, one of Martin's three Judgement pictures which were widely acclaimed when exhibited and sent on tour through England and the U.S.A. for twenty years.

Nineteenth-century, particularly Victorian, genre painting forms an interesting section of the Tate collection. David Wilkie, who survived only a few years into the reign of Victoria, captured public taste with works like *The Blind Fiddler*. William Mulready persisted in the vein with works like *The Last In*, and it continued in different forms until late in the century with works like Augustus Egg's *Past and Present*, Nos 1, 2, and 3 of 1858—a representation of the Fall, heavily laced with symbolic emblems; W. P. Frith's *Derby Day*, 1858, and Robert Martineau's *The Last Day in the Old Home*. The Pre-Raphaelite movement, the most important movement of the mid-century, is well represented. Millais's *Christ in the House of his Parents*, exhibited at the Royal Academy in 1850, was virulently attacked by the critics, among them Charles Dickens in his magazine *Household Words*. Others of his works here include *Ophelia*, 1851-2, for which Elizabeth Siddal posed; *The Order of Release*, and *The Vale of Rest*. From Holman Hunt come *Claudio and Isabella*, and *Our English Coasts (Strayed Sheep)* of 1852. By Rossetti are two works from the earliest point in his career, *The Girlhood of Mary Virgin*, and *Ecce Ancilla Domini*, 1849; later works are *Monna Vanna*, *Beata Beatrix*, and *The Wedding of St George and Princess Sabra*. There are several works by Ford Madox Brown; a version of *The Last of England*; *Christ Washing Peter's Feet*; *Carrying Corn*; and the extraordinary unfinished *Take Your Son, Sir!* William Dyce's *Pegwell Bay* should not be overlooked and there are numerous other works by associates of the original Pre-Raphaelites. From Arthur Hughes come *April Love* and *The Eve of St Agnes*. From William Morris his only surviving easel painting, *Queen Guinevere*. From Burne-Jones *King Cophetua and the Beggar Maid*, *Love and the Pilgrim* and *The Golden Stairs*. Other paintings of the period which should be mentioned include Philip Hermogenes Calderon's *Broken Vows;* W. L. Windus's *Too Late;* Henry Wallis's *Death of Chatterton* (the model for this was the novelist George Meredith—and two years later Wallis eloped with his wife); Richard Dadd's fantastic *Fairy Feller's Master Stroke*, painted in Broadmoor, where Dadd spent his life after murdering his father in 1843; G. F. Watts's *Hope* and *Eve Tempted*. Other works are by James Collinson, John Brett, Lord Leighton, Albert Moore, J. F. Lewis, Alfred Stevens, Alma-Tadema.

From the late 19th and early 20th century come an impressive selection of portraits by John Singer Sargent, among them *Sir Philip Sassoon* and *Vernon Lee;* several works by his compatriot Whistler such as *Old Battersea Bridge* and *Nocturne in Blue and Gold; The Ball on Shipboard* by the French-born James Tissot, as well as paintings attempting a certain social realism such as those by Luke Fildes and Frank Holl. Examples of new trends in British painting are to be found in a number of works by Sickert and Wilson Steer: by the former are a version of

Ennui; Café des Tribuneaux, Dieppe; and a portrait of Aubrey Beardsley; by the latter are *The Beach at Walberswick; Girls Running, Walberswick Pier;* and *Boulogne Sands.* Harold Gilman is represented by *Edwardian Interior, Leeds Market* and others, and other painters of the Camden Town Group such as Spencer Gore, Robert Bevan, Charles Ginner are also here. Outstanding are works by Stanley Spencer, including two versions of *The Resurrection: Cookham; Apple Gatherers;* and *Christ Carrying the Cross.* Another group of artists displayed includes members of the Bloomsbury group and their associates; painters such as Duncan Grant, Vanessa Bell, Mark Gertler and Augustus John, whose sister Gwen John is also represented. From the Vorticist group also come a number of works, among them David Bomberg's *In the Hold* and Wyndham Lewis's *Portrait of Ezra Pound;* C. R. W. Nevinson, Edward Wadsworth and William Roberts are also represented. Other artists of the 20th century here include Matthew Smith, Victor Pasmore, Christopher Wood, Ben Nicholson, Paul Nash, John Nash, Edward Burra, David Jones, Ivon Hitchens, William Coldstream, Graham Sutherland, John Piper, John Craxton, John Minton, Bridget Riley, Keith Vaughan, Lucian Freud, Alan Davie, Patrick Heron, Lowry, Gillian Ayres, William Scott, and others. Worthy of the closest attention are a group of paintings by Francis Bacon, among them *Three Studies for Figures at the Base of the Crucifixion; Figures in a Landscape; Study of a Dog; Seated Figure.*

The collection of modern foreign painting begins with a group by the Impressionists and Post-Impressionists. Here are Manet's *Woman with a Cat* (a portrait of his wife); Monet's *Poplars on the Epte* and *The Seine at Port-Villez;* Sisley's *The Small Meadows in Spring;* Degas's *Woman at her Toilet;* Toulouse-Lautrec's *The Two Friends;* together with several Cézannes: *The Gardener* of about 1906, the *Avenue at the Jas de Bouffan,* and the unfinished *Still Life with Water Jug;* a Seurat, *Le Bec du Hoc, Grandcamp;* several Van Gogh works: *View at Auvers, The Chair and the Pipe;* and by Gauguin, *Harvest: Le Pouldu* and *Faa Iheihe. Flowers* by Henri 'Douanier' Rousseau is also here. By Bonnard and Vuillard, both members of the group called *Les Nabis* (from the Hebrew—'Prophet') in their early days are, by the former: *Interior at Antibes; Bathing Woman Seen from the Back; La Table;* and by the latter: *The Red Roof* and *Girl in an Interior.* Utrillo is represented by several works, Modigliani by sculpture and *Portrait of a Girl* and *The Little Peasant.* French expressionism is illustrated by Rouault's *Les Trois Juges* and *Aunt Sallys,* and by Soutine's *Landscape at Ceret.*

There is a room devoted almost entirely to the work of Matisse. Among the works to be found here are *Nude Study in Blue,* 1900; *Standing Nude,* 1907; *Portrait of André Derain* (here too is one of Matisse by Derain painted when they were in Collioure together); *The*

Inattentive Reader, 1919; *Reading Woman with a Parasol,* 1921, of which Matisse wrote when it was bought by the Tate, 'The painting selected is the result of prolonged effort and will represent me as well as possible—moreover I think it won't frighten the acquisitions committee of the Modern Museum in London.' The large composition of cut-outs entitled *The Snail* was done in 1953 when Matisse was too crippled to hold a brush or move from his chair. This new abstract technique is composed of coloured paper cut into shapes and pasted into forms by assistants under Matisse's direction. The four bronze studies of *The Back,* done over a period of twenty years, are also of considerable interest.

Picasso is equally well represented in the various phases of his career. An example of his early Blue Period of about 1905 is *Woman in a Chemise* and from the period of analytical Cubism come *Bust of a Woman, Seated Nude,* and *Guitar, Glass and Bottle* of 1912. His return to classical representational painting is illustrated by *Seated Woman* of 1923 but the rejection of this approach is witnessed by such paintings as *The Three Dancers,* 1925; *Seated Woman with Hat; Dora Maas Seated; Nude Woman in a Red Armchair.* A post-war painting is *Goat's Skull, Bottle and Candle.* Other Cubist works and paintings of those associated with the movement include *The Guitar, Fish, Guitar and Jug* by Braque; *The Sunblind* by Juan Gris; *Windows Opening Simultaneously* by Robert Delaunay; *Still Life, Leaves and Shell* and *Two Women Holding Flowers* by Fernand Léger. There are several works by Giacomo Balla, Umberto Boccioni, and Severini, painters belonging to the group known as the Futurists, founded in 1909. German Expressionism is to be seen in the work of Munch—*The Sick Child;* of Emil Nolde—*The Sea B,* 1930; and of Schmidt-Rottluff—*Woman with a Bag* and *Dr Rosa Schapiro.* And by Oscar Kokoschka are a portrait of the one-time Russian Ambassador to London, *Maisky,* and a view of Polperro, Cornwall which was given by the former Czech President Eduard Benes. Painters who represent the European movements of Dada and Surrealism are also to be found. *The Poet Reclining* by Chagall was painted in 1915 during the honeymoon following his first marriage. Of *Bouquet with Flying Lovers,* painted between 1934 and 1947, he said, 'Say that I work with no express symbols but as it were subconsciously. When the picture is finished everyone can interpret it as he wishes.' From Paul Klee comes *Walpurgis Night;* from de Chirico, *The Painter's Family;* from Max Ernst, *Forest and Dove* and *The Entire City;* from Magritte, *The Reckless Sleeper;* from Paul Delvaux, *Venus Asleep,* done in 1944 during bombing raids; and there are also paintings by Miró, Dali, André Masson, Man Ray, Tanguy. Abstract painting in Europe is illustrated by such works as *The Battle* by Kandinsky; *Composition with Red, Yellow, and Blue* by Mondrian, and the perhaps less stringently abstract paintings of such

artists as Jean Dubuffet, Hans Hartung, Nicolas De Stael, Pierre
Soulages, Antonio Tapies, and Serge Poliakoff.

A small room is devoted to the sculpture and paintings of Giacometti
and nearby is a room filled by a series of works by Mark Rothko, one of
the foremost American Abstract Expressionists. These works were
originally done for the Four Seasons restaurant in the Seagram building
in New York but the artist judged them to be unsuitable. The Abstract
Expressionist movement, mainly American, is also represented by works
by Jackson Pollock, Arshile Gorky, Franz Kline, De Kooning, Barnett
Newman and others. Other modern movements such as Op Art, Kinetic
Art, Pop Art and Post-Painterly Abstractions are represented by such
painters as Vasarely, Josef Albers, Morris Louis, Kenneth Noland, Frank
Stella, Bernard Cohen, David Hockney, Jasper Johns, Robert
Rauschenberg, Roy Lichtenstein, Andy Warhol, and others.

Sculpture in the Tate includes Rodin's *The Kiss*, Henry Moore's
Recumbent Figure and *Family Group*, Barbara Hepworth's *Three Forms*,
Marino Marini's *Horseman*, Jean Ipousteguy's *Earth*, and works by
sculptors as various as Epstein, Maillol, Degas, Lipschitz, David Smith,
Lyn Chadwick, Eduardo Paolozzi, Gaudier-Brzeska, Reg Butler, Ken-
neth Armitage, Anthony Caro, Jean Arp, Naum Gabo, Antoine Pevsner,
Kenneth Martin, Mary Martin.

Victoria and Albert Museum, Cromwell Road, London S.W.7
Tel.: 01-589 6371
Open weekdays 10-6; Sunday 2.30-6

The Victoria and Albert Museum is a repository of magnificent treasures
belonging to the fine and applied arts of all countries, styles and periods.
Paintings and sculptures form but a part of the collection though by no
means an inconsiderable one. The foundation of the Museum is owed to
Prince Albert whose name it partly bears and to Sir Henry Cole, its first
Director, whose portrait in mosaic is to be seen on one of the staircases.
The sources of the original collection were the Great Exhibition of 1851,
where contemporary works were purchased, and the Government School
of Design, which possessed a varied selection of objects of all periods.
These collections were originally held by the Museum of Manufacturers
which, on its removal to South Kensington in 1857 to become part of the
new South Kensington Museum, became known as the Museum of
Ornamental Art. The collection rapidly grew through purchase and
through the acquisition of such gifts as the Sheepshanks collection of
British painting, and in 1891 a competition was held for the design of

new, much larger buildings. The competition was won by Aston Webb and in 1899 the foundation stone was laid by Queen Victoria, who requested that the new building should be called the Victoria and Albert Museum. The building was opened in 1909 and the scientific part of the collection was set aside to form the new Science Museum. Before dealing with the painting and sculpture to be found in the Museum mention must be made in passing of some of its other attractions, for example; the Musical Instruments Gallery; the Costume /Court, which provides a visual history of European dress; the Cast Court, where casts of many major European sculptures are to be seen; the galleries dealing with medieval and Far and Near Eastern Art; the Gothic Tapestry Court with its outstanding set of Devonshire Hunting Tapestries.

Among the paintings in the Museum pride of place must be given to the Raphael Cartoons which are to be found in Room 48 on the ground floor. These are the most important examples of High Renaissance art to be seen in England and were painted by Raphael in 1515-16 as designs for tapestries commissioned by Pope Leo X for the Sistine Chapel. They were acquired by Charles I when Prince of Wales in 1623 and were placed on loan in the Museum by Queen Victoria in 1865, which loan is continued by the present Queen. The original set of tapestries woven from these designs is now on display in the Vatican Picture Gallery. One tapestry woven at Mortlake in the 17th century from the design for *The Miraculous Draught of Fishes* also hangs here. Originally there were ten cartoons but only seven have survived. The sequence of subjects is as follows: *The Miraculous Draught of Fishes, Christ's Charge to Peter, The Healing of the Lame Man by St Peter and St John at the Beautiful Gate, The Death of Ananias.* All these are on one wall and opposite are scenes from the life of St Paul: *The Blinding of Elymas the Sorcerer, The Sacrifice of Lystra, St Paul Preaching at Athens.*

There are several other Italian paintings of interest, the earliest being a large *Christ on the Cross* in tempera probably painted in central Italy about 1200. From the 14th century come works by the Florentine artist Nardo di Cione and the Genoese Barnaba da Modena; and from the 15th-century examples of the work of Botticelli and Crivelli. *The Conversion of St Paul* is by the Sienese Mannerist painter Domenico Beccafumi and there are examples of fresco painting by Perino del Vaga and Lodovico Carracci—*Hercules and the Hydra* by the latter is an unusual example of his work to be found in England. Numerous *cassone* or wedding chests also illustrate Florentine and Sienese painting and another facet of Florentine art is to be seen in the etchings of Stefano della Bella, a 17th-century artist influenced by Jacques Callot and one of the greatest Italian etchers. Besides the Crivelli already mentioned Venetian art is represented by a self-portrait by Tintoretto, two *Capricci* with ruins and figures by Guardi, two *Capricci* by Bellotto, several

studies for a ceiling by Giandomenico Tiepolo and a series of oil
sketches by Luca Carlevaris.

German painting is represented by an altarpiece of about 1400, in the
style of Master Bertram of Hamburg, dealing with the subject of the
Apocalypse; and by the large *Martyrdom of St Ursula*, painted about
1495 for a church in Cologne by the artist known only as the Master of
the St Ursula Legend. A portrait, dated 1517, is by Hans Wertinger and
there are several works by the 18th-century artist Johann Georg Platzer.

Of French painting, from the 17th-century comes a painting of
Peasants by Louis Le Nain; and from the 18th century a *Fête Champêtre*
by Pater; *The Swing* and *A Cavalier with Two Ladies* by Lancret; *The
Alarm* by Jean Francois de Troy; *Girl with Birdcage* by Greuze; and
several works by Boucher including a portrait of Madame Pompadour.
From the 19th century come works by Ingres and Delacroix, by the
latter a large sketch for *The Shipwreck of Don Juan* which is in the
Louvre. There are two works by Courbet, *Le Ruisseau du Puits Noir* and
L'Immensité, and here also is the well-known *Wood-Sawers* by Millet.
View on the Landes comes from Théodore Rousseau and other works are
by Corot, Diaz and Fantin-Latour, who has a number of flower and fruit
pieces. Not to be missed is Degas' *Ballet Scene from 'Roberto il Diavolo'*,
painted in 1876.

Certain not to be overlooked is the large altarpiece of *St George* from
Valencia, though it is actually the work of a German painter Andre
Marzal de Sas who was in Spain at the end of the 14th century. It has
recently been regilded and the inspection of its various scenes at close
quarters can provide a fascinating study.

Among Dutch and Flemish works are a small Rembrandt, *The
Departure of the Shunamite Woman; The Garden of Eden* by Jan
Brueghel; several studies by Rubens, including a portrait drawing of
Marie de' Medici; and works by artists such as Adriaen Brouwer, Jan van
Goyen, Philips Koninck, Jan Both, Gerard Ter Borch, Rachel Ruysch
Terborch and others. Many of the paintings from the foreign collection
enumerated here are to be found in the adjoining Rooms 87 and 105
though some of them are scattered throughout the Museum. A considerable number of them derive from the Ionides bequest of 1901, and
many 18th-century works were acquired with the John Jones bequest of
1882.

British painting, to be found in Rooms 104, 104A and 104B, with the
exception of the Constable collection which is in Room 103, is
represented in the Museum through a series of generous bequests,
notably the John Sheepshanks bequest of 1857. One of the earliest works
in the British collection is a portrait of John Donne; from the late 17th
and early 18th centuries come sketches for decorative schemes by
Antonio Verrio and Sir James Thornhill, and from later in that century

come several landscapes by Richard Wilson, his pupil William Hodges, George Morland and Julias Caesar Ibbetson. Gainsborough is represented by his 'showbox', a set of transparencies painted in oil upon glass, and Reynolds by several works including the particularly fine portrait of Mrs Thomas Whetham, and a *Portrait of an Unknown Man.* There is a compelling self-portrait by the Irish painter James Barry and several important dramatic works including Fuseli's *The Fire King,* Benjamin West's *The Choice of Hercules,* John Hamilton Mortimer's *Hercules Slaying the Hydra,* and de Loutherbourg's *The Flood.* Examples of later landscape painting include James Ward's *Bulls Fighting with a View of St Donat's Castle;* John Crome's well-known *View on Mousehold Heath* and *Skirts of the Forest;* Richard Bonington's *St Michael's Mount;* and eight examples of oil-painting by Peter de Wint, a rare medium for this artist. From Turner come several works including *East Cowes Regatta; Line-Fishing off Hastings,* dated 1835; and *Venetian View Showing the Salute and the Dogana.* Other landscape artists represented are John Linnell, J. B. Pyne, and Clarkson Stanfield and, of course best of all, Constable. In Room 103 nine finished oil-paintings and a number of oil sketches, among them full-size studies for *The Hay Wain* and *The Leaping Horse,* are to be found. In Room 106 is a selection of drawings and watercolours which is changed annually. The bulk of the great collection of Constable's works which the Museum possesses was presented by his daughter Isabel Constable in 1888, though several oil-paintings came from the Sheepshanks bequest. Among the oils are two views of Hampstead Heath; *Salisbury Cathedral from the Bishop's Grounds; Boatbuilding near Flatford Mill, Cottage in a Cornfield; Dedham Mill,* dated 1820. Many of the oil sketches include tree and cloud studies, studies done near East Bergholt, and sketches done near Brighton.

Other aspects of 19th-century painting are very well shown in the Museum. There are several works by Wilkie, among them sketches of Sir Walter Scott's daughters and *The Refusal,* a depiction of a scene in Robert Burns's *Duncan Gray.* Most comprehensively represented is William Mulready, son of a maker of leather breeches in County Clare. Among his paintings are *The Fight Interrupted, Shooting a Cherry, The Sonnet, Choosing a Wedding Gown* and many more. Thomas Webster's *The Village Choir* is also here and there is a large group of works by Sir Edwin Landseer. Of *The Old Shepherd's Chief Mourner* which hangs here Ruskin wrote, 'one of the most perfect poems and pictures which modern times have seen'. Here also by Landseer are *The Drover's Departure, The Eagle's Nest,* and *Suspense.* Another artist well represented is Constable's biographer C. R. Leslie, by whom, among other works, are *A Scene in the Artist's Garden, My Uncle Toby and the Widow Wadman,* and *Trissotin Reading his Sonnet to Les Femmes*

Savantes. From Richard Redgrave comes *The Poor Teacher;* from Paul Flaconer Poole *The Last Scene in 'Lear';* and there are also works by painters such as Daniel Maclise and W. P. Frith—there is a portrait of Dickens by the latter, and a fine one of Carlyle by Watts. The Pre-Raphaelite movement is represented by *The Day-Dream* by Rossetti and by Burne-Jones's evocation of the Three Graces, *The Mill.* A large canvas by him, *The Car of Love, or Love's Wayfaring* is to be found in the corridor, where also are to be found two huge frescoes by Lord Leighton, *The Industrial Arts Applied to Peace* and *The Industrial Arts Applied to War.*

The collection of miniatures in the Victoria and Albert is so important that mention must be made of some of the works to be found here in Rooms 55 and 57. The earliest are by Holbein, two portraits of Mrs Bemberton and of Anne of Cleves, the latter commissioned by Henry VIII when he was deciding whether to marry her. Notable among the group by Nicholas Hilliard are a portrait of Queen Elizabeth, one of his wife, and an exquisite work called *A Young Man Leaning against a Tree among Roses.* Among miniatures by Isaac Oliver are one of *Queen Elizabeth in Old Age* and another of Richard Sackville, Earl of Dorset. There are also works by his son Peter Oliver, and later miniaturists represented include John Hoskins and Samuel Cooper. From the collection of foreign miniatures can be picked out a portrait of Marie de' Medici by Francois Clouet. It must be emphasized that just a handful of the miniatures to be seen have been mentioned here.

The superb collection of watercolours can also be mentioned in passing. Only a small portion of it can be shown at any one time, but this group is changed at intervals and any not on show can be seen on application to the Print Room. There are fine examples of the work of Paul Sandby, Thomas Girtin, J. S. Cotman, David Cox, Peter de Wint, Turner, Blake—*Satan among the Rebel Angels,* and, of course, Constable. Thomas Rowlandson, John Crome, Francis Place, Thomas Shotter Boys, William Callow and Samuel Palmer are also among those represented. Examples of 20th-century watercolours are also plentiful and here are to be found works by Wilson Steer, Wyndham Lewis, Paul Nash, Matthew Smith, David Jones, Graham Sutherland, Henry Moore, Ben Nicholson, Keith Vaughan, Roger Hilton, William Scott, Gillian Ayres and numerous others. Foreign watercolours are also in abundance, the 19th century being represented by the work of Daumier, Millet, Decamps, Isabey, Moreau and others. Two works are by Cézanne and from the 20th century come works by Kokoschka, Emil Nolde, Sonia Delaunay, André Derain, and others.

Sculpture is perhaps one of the best-known collections of the Museum. In Room 22 Giovanni Pisano's sculpture of the upper half of the prophet Haggai, from the façade of Siena Cathedral, commands attention. Here is also a large relief of the *Madonna della Misericordia* by the early 15th-century Venetian sculptor Bartolommeo Buon, and there are works by two other Gothic sculptors, Arnolfo di Cambio and Tino di Camaino. Room 27 contains a *Virgin and Child* by the German sculptor Veit Stoss, and the Renaissance Galleries, Rooms 12 to 21, contain outstanding works. Unique outside Italy are the works by Donatello in Room 16. There is a marble relief of *The Ascension with Christ Giving the Keys to St Peter*, executed in the very shallow relief style known as *rilievo stiacciato* and of amazing beauty. Another large marble relief by him is of the *Dead Christ Tended by Angels*. A small bronze relief is a *Lamentation over the Dead Christ* and there is a small bronze figure of a *putto*. Continuing through these Rooms a relief of the *Virgin and Child* by Agostino di Duccio is to be seen—his great work was the sculptured decoration of the Tempio Malatestiano at Rimini. Further interesting works come from the della Robbia family—particularly noteworthy is an armorial roundel by Luca della Robbia and twelve roundels with *The Labours of the Months* by the same artist. Also not to be overlooked are a chimney-piece by Desiderio da Settignano, a portrait bust by Benedetto da Maiano and a bust of Giovanni Chellini, a Florentine doctor, by Antonio Rossellino. There is also another interesting work by this sculptor, a terracotta model of the *Virgin with the Laughing Child*. Another terracotta relief is by Verrocchio, a sketch for the Forteguerri monument at Pistoia and another relief called the *Allegory of Discord* is by the Sienese Francesco di Giorgio. Two small marble reliefs are by Antonio Lombardo and there are numerous small bronzes of great interest. Room 21 contains two famous works of sculpture. *Samson and the Philistine* is a splendid example of the work of Giovanni di Bologna and given pride of place is Bernini's *Neptune and Triton*, originally designed about 1619-20 as the dominating feature of a decorative pond belonging to Cardinal Montalto. Wax models by Michelangelo, Jacopo Sansovino and Giovanni di Bologna should also not be overlooked.

In Room I on the lower floor further important examples of Baroque sculpture are to be found, notably Bernini's bust of Thomas Baker, who took Van Dyck's triple portrait of Charles I to Rome to enable Bernini to work on a portrait bust. Other remarkable works are a bust by Finelli of the poet Francesco Bracciolini, a terracotta bust of St Philip Neri by Bernini and a terracotta model of a bust of Cardinal Zacchia by Bernini's rival Algardi. Two busts of members of the Medici family by Foggini are also here and in the cases are a number of fascinating sketch models. A sketch relief in terracotta of *David Dancing before the Ark* is by Algardi and there is a huge flamboyant bust of Charles II by Honoré Pelle. In Room 7 are busts of Voltaire and Diderot by Houdon which should not be missed.

The Wallace Collection, Hertford House, Manchester Square, London, W.1

Tel.: 01-935 0687

Open weekdays 10-5; Sunday 2-5

The Wallace Collection, housed in the imposing Hertford House, was formally opened to the public by the then Prince of Wales on 22 June 1900. It represents one of the finest collections in existence and was built up from small beginnings by the 1st and 2nd Marquesses of Hertford, both patrons of Sir Joshua Reynolds, to an increasing importance by the 3rd Marquess, who was an intimate of George IV; he bought paintings by Titian, Van Dyck, Canaletto, Rembrandt and others of the Dutch school. But it was his son the 4th Marquess, who became by inheritance an enormously wealthy man and who passed most of his life in Paris, who transformed the Collection into its present greatness as a selection of masterpieces surrounded by other paintings of the highest quality. Not only paintings either; though the scope of the present book is primarily concerned with paintings, mention must be made in passing of the other art objects in the Collection as important in their way as the paintings, amongst them being sculpture, furniture, majolica, enamels, porcelain, armour, and a fascinating collection of medals. Lord Hertford's taste was nothing if not eclectic, though his appreciation of and special interest in French art of the 18th century anticipated that of the brothers Goncourt, who are frequently credited with responsibility for the resurgence of 19th-century interest in that period. With the purchase of Fragonard's *The Schoolmistress* in 1841 for a very low sum, Lord Hertford set the standard for his splendid 18th-century collection, His interests and acquisitions also ranged from Rubens to Poussin, from Andrea del Sarto to Salvator Rosa; he increased the representation of English 18th-century art and did not neglect to purchase works by contemporary artists, both French and English. Lord Hertford did not marry and upon his death in 1870 his fortune and his collection were bequeathed to Richard Wallace, who had lived with him for the past thirty years and appears to have been his natural son. In 1872 Sir Richard and Lady Wallace (he was knighted for philanthropic activities during the Seige of Paris and the Commune) moved with a great part of the collection to London, where it remained on exhibition at the Bethnal Green Museum until Hertford House could be prepared for them to take up residence there. Sir Richard increased the Collection by the purchase of several pictures and by the acquisition of bronzes, goldsmiths' work, majolica and armour. Upon his death in 1890 the Collection was left totally to his wife, a Frenchwoman, who by her will, dated 1894 (she died in 1897), bequeathed it to the British nation upon condition that it should not be broken up and that a special museum should be built to house it. A committee set up to consider the bequest in 1897 recommended that the Collection should remain at Hertford House which should be suitably altered to become such a museum, though it had also been suggested and plans devised that a new gallery should be built adjacent to the National Gallery. Nevertheless Hertford House remained the home of the Collection.

Hertford House was originally built in 1776 by the 4th Duke of Manchester. In 1791, several years after his death, it was leased as the Spanish Embassy, but the lease was acquired by the 2nd Marquess of Hertford in 1797 and he and later his wife lived there until 1834. Neither the 3rd nor the 4th Marquess lived in the house and before Sir Richard and Lady Wallace returned to live there great alterations were made to its structure. Numerous further alterations have also been effected since the house became the gallery of the Wallace Collection.

The Wallace Collection is contained in 22 rooms or galleries; in some of these the greatest interest resides in the collections of art objects other than paintings, so they will be omitted; but in order to make sure of seeing all that there is to be seen it is as well to pass consecutively from one gallery to the next. In the entrance hall are to be seen a life-size portrait of George IV by Sir Thomas Lawrence, a portrait of Isabella Waerbeke by Van Dyck, a bust of Charles I by Roubiliac and one of Queen Caroline by Rysbrack. In Galleries I and II, which form one very large room, are several notable portraits by Sir Thomas Lawrence, among them *The Countess Blessington* and *Miss Siddons,* daughter of the actress; a portrait of George IV as Prince of Wales by John Hoppner; and further works by George Morland and Sir David Wilkie. Of French painting there is a portrait group of Louis XIV and his heirs attributed to Nicolas de Largillière, a portrait of Louis XV by van Loo and two large paintings of dead animals and dogs in landscapes by J. B. Oudry.

Gallery III is remarkable for its art objects, but outstanding also is a portrait of Eleanora of Toledo, Grand-Duchess of Tuscany, by the Mannerist painter Bronzino. Above the fireplace is a portrait of *A Man in a Black Dress* attributed to Bartolommeo Veneto, and also here are some small works by Crivelli, Memling and Corneille de Lyon—by the latter a portrait of the 1st Earl of Hertford. Gallery IV contains two important works by the French 17th-century painter Philippe de Champaigne: a somewhat Baroque religious painting, *The Adoration of the Shepherds* of about 1630; and a portrait of an *Échevin* (alderman) of the city of Paris, a fragment of a larger portrait group which was destroyed during the 1870-1 Commune. In a passage adjoining this gallery is a *Marriage of the Virgin* also by Philippe de Champaigne, dated about 1647-50 and painted for the chapel of the Palais Royal. Besides this artist's works Gallery IV also contains a portrait of Cardinal Fleury by Hyacinthe Rigaud, a terracotta bust of Charles Lebrun by Antoine

Coysevox and in show-cases numerous Italian drawings by, among others, Polidoro da Caravaggio, Pollaiuolo, and Carlo Maratta. The back corridor contains paintings by French artists of the 19th century working in an academic tradition. Here are *Judah and Tamar* by Horace Vernet and works by among others Meissonier, Prud'hon, Decamps, Delaroche. Several galleries now contain armour etc. until the Founders' Room is reached where hang portraits of the Hertford family by Sir Joshua Reynolds and tinted portrait drawings by John Downman.

Gallery IX contains a portrait by Allan Ramsay of George III in coronation robes and views of Venice by Canaletto and Guardi. The corridor adjoining contains a number of interesting watercolours by Richard Parkes Bonington; especially notable is the *Interior of Sant' Ambrogio, Milan.* There are also four early watercolours by Turner. Gallery X is notable for its Italian works, including *Saint Catherine of Alexandria* by Cima da Conegliano; *Virgin and Child with Angels* by Andrea del Sarto; *Venus and Cupid,* doubtfully attributed to Titian; *The Young Cicero Reading,* a fragment of a fresco by the Milanese painter Vincenzo Foppa; several works including a *Virgin and Child* by Bernardino Luini; *The Mystic Marriage of St Catherine* by Sassoferrato; and *Virgin and Child with Saints,* attributed to the 14th-century Sienese painter Fransesco di Vannuccio. A portrait of Robert Dudley, Earl of Leicester, is by an unknown artist but that of *An English Nobleman* is by Hans Eworth.

In Gallery XI Murillo is represented by some very fine works, among them *The Adoration of the Shepherds, Joseph and his Brethren,* and *The Charity of St \Thomas of Villanueva,* all of which were formerly in a Genoese convent. Two smaller works by him are *The Marriage of the Virgin* and *The Virgin in Glory.* A circular *Virgin and Child* is by Sassoferrato and *Venus and Cupids* is by the Bolognese painter Francesco Albani. In this room also is a beautiful collection of miniatures, mainly French and mainly 18th- and 19th-century, but among them is a splendid self-portrait by Holbein, dated 1543.

The staircase leading to the galleries on the first floor is hung with important works by Boucher, of whom the Goncourt brothers wrote, 'Boucher is one of those men who signifies the taste of a century, who explains and personifies it.' Here he is to be found perhaps at the peak of his achievement with two large paintings, *The Rising* and *The Setting of the Sun,* which were painted in 1753 and intended as designs for Gobelins tapestries; they were later owned by Madame de Pompadour. Two other Bouchers, *The Rape of Europa* and *Mercury Confiding the Infant Bacchus to the Nymphs,* are on the side walls and several pastoral scenes are to be found on the landing. Also to be seen on the staircase are three marble busts: of King Louis XIV by Coysevox; of Madame Victoire de France, 5th daughter of Louis XV, by Houdon; and of Madame de Serilly, also by Houdon.

Gallery XII is distinguished by some very fine paintings of Venetian scenes by Guardi: *San Giorgio Maggiore, The Dogana, Santa Maria della Salute,* and *The Rialto.* These large works are accompanied by smaller views by the same artist while at the other end of the gallery are to be found two large scenes by Canaletto: *Bacino di San Marco* and *The Fête on the Piazetta.*

In Gallery XIII is to be found a very interesting group of works by Rubens. There is a dramatic *Christ on the Cross* but equally fascinating are a number of his oil sketches such as two sketches of an *Adoration of the Magi,* one for the altarpiece in Antwerp Museum, the other for that now in King's College Chapel, Cambridge. Also here are three sketches for Rubens's proposed decoration of a second gallery in the Luxemburg Palace in Paris which owing to political disturbances proved an abortive undertaking, and there is a further sketch for *The Defeat and Death of Maxentius.* Gallery XIII also contains a self-portrait by Rembrandt but it is now disputed whether the painting and etching of *The Good Samaritan* are indeed from his hand. Other paintings here are by Ferdinand Bol, Van der Neer, Paulus Potter, Dou and Mierevelt.

Genre painting in Holland is widely illustrated in Gallery XIV, where are to be found *The Harpsichord Lesson, The Lute Player,* and *The Village Alchemist* by Jan Steen; the beautiful *Lady Reading a Letter* by Gerhard Terborch; *The Lacemaker,* dated 1664, by Caspar Netscher; *Interior with a Woman Cooking,* dated 1656, by Esaias Boursse; *A Boor Asleep* by Adriaen Brouwer; and works by, among others, Gabriel Metsu, David Teniers the Younger and Nicolaes Maes. Gallery XV continues with Dutch painting but here the land and seascape tradition manifests itself in four excellent works by Meindert Hobbema including *A Watermill* and *Landscape with a Ruin;* three by Jacob Ruisdael, among them *Landscape with a Village;* and two by Albert Cuyp, *The Avenue at Meerdervoort, near Dordrecht* and *The Ferry Boat on the Maes.* Among other paintings which should not be overlooked are *A Waterfall* by van Everdingen, *Canal Scene by Moonlight* by Aert van der Neer, *A Dutch Man-of-War Saluting* by Willem van de Velde; and other works by Adam Pynacker, Nicolaes Berchem, Jan Both, Wouwerman, Isaac van Ostade, Karel Dujardin, and others. *Landscape with a Coach* is attributed to Rembrandt though perhaps the attribution is doubtful.

Gallery XVI contains almost an embarrassment of masterpieces. If portraiture interests the visitor paintings of the highest quality vie for attention. From Velazquez comes *A Lady with a Fan,* a magnificent work thought by some to be a portrait of his daughter, and a portrait of Don Balthasar Carlos, son of Philip IV, when a child. Also hanging here is the universally-known *The Laughing Cavalier* by Frans Hals, dated 1624. Less well-known but of the highest quality is Van Dyck's *Philippe Le Roy, Seigneur de Ravels,* dated 1630, here together with a less beautiful companion portrait of the sitter's wife Marie de Raet. From Rembrandt comes the moving portrait of his son Titus painted about 1657 when the lad was about 16; and also by him are two portrait groups of Jean Pellicorne with his son Gaspar, and of his wife Susanna van Collen with her daughter, both probably painted about 1635. By Rubens there is a portrait of his first wife Isabella Brandt, and not to be overlooked is a *Self-portrait as The Shepherd Paris* by Van Dyck. English portraiture represented here is also remarkable. From Reynolds come a splendid portrait of the well-known beauty Nelly O'Brien, painted in 1763; *Miss Jane Bowles with her Dog; The Strawberry Girl*, a portrait of his niece Theophila Palmer; *Mrs Richard Hoare and her Son; Mrs Carnac;* and *Mrs Robinson*, a profile portrait of the actress. Gainsborough's beautiful full-length portrait of the same *Mrs Robinson as Perdita* is also in the gallery. She was mistress of George IV when Prince of Wales, and here she holds a miniature in her hand. Another fine portrait of her by George Romney also hangs here, and there is another portrait by Gainsborough of *Miss Haverfield*, painted in the early 1780s.

The interest of this gallery is by no means confined to portraiture. One of the greatest of Rubens's landscapes, the *Rainbow Landscape* of 1636-8, painted near his country home at Malines, is here and repays the closest attention. It can be compared with other find landscapes hanging nearby: Jacob Ruisdael's *Rocky Landscape;* Cuyp's *River Scene with a View of Dordrecht;* and the very fine work by Salvator Rosa, *Landscape with Apollo and the Cumaean Sibyl.* Other landscapes in the gallery are *Italian Landscape*, dated 1658, by Claude, *The Falls at Tivoli* by Gaspar Dughet, and *A Stormy Landscape* by Hobbema.

Among the other great works in this room is *Perseus and Andromeda* by Titian, painted about 1554 as one of a series of mythologies for Philip II of Spain. Van Dyck is said to have owned it at one time and it was later in the Orleans collection. A companion work, *The Rape of Europa,* is in the Isabella Stewart Gardner collection in Boston. Here too are an allegorical painting, *A Dance to the Music of Time,* from the late 1630s, by Poussin; an extremely large *Annunciation* by Philippe de Champaigne; two exquisite interiors by Pieter de Hoogh, *A Woman Peeling Apples* and *A Boy Bringing Pomegranates;* two important religious works by Rubens, *Christ's Charge to Peter* and *The Holy Family with St Elizabeth and John the Baptist; The Halt during the Chase,* a large work painted in 1720 by Watteau; *The Persian Sibyl* by Domenichino; *The Centurion Cornelius* attributed to Rembrandt; *The Annunciation* and *The Holy Family with John the Baptist* by Murillo; *The Christening Feast* by Jan Steen; and works by Alonso Cano, Frans Snyders, Jan Weenix, Jan Davidsz de Heem, Pieter Pourbus, Jacob Jordaens, and others.

Gallery XVII, which leads off this main gallery of the Museum, again provides a view of French art before the advent of the Impressionists.

17 Head of an Arab
(LORD LEIGHTON)
Leicester Museums and
Art Galleries

18 Hireling Shepherd
(W. HOLMAN HUNT)
City of Manchester
Art Galleries

19   Nelly O'Brien   (REYNOLDS)
The Wallace Collection, London

The greatest artist here is Delacroix, represented by *The Execution of the Doge Marino Faliero,* which was exhibited at the Salon of 1827 along with his *Death of Sardanopolos.* Stendhal wrote of the young Delacroix at that time that he could make mistakes but he had the courage to be himself. The painter Prud'hon whom the Goncourts admired is well represented here with, among others, a large *Venus and Adonis,* and a fine portrait of the Empress Josephine. There is also a large group of works by Meissonier, among them *An Artist Showing his Work, The Roadside Inn* and *Polichinelle,* which last was painted in 1860 on a door panel in the apartment of Madame Sabatier, who cultivated a circle of artistic admirers and whom Baudelaire vainly loved. Other artists represented include Horace Vernet—*The Arab Tale Teller;* Paul Delaroche—*Edward V and the Duke of York in the Tower;* Thomas Couture, Decamps, Géricault, Isabey, Gerôme, and members of the Barbizon School such as Troyon, Diaz, Rousseau and Corot. *Macbeth and the Witches* is by the latter. There are two British works: *Highland Scene* by Landseer; and *Interior of Saint Gommar, Lierre, Belgium* by David Roberts.

Gallery XVIII appropriately enough presents a range of 18th-century painting and here is to be found an extensive selection of the paintings of Watteau, among them the delightful *Music Party; The Music Lesson; A Lady at her Toilet; Les Champs Elysées; Gilles and his Family; Harlequin and Columbine.* Fragonard is also superbly represented by the beautiful *The Swing,* painted about 1766; the fine landscape, *The Gardens of the Villa d'Este, Tivoli; The Souvenir; The Schoolmistress,* and a number of other works. There are also works by Nicolas Lancret and J. B. Pater; particularly notable by the former are *La Belle Grecque, Mademoiselle Camargo Dancing,* and *The Bird Catchers;* and *Watching the Dance,* and *Les Vivandières de Brest* by the latter. Boucher is here again with a number of pictures in his characteristic manner and there is a fine portrait, *The Comtesse de Tillières,* by Jean Nattier. In this gallery too the visitor has the opportunity to see several fine portraits by Greuze; *Mademoiselle Sophie Arnould; Girl in a White Dress; A Lady; Girl with Doves.* A portrait of the Comte d'Espagnac is a good example of the work of Madame Vigée-Lebrun.

In Gallery XIX Boucher and Greuze are again excellently represented; Boucher by his famous portrait Madame de Pompadour and four decorative panels dealing with myths in which the depiction of Venus plays the most important role—the sort of paintings which prompted the Goncourts to write, *'Qui a déshabillé la femme mieux que lui?'* Two fine illustrations of Greuze's talent are *The Broken Mirror* and *The Inconsolable Widow.* Gallery XX is most worthy of attention because of the large collection of oil-paintings by Bonington who, with the addition of numerous watercolours, is extremely well represented in the Wallace

Collection. Among other paintings are *Sea Piece, Landscape with Timber Wagon; France, Coast of Picardy* and examples of his literary and historical works such as *Henry III and the English Ambassador; Francis I and Marguerite of Navarre.* In this room too is a portrait of *Mrs Bradyll* by Sir Joshua Reynolds. In the corridor leading to Gallery XXI are watercolours by Bonington. The gallery itself contains still life and animal paintings by Oudry and Desportes but it is particularly notable for the attractive *Italian Comedians by a Fountain* by Lancret.

Gallery XXII contains further works by Pater, but of chief interest here are the works of Greuze: *Votive Offering to Cupid,* an important example of his work; *A Girl with a Gauze Scarf;* and *A Boy with a Dog.*

Wellington Museum, Apsley House, Hyde Park Corner, London W.1

Tel.: 01-499 5676
Open weekdays 10-6; Sunday 2.30-6

The collection of treasures amassed during the course of his career by the first Duke of Wellington is housed in the building known as Apsley House, which is to be found in an outstanding position in the heart of London at Hyde Park Corner. The house derives its name from its original owner Baron Apsley, for whom it was built by Robert Adam, being completed by 1778. It was bought by the Duke's elder brother in 1805 and was sold by him to the Duke in 1817; it belonged to his family until in 1947 it was offered to the nation by the 7th Duke, several apartments in it being retained by the Wellington family. In 1828-9 the Duke of Wellington had extensive alterations carried out on the building, the large Waterloo Gallery being constructed then as well as the massive portico, and the whole structure being faced with Bath stone in place of its original red brick. The house was completely renovated after the Second World War as it had suffered considerable bomb damage and in 1952 the Wellington Museum, under the administration of the Victoria and Albert Museum, was opened to the public. The paintings in the Museum fall into two categories: those purchased by or given to the Duke either in England or in France, and those captured from Joseph Bonaparte, Napoleon's brother whom he had made King of Spain, after the battle of Vitoria in 1813 at the conclusion of the Peninsular War. Though the Duke apparently had the intention of returning these to Spain he was urged to keep them by the Spanish monarch, a gesture which was indeed fortunate for those of us who are privileged to visit the Museum, for the outstanding paintings there are for the most part those which formerly belonged to Spain.

The ground floor of the house is devoted principally to paintings of Wellington and his political and military associates or of scenes con-

nected with his life. By this token they are on the whole of greater
historical than artistic interest, though Turner's *Tapping the Furnace*,
which represents the casting of an equestrian statue of the Duke, and
Landseer's *Dialogue at Waterloo* must be mentioned. The staircase
vestibule is remarkable for a huge nude statue of Napoleon carved in one
block of marble by Canova. Napoleon disliked the finished work and in
1816 it was bought by the British Government. Surrounding it on the
walls are a number of paintings of Napoleon and his family.

Among other paintings on the first floor landing are a portrait of
Charles X of France by Baron Gérard and Sir David Wilkie's *Chelsea
Pensioners Reading the Waterloo Despatch*, which Wellington commissioned from Wilkie. Wilkie gives a vivid description of the Duke's visit
to his studio in a letter to B. R. Haydon, concluding, 'The subject he has
chosen seems to reflect on him, from its reference to the good old
English companions of his victories: and to me it is a gratification to find
that even my peaceful style of Art should be felt necessary as a recreation
to a Wellington.'

In the room known as the Piccadilly Drawing-Room on the first floor
is a fine selection of mainly Dutch and Flemish pictures, the majority of
them coming from the Spanish collection. Outstanding perhaps for its
gem-like beauty is *Judith and Holofernes* by the German painter Adam
Elsheimer, whose work, small though it was, was seminal for much
better-known 17th-century painters. Not to be missed are *Agony in the
Garden* by Correggio and the gruesome *La Carcasse* by Ribera. Other
paintings of considerable interest are *Landscape with St Hubert and the
Stag* by Paul Brill; *The Crucifixion* and *Angels Guiding the Shepherds to
the Nativity of Christ* by Cornelis van Poelenburgh; *The Physician's Visit*
by Jan Steen; *The Smokers* by Adriaen Brouwer; *The Milkwomen* and
Lovers with a Woman Listening by Nicolaes Maes; *A Cavalier Talking
to a Lady* by Pieter de Hooch; *Landscape with Ruins and Figures* by
Bartolomeus Breenbergh; *A Lady at her Toilet* by Caspar Netscher; and
several scenes by Jan Brueghel the Elder.

In the Portico Room there are several scenes with peasants by David
Teniers the Younger and several ebullient scenes such as *A Wedding
Party* and *The Dissolute Household* by Jan Steen. Also here are *A Musical
Party* by Pieter de Hooch; *View over a Bay* by Claude Joseph Vernet;
and *St Paul at Malta* and *St Paul at Athens*, dated 1735 and 1737, by
G. P. Panini.

The Waterloo Gallery, the great room where the Duke held all-male
banquets in commemoration of the battle of Waterloo from 1830 to
1852, still contains the original banqueting-table and chairs, Portuguese
silver and silver-gilt service, and cut-glass chandelier. A considerable
number of the paintings on the walls were captured at Vitoria. Among
them are two works by Murillo, a *Portrait of an Unknown Man* and *St*

Francis Receiving the Stigmata; two by Ribera, *St John the Baptist* and *St James the Great; St Rosalia* by Van Dyck; a battle scene by Salvator Rosa; and two works by the Cavaliere d'Arpino, *The Marriage of St Catherine* and *The Expulsion from Paradise. Landscape with a View of the Ponte Molle,* ascribed to Claude, is a studio version of a painting to be found in Birmingham Art Gallery. There is an interesting portrait of the Duke in the Spanish equestrian tradition by Goya, though it is hardly in the first rank of that artist's work. Also here are some examples of Italian Baroque art, *St Joseph* by Guido Reni; *Mars* and *Venus and Cupid* by Guercino, *The Virgin and Child* by Sassoferrato, *The Holy Family with S. Carlo Borromeo* by Francesco Trevisani. *Head of an Old Man* is attributed to Rubens and there are also works by Ludolf Bakhuysen, Luca Giordano, Mengs and a *Flight into Egypt* by Sir Joshua Reynolds.

The Yellow Drawing-Room contains the masterpieces of the collection: the magnificent *Waterseller of Seville* by Velazquez, and *A Spanish Gentleman* and *Two Young Men Eating at a Humble Table* by the same artist. Ascribed to a member of his studio is the portrait of the poet Don Francisco Gomez de Quevedo y Villegas. By Rubens there is a portrait of Ana Dorothea, daughter of Rudolph II, *A Nun at the Convent of the Descales Reales, Madrid,* painted in 1628. *Isaac Blessing Jacob* is by Murillo and there are two hunting pictures by Philips Wouwerman.

The remaining major rooms contain portraits of chiefly historical or biographical interest by such artists as Sir Thomas Lawrence, Baron Gérard and Jan Willem Pieneman, and there are portrait busts by Nollekens and Sir Francis Chantrey.

The Whitehall Banqueting House, Whitehall, London S.W.1
Open weekdays 10-5; Sunday 2-5 (Closed Monday in Winter)

Strictly speaking this building is not a gallery in the ordinary meaning of the term, but as the finest set of ceiling paintings in Great Britain is to be found there, paintings which illustrate an invaluable aspect of the art of Rubens, the Banqueting House should be mentioned in a book such as this. In 1619 the Banqueting House at Whitehall was burnt down and the present building, designed by the great architect Inigo Jones, was constructed to replace it between 1620 and 1622. This Banqueting House was of great architectural importance, being influential on much future building. The ceiling paintings, for which Rubens was paid a fee of £3,000, were commissioned by Charles I and were designed to celebrate the reign of his father James I in allegorical terms. Rubens executed them in Antwerp and they were brought to England and set in position in 1635. The breadth and splendour of Rubens's powers of imagination and composition are here fully displayed. No other ceiling paintings by him are extant, so a visit to the Banqueting House provides a unique revelation of his genius.

William Morris Gallery, Lloyd Park, Forest Road, London E. 17

Tel.: 01-527 5544 Ext. 390

Open weekdays 10-1, 2-5 (Summer Tues. and Thurs. 10-1, 2-8); First Sunday in each month 10-12, 2-5

This beautiful Georgian house, known as the Water House, was lived in by William Morris as a boy from 1848 to 1856. Here are kept and displayed a collection of objects related to Morris and his work together with a selection of paintings, drawings, prints and sculpture donated by the painter Sir Frank Brangwyn and a collection of furniture and ceramics given by the architect A. H. Mackmurdo. The Morris collection, of course, deals with many types of activity besides painting; there are examples of textiles, tapestries, embroidery, wallpaper, ceramics, stained glass, books and manuscripts. Paintings and drawings are for the most part by members of the Pre-Raphaelite group or the circle associated with them.

There are a number of works by Rossetti, mostly sketches in chalk or pen and ink; notable are a self-portrait, a sketch of Jane Morris seated on the floor, and a drawing of Elizabeth Siddal. There is a fine pencil and watercolour drawing of Rouen Cathedral by John Ruskin, two sketches for lunettes by Millais and a drawing by him of Alex Munro. There are several watercolours by Burne-Jones, one of *St George and the Dragon*, another entitled *Summer Snow*, and a charming caricature of William Morris weaving. Ford Madox Brown has a painting, *Jacopo Foscari in Prison*; there are pages from a sketchbook by Simeon Solomon and a self-portrait drawing by William Bell Scott. One room is devoted to the paintings of Sir Frank Brangwyn and also here are cartoons of *The Parable of the Vineyard* done by Rossetti for stained glass for the windows of St Martin's Church, Scarborough.

MAIDSTONE
Maidstone Museum and Art Gallery, St Faith's Street

Tel.: 0622 54497

Open weekdays April-September 10-6; October-March 10-5

This gallery is situated in a beautiful Elizabethan manor house which contains many other objects besides paintings. Among Italian artists represented here are Michel Cerquozzi, Carlo Maratta, Salvator Rosa,

Bernardo Strozzi, Francesco Zuccarelli. Flemish painting is represented by *Classical Landscape* by Jan van Bloemen (called Orizzonte); *Flight into Egypt,* attributed to Jan Brueghel; and there are works by Dutch painters such as Poelenbergh, Frans Snyders, Jan van Goyen. Among the English paintings of considerable interest is a portrait of William Hazlitt by his brother John. Other artists represented include John Opie, John Hoppner, James Northcote, Arthur Hughes, Landseer, David Cox, Thomas Girtin and John Brett.

MANCHESTER
Manchester City Art Gallery, Mosley Street
Tel.: 061 236 2391/2

Open weekdays 10-6; Sunday 2.30-5

The Manchester Institute designed to aid the promotion of the arts was founded in 1823 and a building in the Greek revival style was erected, designed by the young Charles Barry, and opened in 1829. The casts of the Elgin Marbles, still visible on the upper walls of the entrance hall, were donated by George IV. The Institute was handed over by its Governors in 1882 for the purpose of becoming the City Art Gallery; this was endowed with a nucleus of works of art formed since the Institute's inception and a provision was made that for the next 20 years, £2,000 should be set aside from the rates for the purchase of works of art. At intervals over the next 50 or 60 years strenuous efforts were made to promote the building of a new gallery but these were all defeated by a combination of circumstances. The Gallery was extended however in 1938 by the purchase of an adjoining building and the collection was continually expanded by gifts from local benefactors, the most recent of which has been the magnificent Assheton Bennett collection of silver and of 17th-century Dutch paintings. As well as the main City Gallery which houses the major works of art Manchester also possesses a number of branch galleries, each of which specializes in some aspect of art, such as drawings, costume and applied art.

Though the collection of paintings belonging to foreign schools is not large there are some works of the greatest interest. Of early Italian works there is a *Crucifixion* by the Sienese artist Matteo di Giovanni and a large circular *Adoration* which perhaps doubtfully has been attributed to the Florentine artist Piero di Cosimo. Also to be seen are four long panels from the Central Italian School of Lo Spagna (Giovanni di Pietro) consisting of *The Annunciation, The Nativity, The Adoration* and *The Presentation in the Temple.* Seventeenth-Century Italian works include a splendid *St John the Baptist* by the great illusionist painter Gaulli; *Portrait of an Actor* by Domenico Feti; and works attributed to Annibale Carracci, Pietro da Cortona and Sebastiano Ricci. From the Assheton

Bennett bequest comes a beautiful group of small views by Guardi.

Of Flemish pictures there are an early *Madonna and Child* and a *Holy Family* by Van Dyck; a glowing landscape by Jan Brueghel the Elder; *Peasants Eating Mussels* by Adriaen Brouwer; and two lively works by David Teniers the Younger. All are from the Assheton Bennett bequest. From the same collection come some excellent Dutch works: two portraits of Dutch dignitaries by Gerhard Terborch; a small *Fisherboy* by Hals; *Portrait of a Girl* by Gerard Dou; two interiors by Pieter de Hooch; *A Woman Smoking a Pipe* by Gabriel Metsu; *Two Peasants Fighting* by Adriaen van Ostade; four charming works by Jacob Ochtervelt; and a small picture, *The Rommelpot,* by Jan Steen. Of land and seascapes there are works by Jacob Ruisdael, *Storm off the Dutch Coast* and *Woman and Child Walking along a Country Lane,* and from his uncle Salomon Ruisdael, a *River Scene* and *Winter Scene with Skaters;* from Jan van Goyen there is also a *Winter Scene* and from Albert Cuyp a delightful *River Scene.* Other Dutch painters represented include Avercamp, Cabel, Jan van de Cappelle, Jan van der Heyden, Philips Koninck, Philips Wouwerman, Aert van der Neer, Jan Wynants, Isaak van Ostade, Paulus Potter, Willem Kalf.

From France comes a landscape by Gaspar Dughet and then works by members of the Barbizon School and their associates. *Pasturage in Normandy* is by Troyon; *Sunset, Figures under Trees* by Corot; and there is a landscape by Courbet, *Le Ruisseau du Puits Noir.* From the Impressionists come *Trouville Harbour* by Boudin; a penetrating self-portrait and other works by Fantin-Latour; *A Village Street, Louveciennes* and *Bridge at Bruges* by Camille Pissarro. *Normandy Farm* by Sisley; *The Castle of Clisson* by Harpignies; an early Impressionistic view of *Dieppe Harbour* by Gauguin; and the striking *Dancers in the Wings* by Forain should also not be missed. Degas's lovely work *Woman Washing* recalls his remark to George Moore, 'The nude has always been represented in poses which presuppose an audience but these women of mine are honest, simple folk, unconcerned by any other interests than those involved in their physical condition.' Also here and of great interest are Van Gogh's *Springtime;* Vlaminck's *Road through the Trees;* a Derain portrait; *Painting 1926* by Fernand Léger; and *La Ville Petrifée* by Max Ernst.

It is in British painting that the Manchester collection is richest and most comprehensive. One of the earliest portraits is of Elizabethan date, a stiff but charming representation of *Mary Cornwallis* possibly by George Gower, a painter of gentle birth. An outstanding painting, probably dated 1635, is that of Sir Thomas Aston at the deathbed of his first wife by John Souch, a painter from Chester. Lacking in all sense of perspective and replete with symbolic references, this painting is a fascinating example of English provincial work. Of a completely different level of accomplishment are the portraits of the *1st Earl of Inchiquin* by Michael Wright and of *Lady Whitmore* by Sir Peter Lely. From the 18th century come a portrait of *Admiral Lord Hood* by Reynolds; a small *Landscape with Figures* by Gainsborough; two characteristic works, *Cicero's Villa* and *A Welsh Valley* by Richard Wilson; a self-portrait by Nathaniel Hone; and a religious work, *The Pool of Bethesda* by William Hogarth. There is an excellent portrait of *Captain Williams* by Romney and *The Farrier's Forge* by George Morland, and *A Scene from 'Twelfth Night'* by Francis Wheatley should also not be overlooked. There is a fine portrait by Lawrence, but of exceptional interest are eighteen portraits of famous men by William Blake. These were painted for the library of his patron William Hagley and consist of idealized conceptions of great figures such as Homer and Voltaire, each surrounded by a wreath of leaves with incidents from the life or the works of each writer incorporated in the design. A fine acquisition of recent years is George Stubbs's *Cheetah and Stag with Two Indians.*

Works by 19th-century artists are perhaps the richest aspect of the Gallery's collection. There is a large marine painting, *Now for the Painter,* by Turner, as well as some very fine watercolours; among them the superbly colourful *Heidelberg Sunset* and *A Distant View of the Town of Exeter.* Ordinarily most of the Turner watercolours and other works in that medium are on view in the Fletcher Moss Branch Gallery at East Didsbury. Constable is also represented by some small works, among them *Harrow from Hampstead Heath* and *Cottage in a Cornfield.* There is a selection of landscapes by other artists: an Impressionistic study, *Rhyl Sands* by David Cox; *View over Flat Country* by Peter de Wint; *Bolton Abbey* by Sir Edwin Landseer; and a number of other works. In a different vein are the highly romantic paintings of William Etty, among them *The Storm, Ulysses and the Sirens, An Israelite Indeed,* a self-portrait, and several nudes. Sir David Wilkie's *Portrait of Sir Alexander Keith during the State visit of George IV to Scotland,* 1822, and an Irish scene give some inkling of his work. Later Victorian artists represented include Daniel Maclise with *Winter Night's Tale* and *The Origin of the Harp;* Lord Leighton with *The Captive Andromache,* exhibited at the Royal Academy in 1888, and *The Last Watch of the Hero;* J. W. Waterhouse with *Hylas and the Nymphs;* and W. P. Frith with a replica of his famous *Derby Day* which he considered to be better than the original.

Most notable, however, is the collection of the Pre-Raphaelite artists and their followers. Holman Hunt is represented by some of his major works, among them: *The Shadow of Death,* which he painted in Bethlehem and Jerusalem between 1869 and 1872; *The Hireling Shepherd,* which is full of moral and religious meanings and which was exhibited in the Royal Academy of 1852; *The Lady of Shalott*, which developed from an illustration he did for Moxon's edition of Tennyson's poems published in 1857; *The Light of the World*, which is the original sketch of the larger work in Keble College, Oxford—there is yet another version in St Paul's Cathedral; *The Scapegoat*—this is the smaller version of the painting in the Lady Lever Gallery and here the goat is black and there is a rainbow on the right of the picture. Millais is represented by his famous *Autumn Leaves;* the models he used here (it is dated 1856) were his sisters-in-law Alice and Sophie Grey and two other girls. Ruskin wrote that it was 'by much the most poetical work the painter has yet conceived; and also, as far as I know, the first instance existing of a perfectly painted twilight'. Also by Millais are two lesser works, *Only a Lock of Hair* and *Portrait of Mrs Charles Freeman*. By Rossetti are several works: *The Bower Meadow; Astarte Syriaca*, 1877—the principal figure is that of Mrs William Morris; and *Joli Coeur*. Here too are *Sibylla Delphica* by Burne-Jones; *Answering the Emigrant's Letter* by James Collinson; *Ophelia* by Arthur Hughes (this was exhibited in 1852, the same year as Millais' Ophelia; the artists were unaware that they had chosen the same subject until varnishing day); *The Outlaw* by W. L. Windus; *The Artist's Wife in a Red Cape* by R. B. Martineau; *The Pedlar* by Charles Collins; *Eve Tempted* by Spencer Stanhope; and *At the Golden Gate* by Val Prinsep. Most widely represented of all however is Ford Madox Brown, who had close associations with Manchester, having executed decorations for the Town Hall there. Outstanding is his famous painting, *Work*, which is set in Hampstead near the Heath. The painting bears the text, 'Seest thou a man diligent in his business! He shall stand before Kings. I must work while it is day for the night cometh when no man can work.' Madox Brown wrote about the painting as follows, '. . . at that time extensive excavations were going on in the neighbourhood, and, seeing and studying daily as I did the British excavator, or *navvy*, as he designates himself, in the full swing of his activity . . . it appeared to me that he was at least as worthy of the powers of an English painter as the fisherman of the Adriatic, the peasant of the Campagna, the Neapolitan lazzarone . . . at the further corner of the picture are two men who appear as having nothing to do. These are the brain workers, who, seeming to be idle, work, and are the cause of well-ordained work and happiness in others . . . ' These latter figures are in fact portraits of the Christian Socialist reformer Frederick Denison Maurice and Thomas Carlyle. Inspired by Byron's poem *Manfred* is the strange painting *Manfred on the Jungfrau*, and another work is called *Byron's Dream*. Other paintings by Brown include *Crabtree Watching the Transit of Venus, The Stages of Cruelty, Cromwell, Protector of the Vaudois*, and a portrait of his son, Oliver Madox Brown.

Interesting among later works is Sir William Orpen's *Homage to*

Manet painted 1909, in which are depicted Sickert, Wilson Steer and George Moore. There are numerous examples of the work of Sickert here, among them being *The Blue Hat, Victor Lecour, The Grey Dress, Reclining Women;* Wilson Steer is also well represented by such works as *The Mauve Dress, The Horseshoe Bend of the Severn, The Deserted Quarry, Ironbridge, The Embarkment.* Other members of the Camden Town Group figure here such as Harold Gilman, Spencer Gore, and Robert Bevan, and there are some good pictures by Augustus John, notably his portraits of W. B. Yeats and Signorina Estella Cerutti. Indeed it must be said that nearly every painter of note in the art scene in 20th-century Britain is represented: there are works by Wyndham Lewis, C. R. W. Nevinson and William Roberts representing the Vorticist movement, and from the Bloomsbury group there are paintings by Duncan Grant (*Window, South of France*), Vanessa Bell and Mark Gertler, while there are important works by John Nash and Paul Nash (*Nocturnal Landscape*) from a later generation which includes Gilbert Spencer, Stanley Spencer, L. S. Lowry, Henry Lamb, Matthew Smith and Edward Wadsworth. *Au Chat Botté*, a well-known work by Ben Nicholson, is here as is *Bird in Landscape* by Graham Sutherland, and other works are by painters such as Victor Pasmore, Carel Weight, John Piper, David Jones, Josef Herman and Lucian Freud.

Of sculpture there is a terracotta portrait of his wife by Roubiliac, a bronze *Eve* by Rodin and a bronze *Pomona* by Aristide Maillol together with the large figure, *Youth Advances*, executed for the 1951 Festival of Britain by Epstein. Here too are several portrait busts by him including one of C. P. Scott, the famous editor of the *Manchester Guardian*, and also of Vaughan Williams and Joseph Conrad. There is a *Mother and Child* in stone by Henry Moore and also works by Gaudier-Brzeska, Barbara Hepworth, Eric Gill and others.

Whitworth Art Gallery, Oxford Road
Tel.: 061 237 1880
Open weekdays 10-5 (Thursdays 10-9)

The Whitworth Institute and Gallery was founded in 1889 as a memorial to Sir Joseph Whitworth, inventor and toolmaker, to be 'a source of perpetual gratification to the people of Manchester, and at the same time a permanent influence of the highest character in the direction of technical education and of the cultivation of taste and knowledge of the arts of painting, sculpture and architecture'. It was financed by part of the huge fortune Sir Joseph Whitworth had left. (Another portion of his wealth benefited the University.) By 1892 the administration of the Institute had been handed over to the Manchester Corporation but the Gallery remained in the hands of the committee set up by Sir Joseph's legatees, among whom was Robert Dunkinfield Darbishire, himself a considerable benefactor of the Gallery. Grove House, bought for the purpose, opened in 1889 with a small collection including 72 prints of Turner's *Liber Studiorum*, the record he made of his own work, and the large *Love and Death* by G. F. Watts, given by the artist. In 1892 the editor of the *Manchester Guardian*, John Edward Taylor, presented the Gallery with over 140 early English watercolours. Other gifts of water-colours followed which resulted in the decision to develop the Gallery to become one of the finest collections of watercolours in the provinces. Early in the 1920s Grove House was pulled down and new galleries were built. In 1958, after years of financial and organizational difficulties, the Whitworth Art Gallery was handed over to Manchester University and thus began a new vital role in serving the teaching of the history of art. Oil-paintings and modern works of art were purchased and the textile collection which had always been considerable was expanded. During the 1960s the interior of the building was reconstructed with great success and the Whitworth Gallery is now one of the finest buildings organized for the display of art in Britain although its previous red brick exterior remains untouched.

Before the acquisition of the Gallery by the University there had been no serious effort to collect oil-paintings and thus it is still hardly meaningful to divide what has been acquired into various schools. One of the first new purchases was *View of Tivoli* by Gaspar Dughet, followed by several other classical landscapes, for example, *Classical Landscape* by John Wootton, who spent some years in Rome and much admired Dughet and assisted in introducing landscape painting of this type into England. Other landscapes include a *Capriccio with Classical Ruins* by Charles Clérisseau; *The Casino at Marino, near Dublin* by William Ashford; *Landscape with Travellers* by Joos de Momper, the most important of a family of Flemish painters; and *Landscape with Mythological Figures* by Cornelis van Poelenburgh. By Sir Thomas Lawrence there is a splendid portrait of the critic and connoisseur Richard Payne Knight. Also to be mentioned are a small *Study of Clouds* by Constable, two small works by Edward Calvert, described by Samuel Palmer's son as 'a dreamy intellectual dallying with art', and small works by David Cox, Landseer and Corot.

Apart from Watts's *Love and Death* other 19th-century works include J. F. Lewis's *Indoor Gossip, Cairo*, Ford Madox Brown's *Execution of Mary, Queen of Scots* and a study by Millais for his *Black Brunswicker*.

The collection of modern paintings in oils is still small but it is continually being increased. There is a large work, part of a triptych, *The Philosopher* by de Chirico, together with accompanying drawings. Here too are *Lake Landscape* by L. S. Lowry, *Landscape* by Paul Rebeyrolle, and works by Alan Davie, Roger Hilton and others. The interesting selection of modern sculpture includes works by Epstein (*Genesis,* 1931), Henry Moore, Barbara Hepworth, Lynn Chadwick, Elizabeth Frink, Kenneth Armitage, Edward Paolozzi, Frank Auerbach.

But the importance of the Whitworth at the moment still resides in its collection of watercolours, prints and drawings. Among the watercolours are to be found William Blake's *Ancient of Days,* which, according to its original owner, was done on his deathbed; J. R. Cozens's *Lake Nemi; The West Front of Peterborough Cathedral* by Thomas Girtin; *Coniston Fells* by Turner; *En Bretagne* by Gauguin; Van Gogh's *The Ramparts, Montmartre;* and Picasso's *Poverty.* Prints, engravings and etchings include examples by Schongauer, Dürer, Mantegna, Pollaiuolo, Rembrandt, Raimondi, Ribera, as well as Turner's *Liber Studiorum* series. The number of artists represented in the drawings collection is too great to specify; also of the greatest interest is the collection of textiles, which includes tapestries designed by William Morris and Burne-Jones.

MIDDLESBROUGH
Middlesbrough Art Gallery, Linthorpe Road
Tel.: 0642 83781

Open weekdays 10-6

Undoubtedly the finest object in the Gallery, which is one of the Teesside Museums, is the painting by Georges de La Tour, *The Dice Players.* This picture, though signed by de La Tour, was only discovered to be an authentic work in recent years. It was bequeathed to the Museum in 1930 by Annie Elizabeth Clepham along with a number of other works, among which are a watercolour by Delacroix *Abélard and Héloïse, River View* by Thomas Girtin, and *Lydgate, Devon* by Copley Fielding.

Other works of interest include *The Gorge, Ronda, Spain,* dated 1935, by David Bomberg; *The Romans Leaving Britain* by Sir John Millais; *Old Town Hall and St Hilda's Church* by L. S. Lowry; *Morning* by Josef Herman; *Green Glade* by Ivon Hitchens; and works by, among others, Victor Pasmore, Ceri Richards, Philip Sutton.

Examples of sculpture in the Gallery are a bronze bust of Somerset Maugham by Epstein, and a bronze *Horse's Head* by Elizabeth Frink.

NEWCASTLE-UPON-TYNE
The Hatton Gallery, The Quadrangle, University of Newcastle-upon-Tyne
Tel.: 0632 28511 Ext. 3647

Open weekdays 10-6

The Hatton Gallery is part of the University of Newcastle-upon-Tyne and contains a number of paintings by Italian and other old masters and an interesting group of 20th-century works. Outstanding among the former are a Florentine saint from the 14th-century; *Descent from the Cross* by Domenichino; *Soldiers and Peasants in a Rocky Landscape* by Salvator Rosa; *St Mark* by the Venetian Palma Giovane; *The Drunkenness of Noah* by the Milanese artist Camillo Procaccini; *Pietà* by Lorenzo Sabbatini; *Portrait of a Gentleman* by Rembrandt's successful contemporary Govaert Flinck; and *View of Tivoli* by Gaspar Dughet. John Linnell's self-portrait is worth noting also.

Of great interest to students of modern art will be the *Elterwater Merz* construction by the German artist Kurt Schwitters. This was the third *Merzbau* Schwitters made, the two earlier ones being in Hanover and Norway; he had to flee from both these places because of the Nazis. The *Merzbau* and other collages were Schwitters's version of Dada. This one was constructed in a barn in 1947 and the whole wall was moved to its present position in the Hatton Gallery.

Among the 20th-century British works are a characteristic painting by William Roberts, *Bank Holiday in the Park; Composition* by David Bomberg; two landscapes by Keith Vaughan; and a large painting, *Study for Figure No. 6* (1956) by Francis Bacon.

Laing Art Gallery and Museum, Higham Place
Tel.: 0632 27734 or 26989

Open weekdays 10-6 (Tuesday and Thursday 10-8); Sunday 2.30-5.30

The Laing Art Gallery was built and opened in 1904 on receipt by the Council of a large bequest from Alexander Laing, a local businessman. At that time the Gallery did not possess a single work of art but depended entirely on loan exhibitions. Its important collection has been built up since then by means of purchases, gifts and bequests. The Gallery has continued to be the site of many important exhibitions and an active centre for the dissemination of knowledge concerning art. The collection of oil-paintings centres mainly upon British painting since the early 18th century to the present day although there are occasional examples of Continental work.

Among the British works are several portraits by Thomas Hudson, notably a larger-than-life depiction of *Anne, Countess of Northampton,* and a portrait of *Sir William Middleton.* From Sir Joshua Reynolds comes a full-length portrait of *Elizabeth Riddell* and attributed to him is a picture of *Mrs Robinson as Perdita.* There is a portrait of *James Adam,* brother of Robert, with an architectural drawing in his hand, by Allan Ramsay, and a portrait of *Lady Catherine Henry* is also attributed to him. From Sir Henry Raeburn comes a portrait of *Robert Allan,* and from Sir

Thomas Lawrence a portrait group and a single depiction of *Mrs Littleton*. On loan is *Rustic Children* by Gainsborough and there is a genre scene by George Morland, *Paying the Ostler*. *The Alban Hills* by Richard Wilson does not seem in very good shape but there is a version of *Salisbury Cathedral* by Constable and several striking pictures by John Martin. Martin was a local artist, born at Haydon Bridge, who created fantastic large scenes, drawn mainly from the Bible; these had enormous success for many years before fading into the oblivion from which they have just recently begun to be rescued. Here are a huge architectural, apocalyptic fantasy, *Belshazzar's Feast*, which had a great success when first shown in 1821; a fantastic mountain scene, *The Bard;* and another highly colourful creation, *The Destruction of Sodom and Gomorrah*. This painting was exhibited at the Royal Academy in 1852, the same year as Daniel Maclise's *King Alfred in the Camp of the Danes,* which is also in the Gallery. There are several Pre-Raphaelite paintings to be seen: Holman Hunt's *Isabella and the Pot of Basil,* inspired by Keats's poem derived from Boccaccio's *Decameron* but actually begun as a portrait of the artist's wife in Florence in 1866-7; Arthur Hughes's *The Potter's Courtship;* Rossetti's *Fazio's Mistress* or *Aurelia* (on loan from the Tate); William Bell Scott's *Entry of Charles II into London;* Sir Noel Paton's *The Man of Sorrows;* and several studies for stained-glass windows by Burne-Jones and William Dyce. Other Victorian paintings are: *Love in Idleness* by Alma-Tadema; *The Catapult,* dated 1872, by E. J. Poynter; and works by J. B. Pyne, Thomas Creswick, T. S. Cooper, Atkinson Grimshaw.

Paintings of this century include Sickert's *St Mark's Square, Venice,* 1903; Dame Ethel Walker's *The Forgotten Melody;* Duncan Grant's *The Hammock,* dated 1921-3; Matthew Smith's *Creole Girl;* C. R. W. Nevinson's *Notre Dame de Paris;* Augustus John's *Two Gitanas;* Dame Laura Knight's *The Fair;* and Harold Knight's *At the Piano.* Interesting paintings also are Stanley Spencer's *The Lovers* or *The Dustman;* Mark Gertler's *Portrait of Thomas Balston;* Victor Pasmore's *Girl with Mirror;* Christopher Wood's *Sleeping Fisherman;* S. J. Peploe's *Yellow Tulips and Statuette;* and John Nash's *Mill Pond, Evening,* 1946. Other painters represented include Edward Wadsworth, Ivon Hitchens, L. S. Lowry, William Gear, Alan Davie.

European paintings include a *Landscape with Ruins and Figures* by van Poelenburg; a portrait by Pompeo Batoni; and, rather surprisingly, *Bretons et Moutons* by Gauguin.

The collection of watercolours is very comprehensive, including works by Francis Barlow, Thomas Shotter Boys, Peter de Wint, J. R. Cozens, David Cox, Edward Dayes, Gainsborough, Girtin, de Loutherbourg, Samuel Palmer, Turner, Paul Sandby, Wilson Steer, Graham Sutherland and many others.

NEWPORT (MONMOUTH)
Newport Museum and Art Gallery, John Frost Square
Tel.: 0633 65781
Open weekdays 10-5.30

Most of the paintings in the permanent collection of this gallery are by English and Welsh artists, with the concentration mainly on the 20th century. Representative of other times are *A Backwater of the Severn* by Richard Wilson and *Offering to Isis* by Sir Edward Poynter. From this century come *Reading Room* by William Roberts, *Sausage Shop* by Stanley Spencer, *Anticyclone* by Edward Wadsworth, *The Top Floor* by Robert Medley, *Welsh Hills* by Fred Uhlman, *Goat Head* by Julian Trevelyan, *Mumbles Gone West* by Alfred Janes, *Field Workers* and *Women in the Fields* by Josef Herman and works by, among others, John Minton, Christopher Wood, Carel Weight, L. S. Lowry, Kyffin Williams, Evan Walters, Morland Lewis and Lawrence Gowing.

The Gallery also possesses an interesting group of Old Master drawings and a selection of watercolours by artists such as George Barret, J. S. Cotman, Peter de Wint, Nicholas Pocock, David Roberts, John Nash and Ceri Richards.

NORTHAMPTON
Northampton Central Museum and Art Gallery, Guildhall Road
Tel.: 0604 34881
Open weekdays 10-6 (Thursday and Saturday 10-8)

In addition to its interesting collection of pictures Northampton Museum and Gallery is also remarkable for its collection of shoes and examples of shoe design through the ages which, of course, is fitting in a town noted for its shoemaking industry. An examination of the pictures in the gallery reveals that those responsible have been pursuing a definite policy with regard to their purchases for much of the collection consists of Italian works of the 17th and 18th centuries. Some of these are on extended loan to the Gallery; others have been purchased to augment the importance of the collection.

Among these Italian works are: *The Assumption of the Virgin* by Antonio Pellegrini, a decorative painter who spent part of his life in England and decorated Castle Howard among other places—other works by him here are *Venus and Cupid* and *Jason Rejecting Medea; Still Life with Fish* by the 17th-century Neapolitan Giuseppe Recco, who specialized in such subjects; *St John the Baptist Preaching* by Luca Giordino, an 18th-century Neapolitan who painted all over Europe; *The Vision of St Rosalie of Palermo* by Sebastiano Conca, a Neapolitan who had great success in Rome during the middle years of the 18th century. From 18th-century Venice come *Interior of a Venetian Palace* by Michiel Marieschi, a painter who was probably a pupil of Canaletto but who himself had a formative influence on Guardi; *The Abduction of Helen* by Antonio Molinari; *The Holy Family* by Francesco Trevisani, whose sweet Madonnas and children were very popular throughout Europe; *A Young Girl Warming Herself at a Brazier* by Jacopo Amigoni, whose light-hearted art was welcomed in courts and large houses in Germany, Italy, England and Spain; and a painting of *The Piazza San Marco* by Guardi himself. One interesting feature of this work is that it appears to have been executed on top of another one and it is just possible to see in the sky the shape of a horse's head which must derive from the first picture. Also to be noted, not only for its own merits but because it is probably the only one of his works in a public collection in Britain, is the Venetian Francesco Fontebasso's *Belshazzar's Feast.* This artist was much influenced by Tiepolo and spent part of his working life in Russia. By Francesco Solimena, who was the unchallenged leader of the Neapolitan School during the first half of the 18th century, are two works, *Minerva* and *The Nativity,* both in his typical shadowy style. Not to be overlooked are a classical landscape by the Roman painter Panini, *The Meeting of Isaac and Rebecca* by Micco Spadaro, a 17th-century Neapolitan, and a ceiling sketch for Burleigh House by Antonio Verrio.

An *Entombment* which derives from the collection at Hamilton Palace and is attributed to Titian is possibly a late work from his school. Notable also are a *Madonna and Child with St Catherine* by the Master of the 1518 Antwerp School, and an intriguing triptych of the marriage of Edward IV and Elizabeth Woodville—at what date this was painted and whether by an English painter is not known.

Modern works include *Yellow Flowers in a Blue Vase* by Fernand Léger, *Stockholm Harbour* by Albert Marquet, *Standing Form* by Graham Sutherland and works by artists such as C. R. W. Nevinson, Frank Brangwyn, John Bratby and others.

NORWICH
Norwich Castle Museum
Tel.: 0603 22233
Open weekdays 10-5; Sunday 2-5

Norwich Castle goes back originally to the years soon after the Norman conquest when it was a wooden structure, though the present Keep was built about 1130. Soon after this the Castle became a gaol and it was used as a prison until 1887, some of the prison buildings constructed in the early 19th century being now used as exhibition galleries. The Castle was opened as a museum in 1894. Before that time, though the city had possessed a number of pictures, there had existed no gallery in which to display them. The backbone of the collection was then, as it is now, works by artists of the Norwich School. In 1898 Jeremiah James Colman bequeathed a number of paintings of this school to the gallery. Another bequest of the same ilk came from Sir Henry Holmes, and in 1946 R. J. Colman, son of the former benefactor, bequeathed the whole of his collection which included a large number of oils and watercolours by John Sell Cotman. Together with these he gave a large sum of money for the construction of galleries to house the collections donated by him and his father. These two galleries, known as the Cotman and the Crome Galleries, were completed in 1951 and now lead off the Rotunda, the central building of the Museum, which was completed in 1969.

The Crome Gallery contains an excellent selection of works by John 'Old' Crome, who founded the Norwich Society of Artists in 1803. He was influenced by the 17th-century Dutch painters of landscape and by Richard Wilson, but above all by the landscape he set out to paint. *Carrow Abbey,* exhibited 1805, is an early work; *Back of the New Mills* and *The Yare at Thorpe, Norwich* are two river scenes; *Yarmouth Jetty* (a subject which he painted six times between 1807 and 1819) is illustrative of his advice to his follower, James Stark, ' ... give the sky, which plays so important a part in all landscape, and so supreme a one in our low level lines of distance, the prominence it deserves ...' *Landscape: Grove Scene* is a different aspect of Crome, as is *Bruges River, Ostend in the Distance—Moonlight,* painted on his only trip abroad in 1814. His son, also John Crome, is represented here too with *Burgh Castle, near Yarmouth* and a *Yarmouth Jetty* painting. Elsewhere in a small reserve gallery in the Museum are further paintings by Crome not derived from the Colman collection. Among them are *New Mills—Men Wading,* and *The Boulevard des Italiens* and *Fishmarket at Boulogne* also painted on the 1814 trip and on long loan to the Gallery. Here too is *The Thames at Twickenham* by Richard Wilson, and two fine conversation pieces by Henry Walton and J. H. Mortimer, the former a pupil of Zoffany, the latter a pupil of Thomas Hudson.

The Cotman Gallery contains works by John Sell Cotman and his two sons. Here is the early *After a Storm* but particularly remarkable are four oil paintings from about 1827-9: *The Baggage Wagon; The Mishap; Silver Birches; Normandy River. Old Houses at Gorleston* is a serene architectural study. There is an incomparable collection of his watercolours. From early visits to Yorkshire and the North in the years 1803-5 come *Durham, Trentham Church* and the superb *Devil's Elbow, Rokeby Park.* From later visits to Normandy and other parts of the Continent derive *Abbatial House, St Ouen, Rouen,* and *Schaffhausen,* and *The*

Gateway of the Abbey Aumale. Dramatic colour fully asserts itself in works such as *Storm on Yarmouth Beach* and *St Benet's Abbey* of 1831. *Boats on the Medway* is a notable oil by his son Miles Edmund, some of whose watercolours are almost worthy of his father; a few works by the younger son, Joseph John are also of interest.

In the various galleries devoted to their work is to be found an invaluable selection of paintings by other members of the Norwich School. Notable are *The Forest Gate* by James Stark; *Trowse Meadows* by George Vincent; *Thorpe Water Frolic* by Joseph Stannard; *Bishops Bridge, Norwich* by Robert Ladbrooke; and watercolours by Cotman's brother-in-law John Thirtle. There are many more fine works by artists such as Henry Bright, the Reverend Edward Thomas Daniell and many others.

Represented in the Gallery also is the Norwich-born Frederick Sandys, who, as is demonstrated in the painting *Autumn,* was influenced by the Pre-Raphaelites. An *Annunciation* in tempera by Burne-Jones also hangs here as well as a number of portraits by Gainsborough and John Hoppner.

NOTTINGHAM
Nottingham City Art Gallery and Museum, The Castle
Tel.: 0602 43615

Open April-September weekdays 10-6.45; Fridays 10-5.45; Sunday 10-4.45; October-March weekdays 10-dusk; Sunday 10-4.45

Nottingham Art Gallery and Museum is to be found in Nottingham Castle, once a fortress used as a stronghold by several kings of England, perhaps most notably Richard I and King John, round whose occupation of the Castle the stories of Robin Hood were woven. Edward IV, Richard III and Henry VII also used the Castle but it was demolished in 1651 under Oliver Cromwell and nothing of the original building now remains. The present Castle was built by the 1st Duke of Newcastle in the 1670s and was burned down by rioters at the time of the agitation for reform of the Houses of Parliament in 1831. It was restored some decades later and opened in July 1878 as the first Provincial Museum of the Fine and Decorative Arts by the then Prince and Princess of Wales.

In the Museum is a wide variety of objects—antiquities, pottery, glass, alabaster carvings, silver, etc. Of the paintings from European schools here on display the earliest seem to be some 14th-century works in tempera depicting various saints and a *St Jerome* of the South German school dated 1515. But the 17th and 18th centuries are more widely represented. Of great interest is a painting, *Hercules and Diomedes* by Charles Lebrun, virtually dictator of the arts under Louis XIV; this work, executed while he was still training in the studio of Simon Vouet, is thought to have been painted for Cardinal Richelieu. *Man with Broken Eggs* is a good example of the work of the Utrecht Mannerist painter Abraham Bloemaert. Also here is *The Flight into Egypt* by Jan Brueghel and Hendrick van Balen.

Turning to British painting there is an *Allegory of the Restoration of Charles II* by Michael Wright, who spent some time studying in Rome as a member of the famous Academy of St Luke. Two good portraits of Eleanor Dixie and Sir Wolston Dixie are by an 18th-century English painter, Henry Pickering, who also studied in Rome. Most important however in the section of British painting are two groups of works by Paul Sandby and Richard Parkes Bonington. The former, primarily a watercolourist, was referred to by Gainsborough as 'the only man of genuis' to paint 'real views from Nature in this country'. Among Sandby's works here are drawings from his *Cries of London* series, a delightful *Tea at Englefield Green, Landscape with Farmyard near Windsor* and many others. Even more outstanding is the collection of works by Richard Bonington, who was a native of the city of Nottingham but went to France and trained there, becoming a friend of Delacroix. To name but a few, here are *The Grand Canal, Venice, Fisherfolk on the Normandy Coast, Don Quixote in his Study, A Cornfield,* and *The Undercliff*—his last watercolour, according to the inscription on the back by his mother; he died at the age of 26 or 27.

There are some works by George Morland: a typical *Two Pigs in Straw,* a less typical *Artist in his Studio,* and *The Wreckers.* There is also a portrait of him as a boy by his father Henry Morland and some works by his brother-in-law James Ward, among them *A Dewy Morning—The Duel of the Stags.* John Crome is represented by a delightful work, *Willow Tree with a Horseman* and *Woman on a Road,* Richard Wilson by a carefully composed Welsh scene, *Snowdon from Llyn Nantile,* and there is a good small painting by David Wilkie, *The Soldier's Grave.* Very interesting are several studies of figures by Henry Fuseli and, though small in size, there is a typically grandiose conception of the *Crucifixion* by John Martin. Francis Danby's *The Israelites Led by a Pillar of Fire by Night* is here, and there is a tender *Virgin and Child* by William Dyce, much influenced by Italian Quattrocento painting and by the German Nazarenes. Two works by Alfred Elmore, *The Origin of the Stocking Frame* and *The Origin of the Combing Machine,* seek to show the sources of inspiration in textile manufacturing. By one of the original—though lesser—Pre-Raphaelites, James Collinson, are two paintings, *View of St Malo* and *For Sale.* Other Victorian painters represented include J. C. Horsley, Marcus Stone, John Brett and W. F.

Yeames, with a version of his well-known painting *The Death of Amy Robsart.*

The Gallery possesses an interesting selection of 20th-century British painting. A group of works by Sir William Nicholson, among them *First Communion* and *Silver,* are very pleasing; and there is an abstract work, *Bistre II,* by his son Ben Nicholson. *Moorish Wall, Cyprus* is by David Bomberg and *Storm in the Jungle* is an impressive work by Edward Burra. Other paintings not to be missed are *Noctes Ambrosianae* by Sickert, *Green Landscape with Gate* by Victor Pasmore, *Still Life* by Matthew Smith, *River Pool* by Ivon Hitchens, *The Return of Ulysses* by William Roberts, and *The Arrest* and *Industrial Panorama* by L. S. Lowry. Dame Laura Knight also has a group of works here, and there are sculptures by Epstein and Lyn Chadwick.

OLDHAM
Oldham Art Gallery, Union Street
Tel.: 061 624 3633
Open Monday-Friday 10-7; Saturday 10-5

Although the Gallery, like many in the provinces, possesses quite a number of works by Victorian artists, among them Rossetti's watercolour *The First Madness of Ophelia,* its recent policy has been directed towards the purchase of contemporary art and the increasing of its collection of modern prints. Among these modern works are to be found '*As I wend by the shores I know not*' by Carel Weight, one of 60 commissioned by the Arts Council to commemorate the 1951 Festival of Britain, and deriving from some lines by Walt Whitman. Here too is *Vale in Gloucestershire* by Paul Nash, the last large landscape he painted and unfinished at his death. Other contemporary works are by John Craxton, Patrick Heron, Terry Frost, Sandra Blow; and there are watercolours by artists such as Graham Sutherland, Michael Ayrton, Prunella Clough, John Nash.

At Oldham also is the Charles E. Lees collection of watercolour drawings and engravings. Its quality may be judged from the artists represented, who include Turner, with works done in England, Switzerland and Italy; Constable, David Cox, J. R. Cozens, Paul Sandby and Thomas Girtin.

Sculpture includes Epstein's bronze portrait of Sir Winston Churchill, which he did not finish to his satisfaction; Bernard Meadows's *Standing Armed Figure,* and Frederick McWilliam's *The Orator.*

OXFORD
Ashmolean Museum, Beaumont Street
Tel.: 0865 57522

*Open weekdays 10-4; Sunday 2-4. Closed Monday and Tuesday of St Giles'
Fair, Christmas and Easter. (Open Easter Monday.) (Monday and Tuesday
of St Giles' Fair means the first Mon. and Tues. in September providing that
September 1st does not fall on a Sunday.*

The Ashmolean Museum has the distinction of being generally recog-
nized as the oldest museum in Britain. Its name derives from that of its
original founder Elias Ashmole, who was born in 1617 and as a firm
supporter of the Stuarts flourished after the Restoration, being given
various appointments including that of Windsor Herald. Though the
museum he founded was incorporated into the impressive neo-classical
building designed by C. R. Cockerell and erected between 1839 and
1845 which now houses the Gallery as we know it, the name Ashmolean
was not given to the collections, which now included a group devoted to
the fine arts, until 1908. Ashmole was a great antiquarian and a believer
in alchemy and astrology and the collection with which he endowed the
Museum was mostly devoted to objects and curios illustrating the natural
sciences. Pictures in the Museum, which was opened by James, Duke of
York, later James II, in 1683, were confined to portraits of those in some
way connected with the organization of the collections, notably members
of the Tradescant family whose collection Ashmole had inherited. The
most interesting works of this group are a portrait of Ashmole himself
by John Riley, and one of John Tradescant on his deathbed; but others
worthy of attention are ascribed to Emanuel de Critz, who was the son
of a painter and related to the nebulous Gheeraerts family. Though these
early portraits are given a prominent introductory position in the
galleries devoted to painting in the Museum, it was not round them that
the later picture collection grew up but rather round a group of 60
works, the majority of them not very remarkable, brought to the new
building in Beaumont Street from the Bodleian Library. From these
small beginnings the Ashmolean collection was quickly to grow. In 1850
came the gift of some 40 Italian paintings from the collection of the Hon.
William Fox-Strangways, later 4th Earl of Ilchester, a collection he had
formed while in the Diplomatic Service in Italy. (Another group of
paintings he had given to Oxford before the foundation of the University
galleries found its way into Christ Church Library and the paintings may
now be seen in the Christ Church Picture Gallery). Like one or two
other early 19th-century collectors, such as William Roscoe of Liverpool,
Fox-Strangways' taste ran counter to that of his time and he built up a
remarkable collection of Italian primitives. In 1851 the receipt of the
Penrose bequest provided the Gallery with specimens of 17th-century

Dutch and Flemish art. Another extremely important gift was received in 1855, that of Chambers Hall, one of the leading collectors of the time, whose preference in pictures was chiefly for 17th-century Flemish works, 18th-century Venetian views and 18th-century English painting. Numerous other bequests and gifts were received in the 19th century, among them the Combe and Fortnum bequests, and the Gallery's collection has continued to be augmented through the generosity of individuals during the present century.

Among the numerous examples of early Italian painting are *The Birth of the Virgin* by Andrea Orcagna; a panel from an altarpiece predella, *Crucifixion and Lamentation* by Barna da Siena; and *The Virgin and Child,* part of a diptych by Andrea Vanni. *The Meeting of Joachim and Anna* may have formed part of the predella of *The Annunciation* at Munich by Filippo Lippi, and there is an *Annunciation* from the studio of Fra Angelico, variously attributed to Benozzo Gozzoli and Pesellino. *The Baptism of Christ* by Giovanni di Paolo is a predella panel bought by Ruskin's friend and neighbour James Reddie Anderson in Siena in 1875. *St Nicholas Rebuking the Tempest* by Bicci di Lorenzo is a marvellous predella panel for an altarpiece in a Florentine church which derived its composition from a predella by Gentile da Fabriano in the Vatican Gallery. Not to be overlooked either is *Virgin and Child with Saints* by Sano di Pietro. The most fascinating work, however, is undoubtedly Uccello's *The Hunt,* probably painted after 1460. Its delightful vivid figures and its decorative energy hardly seem compatible with the Uccello of 1469 who, filling in his tax return, wrote, 'I am old, infirm and unemployed, and my wife is ill.' Hardly less fascinating is a work of half a century later which hangs nearby, Piero di Cosimo's *Forest Fire.* This may have formed part of a frieze illustrating scenes in the life of primitive man which Vasari described as decorating a house in Florence; companion works are in the National Gallery and the Metropolitan Museum, New York.

Other works which should capture attention among so many treasures are *Ecce Homo* by Andrea Solario; *Virgin and Child* by Bartolommeo Montagna; *Saints Bartholomew and Julian* by Davide Ghirlandaio; *Portrait of a Young Man with a Skull* by Bernardino Licinio; and an unfinished *Virgin and Child* by Lorenzo di Credi. Franciabigio's *Saint Nicholas of Tolentino Performing Miracles* was part of the predella of an altarpiece mentioned by Vasari as being in the Church of S. Spirito in Florence. Also here are a *Virgin and Child* by Pintoricchio, who assisted Perugino with frescoes in the Sistine Chapel, and a *Portrait of a Lady* by Giovanni Santi, father of Raphael. There is also a *Virgin and Child* from the school of Botticelli which was formerly in Ruskin's collection. Other works include *The Sack of Rome and Flight of the Vestal Virgins* by Giovanni Battista Utili, and *St Anthony of Padua* by Francesco Granacci.

Two Venetian works from the beginning of the 16th century are outstanding: *St Jerome in the Desert,* attributed to Giovanni Bellini by Bernard Berenson and certainly a beautiful work, and *Virgin and Child (The Tallard Madonna)* by Giorgione, datable as an early work because of the unfinished Campanile of St Mark's in the background which was in this state between 1489 and 1511. Also from Venice can be named: Tintoretto's *Resurrection of Christ,* which was probably a study for a ceiling painting; Jacopo Bassano's *Christ Disputing with the Doctors;* Leandro Bassano's *Portrait of a Procurator of St Mark;* two companion pictures by Bonifazio de' Pitati (Veronese), *The Finding of Moses* and *The Trial of Moses;* Giovanni Battista Moroni's *Mystic Marriage of St Catherine;* and six scenes from the story of Judith which may be the earliest surviving works of Paolo Veronese. Among 18th-century Venetian works are two early paintings by Canaletto, *View of Dolo on the Brenta,* dated about 1730, and *A Puppet Show on the Piazzetta,* dated 1726-7, but outstanding is a splendid work by Guardi, *Pope Pius VI Blessing the Multitude in the Campo SS Giovanni e Paolo,* one of a set of four pictures commissioned to commemorate the visit of Pius VI to Venice in 1782.

Other Italian works also demand close attention. The portrait of *Don Garzia de' Medici,* third son of Cosimo I, Grand Duke of Tuscany, and his wife Eleanora di Toledo by Bronzino brings to mind Vasari's praise of his portraits, which, he said, were 'most natural, executed with extraordinary care, and finished with a delicacy which left nothing to desire'. A portrait of an *Italian Man of Letters* is by Cristofano Allori, Bronzino's pupil. Another portrait which has been disputed but which is of undeniable interest is the self-portrait by Bernini, probably painted when he was about 18. Among paintings in a different vein are: *An Allegory of the Immaculate Conception* by Vasari; *St Dominic Receiving the Rosary* by Federico Barocci; *Adoration of the Shepherds* by the Bolognese decorative painter Pellegrino Tibaldi; *The Ecstasy of St Francis* by Lanfranco; *Adoration of the Shepherds* by Bernardo Strozzi (a Genoese priest as well as a painter, who spent his last years in Venice); *Raising of the Cross* by Luca Giordano; *Narcissus and Echo* by Pier Francesco Mola; and *Dead Christ Lamented by Angels* by Pietro Testa. Not to be missed is a portrait of David Garrick by Pompeo Batoni from the Bodleian Library collection. It was painted in Rome in 1764 when the actor was 47 and just after a visit to France where he had been acclaimed by Diderot and others.

Paramount among a group of French paintings is Claude's idyllic last work, painted in 1682, the year of his death, for Prince Lorenzo Onofrio Colonna, the greatest collector of Claude's work in his last years, and called *Landscape with Ascanius Shooting the Stag of Sylvia.* The subject comes from Virgil's *Aeneid,* Book VII: Ascanius, son of Aeneas, is out hunting after the Trojans have landed in Latium, and, inflamed by the Fury Alecto, he shoots the pet stag of Sylvia, daughter of Tyrrhus, warden of the herds to King Latinus, an action resulting in war between Latinus and Aeneas and the acquisition of the future territory of Rome. Poussin's *Exposition of Moses,* dated 1654, is also here, as are Gaspar Dughet's *View of Tivoli with Rome in the Distance* and Francois Millet's *Mountain Landscape with Citadel.* There are two works by Simon Vouet, *Portrait of the Poet Strozzi* and a *Virgin and Child,* and an *Allegory of Justice and Vanity* is by Nicholas Tournier. A still life by Chardin, *Marche de Trouper* by Pater and an exquisite Watteau, *Le Repos Gracieux,* illustrate French 18th-century art. By Watteau too there is a copy of Rubens's sketch for the *Apotheosis of James I* done for the Banqueting Hall in the Whitehall Palace. From the 19th century come several landscapes by Corot and a pair of portraits dating from the early 1850s of a merchant of Paris and his wife, M. and Mme Brison. There are two landscapes by Daubigny and two by Courbet, *Winter Scene* and *The Banks of a Stream,* dated 1873. Here also are *View of Notre Dame* by Jongkind; *Jetty at Trouville* and *The Estuary* by Boudin; *Haystack* by Berthe Morisot; *Pansies and Daisies* by Fantin-Latour; *Le Jardin de Montmartre* by Renoir; *Restaurant de la Sirène, Asnières* by Van Gogh; *La Toilette* by Toulouse-Lautrec; and a number of works by Camille Pissarro including *Paysage à Pontoise* dated 1872 and *Le Jardin des Tuileries, Temps de Pluie,* 1899. There are also several works by Lucien Pissarro including *East Knoyle Church:Snow* dated 1919. *Blue Roofs* by Picasso was painted in Paris between June and December 1901; *A Village Street* by Utrillo is dated 1912 and among others are *Nude Model* by Matisse, *Still Life of Plums* by Derain and two works by Bonnard.

Flemish painting commences with *St Catherine of Alexandria,* attributed to Mabuse and Joachim de Patenier's fantastic *Destruction of Sodom and Gomorrah.* There are several sketches by Rubens including landscape sketches and designs for the ceiling of the Jesuit church at Antwerp. From Van Dyck come several grisaille sketches also; one of them, an *Allegory of Charity,* belonged to Reynolds and was retouched by him. *The Deposition* provides a very fine example of Van Dyck's religious painting. *A Man Playing the Flute* is a Caravaggesque work attributed to Ludovicus Finsonius, who was born in Bruges but worked in Italy and France. From the Bodleian Library group comes a *Shorescape* by Adam Willaerts, known chiefly for his studies of fish markets.

Dutch paintings are not numerous in the Ashmolean apart from a very good and varied group of still lives, many of them from the gift made by Theodore Ward in 1940 in memory of his wife. In addition there are *Portrait of a Man* by Ferdinand Bol; *A Man Playing the Bagpipes* by Terbrugghen, dated 1624; *Young Cavalier,* dated 1625, by Pieter Codde, a pupil of Hals; and a large, characteristic *View over Flat Country* by Philips Koninck.

Apart from the portraits already mentioned depicting the founders of the Museum, English painting begins with the portraits that were originally in the Bodleian Library. An early self-portrait is by Robert Walker, famous for his portraits of Cromwell. From Reynolds comes a double portrait of the architect James Paine and his son, dated 1764, an early work which was partnered by a similar portrait of Paine's wife and daughters now in the Lady Lever Gallery. By Reynolds too are portraits of Charles Fitzroy, 2nd Duke of Grafton, Dr Joseph Warton, Head-master of Winchester (painted about 1777), and Mrs Meyrick. The picture which has been declared to be the best existing portrait of the Scottish heroine Flora MacDonald is here, signed by Allan Ramsay and dated 1749. Several of Hogarth's satirical sketches display this aspect of his talent; among them are *The Suicide of the Countess*, probably designed for the last of the *Marriage à la Mode* series; *The Theft of the Watch; The Enraged Musician* and *The Stage Coach*. The serene *View of Lago di Agnano* and *A Weir in the River Po* (1776) represent Richard Wilson; *Portrait of a Young Man* does the same for Wright of Derby. *Coast Scene: Morning*, and *Amy Robsart and the Earl of Leicester*, doubtless inspired by Sir Walter Scott's *Kenilworth*, indicate the variousness of Bonington's abilities. Several works by Constable are here, among them *Watermeadows near Salisbury*, and *Vale of Dedham*, dated 1812. There is a superb selection of Samuel Palmer's work at Oxford, particularly that of his 'visionary' period and in the varying media he used at that time. To mention but a few: *Valley Thick with Corn, Young Man Yoking an Ox, The Rest on the Flight* and the incomparable self-portrait drawing of about 1826.

The selection of 19th-century painting includes several works by William Etty, among them *The Penitent Magdalen* of 1835; Frith's *Before Dinner at Boswell's;* and a number of paintings by G. F. Watts. But it is the Pre-Raphaelite group which is the most remarkable. They come from a bequest by the widow of Dr Thomas Combe, Printer to the University. Combe, a great supporter of the Oxford Movement, was also a good friend of some of the Pre-Raphaelites in their youth, particularly of Hunt and Millais, and their works formed the larger part of his collection. Hunt's early work *A Converted British Family Sheltering a Missionary from the Druids* is here; it was exhibited at the Royal Academy in 1850 and hung there as a pendant to Millais' much-abused *Carpenter's Shop*. Also here are his *Festival of St Swithin* which he bought back and retouched in 1874 and a small version of the *Afterglow in Egypt* of 1863—the larger version is at Southampton. *The Return of the Dove to the Ark,* dated 1851, is the early work of Millais which so much excited the admiration of the young William Morris and Burne-

Jones; there is also a portrait by him of Thomas Combe. Rossetti's watercolour of *Dante Drawing an Angel on the Anniversary of Beatrice's Death,* done in 1853, was highly esteemed by Ruskin. There is a portrait of Mrs Madox by Ford Madox Brown and a reduced version of *Pretty Baa-Lambs,* the original of which is at Birmingham. His *Seeds and Fruits of English Poetry* of 1853 incorporates the earliest version of *Chaucer at the Court of Edward III* in the Tate Gallery. Arthur Hughes was a talented painter much influenced by the Pre-Raphaelites; his *Home from the Sea,* 1862, is here together with a small version of *The Eve of St Agnes* in the Tate. P. H. Calderon's *Broken Vows* is also a smaller version of a Tate picture. Charles Alston Collins's *Convent Thoughts* was severely criticized for its latent 'Popery' when it was exhibited in 1851. Some of Ruskin's firmly-held beliefs about painting are manifested in *Early Spring,* the work of his one-time pupil J. W. Inchbold. Burne-Jones's *The Building of the Brazen Tower* takes us into the era of the later Pre-Raphaelites.

There are some good examples of English painting of the early decades of the 20th century. By Sickert there is *The Lady in the Gondola,* 1905, and a version of *Ennui* painted in Fitzroy Street in 1918 for which there are several studies in the Ashmolean. By Wilson Steer there are two works based on the town of Montreuil. *Interior with Mrs Mounter* is by Harold Gilman and there are also paintings by Spencer Gore, Robert Bevan and Henry Tonks. A portrait of the Emir Faisal by Augustus John once belonged to T. E. Lawrence. Robert Graves thought Lawrence bought it from John with the diamond he had worn as a mark of honour in his Arab headdress.

No account of the Ashmolean Museum would be complete without reference to the incomparable collection of drawings to be found there. The collection of drawings by Raphael is not only numerically the largest in existence but also most representative of all aspects of his development. The collection was formed by Sir Thomas Lawrence, who assiduously sought possession of such works and indeed owned an even larger group than is in the Ashmolean. Part of his collection was bought for Oxford University by public subscription in 1846 while a section of it was acquired by the Prince of Orange, later William II of Holland. At the same time a series of drawings by Michelangelo, also from the Lawrence collection, was acquired and these provide fascinating insights into his work. Among them is an unfinished grisaille of the *Return of the Holy Family from Egypt* which may be by a member of his school. The drawings of Samuel Palmer have already been mentioned but there are many other drawings and watercolours by English masters, notably the collection of works by Turner donated by Ruskin. The remarkable series of drawings by Claude must also be mentioned as well as works by the great German masters, among them a watercolour painted by

Dürer on his way to Venice in 1494. Finally the Gallery possesses a large collection of bronze sculptures, too numerous to mention but of the highest interest.

Christ Church Picture Gallery, Canterbury Quadrangle, Christ Church

Tel.: 0865 42102

Open weekdays 2-4.30. Closed Dec. 24-Jan. 1, week before and including Easter and usually some weeks in Summer.

This collection pleasingly displayed in Christ Church College owes its foundation to a bequest made by General John Guise in 1765—a portrait of him by Reynolds is in the Gallery. He did not want his pictures, prints and drawings to be sold but to be carefully preserved and kept for the use of the college where he had taken his B.A. He collected some of the works in Italy (where his portrait was painted in Rome by Gavin Hamilton) but a large group was brought together in England. Another large group of early works, mainly from Italy, was given to Oxford and placed in Christ Church in 1828 by William Fox-Strangways and this was added to in 1897 by a number of mostly 14th- and 15th-century Italian works bequeathed by Miss Landor and Miss Duke. These were from the collection of Walter Savage Landor who was in Florence after 1821 and may have collected them there in collaboration with Fox-Strangways, who was a diplomat there at that time.

Of the early Italian pictures, from early 14th-century Siena, the school of Duccio, comes a triptych containing scenes of *The Crucifixion, The Virgin and Child.* and *St Francis;* from the 15th century are two works by Sano di Pietro, one of which, *Virgin and Child with Six Saints,* Roger Fry described as 'an early and delicate work of rather an unusual kind'. Also from 15th-century Siena is a *Crucifixion* by Giovanni di Paolo. From 14th-century Florence are *St Peter* by Jacopo di Cione; two works, *St John the Baptist* and *St Dominic,* by the Master of the Straus Madonna; and *St Philip* by Niccolo di Pietro Gerini. 15th-century Florentine works include the *Magdalen,* and *Virgin and Child with Saints* by Raffaellino del Garbo; two paintings of *Five Sibyls Seated in Niches* from the studio of Botticelli; *The Virgin Adoring the Child* by Jacopo del Sellaio; and *A Wounded Centaur* by Filippino Lippi. There are also several early Tuscan works and an Umbrian *Virgin and Child with Three Angels* from the school of Piero della Francesca. Roger Fry wrote of it that he could not 'accept the meagre flaccid forms as his [i.e. Piero's] in spite of the disquieting strangeness of the design and the superb quality of the colour in those parts which have escaped restoration'.

Sixteenth-century Florentine paintings include a *Lamentation over the Dead Christ with St James and St Roch* from the studio of Piero di Cosimo; *Scholar Holding Two Gilt Statuettes* attributed to Pontormo; and two works by Perugino's pupil Bacchiacca, *Christ Preaching before a Temple* and *Christ Appearing to the Magdalen.* From the studio of Andrea Mantegna there is a *Christ Carrying the Cross* formerly in the collection of Charles I. An *Adoration of the Shepherds* is by Girolamo da Treviso, a 16th-century Venetian. Other Venetian works include *The Martyrdom of St Lawrence* and *Portrait of a Gentleman* by Tintoretto; *The Supper at Emmaus* by Lorenzo Lotto; *The Marriage of St Catherine* by Veronese; and *Lamentation* by Palma Giovane. From 18th-century Venice come two works by Francesco Zuccarelli and *The Building of a Classical Temple* by Sebastiano and Marco Ricci.

Of great interest are several works by the Bolognese artist Annibale Carracci: *Man Drinking, Portrait of a Man,* and *Virgin and Child in the Clouds with below a View of Bologna,* a painting once owned by Sir James Thornhill. Most impressive is Carracci's *The Butcher's Shop;* his cousin Lodovico's father was a butcher and legend has it that the various figures depicted represent members of the family at work. There are three paintings by Annibale's great pupil Domenichino, *Landscape with Moses Delivering the Daughters of Raguel from the Shepherds, Landscape with Fishermen and Washerwomen,* and *Studies of the Head of an Old Man;* there is also a *St John the Baptist* by Guercino.

Annibale Carracci did most of his major work in Rome and from Rome too come *Expulsion from Paradise* by the Cavaliere d'Arpino; an interesting copy of Caravaggio's supposedly lost *Martha Reproving Mary Magdalen for Vanity;* and two works attributed to Pieter van Laer, leader of the *Bambocciante* (painters of low life), *The Quack Dentist* and *A Game of Bowls in a Roman Ruin.* From Naples are two works by Salvator Rosa, *Hermit with a Skull* and *The Infant Erichthonius Delivered to the Daughters of Cecrops to be Educated;* and *The Birth of the Virgin* by the 18th-century painter Corrado Giaquinto. Other Italian works include *David and Goliath* and *St Christopher* by Luca Cambiaso; *Judith with the Head of Holofernes* by Bernardo Strozzi; and *The Holy Family* by the Emilian painter Bartolommeo Schedoni, who was painter to the Duke of Parma.

A marvellous Flemish work in tempera on linen is a fragment of *The Lamentation: the Virgin and St John,* presumed to be by Hugo van der Goes, one of the greatest of Early Netherlandish painters. There is a *Diana and Actaeon* by Frans Floris and by Van Dyck there is a painting, *The Continence of Scipio,* and three monochrome sketches, *Martyrdom of St George, Soldier on Horseback,* and *Mars Going to War.*

The Gallery also possesses a large collection of drawings, mainly Italian, but including Flemish, French and German works.

PAISLEY
Paisley Museum and Art Gallery, High Street
Tel.: 041 889 2484

Open weekdays 10-5 (10-8 Tues. 10-6 Sat.)

This gallery and museum is notable for its collection of detailed information on the history of the Paisley shawl. Many specimens of the shawl can be seen together with the sample books, tools and various types of looms. The paintings here are mainly by Scottish artists but there is a small selection of works by Frenchmen and others. Among paintings by members and associates of the Barbizon School are two cattle scenes by Constant Troyon; a landscape by Théodore Rousseau; *Le Couchant de Soleil* by Daubigny; *The Windmill* by Charles-Emile Jacque; and two works by Diaz. Two paintings, *The Mill Stream* and *Un Matin Brumeux*, are attributed to Corot, a *Snow Landscape* is ascribed to Courbet, and there are works by Boudin, Monticelli, Fantin-Latour and Eugène Carrière.

To be noted among the Scottish paintings are a *Portrait of a Lady* by Allan Ramsay; two portraits, *Mrs Forbes* and *John Wilson of Perth*, by Sir Henry Raeburn; and a landscape by Patrick Nasmyth. There is considerable representation from the 19th century: *Church of the Nativity* by David Roberts; *Dark Beauty* by Andrew Geddes; several romantic paintings concerned with the defence of Scotland by David Scott; and paintings by Sir Noel Paton, Sir William Quiller Orchardson, William McTaggart and others. The Glasgow School is represented: one work, *Nethy Bridge*, by William York MacGregor, the pupil of Alphonse Legros (many of whose etchings are here); a group of works by George Henry; and a further collection by Sir James Guthrie. A later generation of painters who studied in Paris and were associated with the Fauves also figure in the Gallery, among them S. J. Peploe and J. D. Fergusson. There are also works by Joan Eardley and Robin Philipson.

PLYMOUTH
Plymouth Museum and Art Gallery, Tavistock Road
Tel.: 0752 68000

Open weekdays 10-6 (Friday 10-8); Sunday 3-5

The permanent collection at Plymouth contains works by many West Country artists, a number of important English painters having been born in or near Plymouth. Most notable among them is Sir Joshua Reynolds, by whom there are several portraits, among them portraits of his father and younger sister from a very early period. A portrait of Mrs Palmer, his elder sister, is a little later and there are also portraits of

Charles Rogers and of George Gibbon, Lieutenant-Governor of Plymouth, done in 1744. Of considerable interest too is a small chalk self-portrait formerly in the possession of Edmund Burke—it was given by Reynolds to Burke's wife. James Northcote, Reynolds's pupil and a very successful portrait painter, was also a native of Plymouth and is represented by, among other works, a portrait of *Dr Yonge* and a self-portrait. Another Plymouth-born painter was Benjamin Robert Haydon, friend of Wordsworth, Hazlitt and Keats; among his works here are a chalk self-portrait aged 60; a large picture painted in 1836, *The Black Prince Thanking Lord James Audley for his Gallantry in the Battle of Poitiers;* and the very big work *The Maid of Saragossa* which was won by Haydon's pupil James Webb in a raffle which netted £525. In 1842, while painting this picture dealing with the besieging of Saragossa by the French forces in 1808-9, Haydon recounts the following incident in his famous diary: 'Painted two hours, finished musket and bayonet. The musket fell down. I did not see it, and ran my foot against it, and the bayonet right ($\frac{1}{2}$ an inch) into my left foot. It bled copiously. As I wanted blood, I painted away on the ground of my Saragossa whilst the surgeon was coming. Never lose an opportunity!' There are works also by Haydon's one-time pupil Sir Charles Eastlake, later Director of the National Gallery and President of the Royal Academy. Here also are paintings and watercolours by Samuel Prout, another native of Plymouth, and by J. W. Abbott and Francis Towne, Devonian artists.

Other artists represented in the Gallery include Burne-Jones with *Venus Concordia,* an unfinished work begun in 1871 and intended as part of a triptych showing the *Story of Troy;* J. W. Waterhouse with *The Hamadryad;* Wilson Steer with *Two Girls on Walberswick Beach;* and John Singer Sargent and Stanhope Forbes.

PORTSMOUTH
Portsmouth City Museum and Art Gallery, Alexandra Road
Tel.: 0705 811527
Open daily May-August 10-9; March, April, September, October 10-6; November-Feb. 10-5

Not surprisingly in this town with its naval traditions a number of views of Portsmouth and its harbour by various artists are to be found in the Gallery. Also here are paintings by the marine painter Dominic Serres, among them *'The Hyena'* and *Admiral Rodney's Action off St Vincent. A Wooded Landscape with Rustic Figures* is by George Smith of Chichester and there is a small work on copper, *Christ Walking on the Water* attributed to Paul Brill.

There are works by Therese Lessore, Sylvia Gosse, and Frances Hodgkins, and contemporary artists represented include Ceri Richards, Bernard Cohen, David Hockney, William Scott, Victor Pasmore and Allen Jones.

PORT SUNLIGHT
The Lady Lever Gallery
Tel.: 051 645 3623
Open weekdays 10-5; Sunday 2-5

The foundation stone of this gallery was laid in 1914 in the year following the death of Lady Lever, to whose memory it was dedicated by her husband the 1st Viscount Leverhulme. The Gallery was opened in 1922 to display the collection which the donor himself had amassed and which thus, in the main, reflects his own taste and discrimination. The massive building itself, constructed of Portland stone and designed in a neo-classical style, is startling to discover among the diminutive domestic architecture of Port Sunlight village.

Though English art is featured for the most part in the Gallery there is also a collection of Chinese porcelain and the Napoleon Room provides a view of the furnishings of the neo-classical period. The collection begins with an impressive group of 18th-century portraits by English and Scottish painters. By Sir Joshua Reynolds there is a noble full-length portrait of *Elizabeth Gunning, Duchess of Hamilton and Argyll,* painted in the year after her marriage. This lady was so noted for her beauty that when she was presented at Court it was said that the 'noble mob in the drawing room clambered on tables and chairs to look at her'. By Reynolds also are a portrait of *The Honourable Mrs Peter Beckford,* and a group portrait of *Mrs Paine with her Two Daughters* which is a companion picture to one of James Paine and his son in the Ashmolean Museum. Also to be seen is a version of Reynolds's *Venus Chiding Cupid.* From Gainsborough come portraits of *Mrs Charlotte Freer,* and *Anne Luttrell, Duchess of Cumberland,* and a landscape, *The Gad's Hill Oak, Rochester.* George Romney's *Sarah Rodbard* is another splendid full-length portrait; his appealing portrait of *Mrs Mary Oliver* features a baby on her lap which was painted in later, having been born after the original work was completed. Allan Ramsay's solemn portrait of *The Dinwiddie Sisters* is an interesting example of his work. The strongly masculine is to be found as a contrast in Sir Henry Raeburn's portrait of the engineer Thomas Telford. John Hoppner's *Lady Elizabeth Howard* and *Jane Elizabeth, Countess of Oxford* should also not be overlooked—the latter lady was a notorious beauty and friend of Byron. Madame Vigée-Lebrun's portrait of *Lady Hamilton as a Bacchante* is also of interest.

The Gallery possesses a number of admirable landscapes. Among them are Richard Wilson's *Castel Gandolfo: Lake Albano,* a fine example of his Italianate work; Turner's *Falls of Clyde,* dated about 1840; Constable's *The Gamekeeper's Cottage* (sometimes called *East Bergholt Mill with Rainbow*); John Crome's *Marlingford Grove,* dated about 1815. Other landscapes are perhaps doubtfully attributed to Turner but here also are John Linnell's *The Woodcutters;* Patrick Nasmyth's *The Miller's Inn, Inverary;* George Morland's *The Piggery, The Soldier's Departure* and *The Soldier's Return;* and Thomas Barker of Bath's *The Woodland Pool.* One group of paintings, to be found in the room known as the Wedgwood Room which is filled with an almost unrivalled collection of Wedgwood pottery, is of great importance and beauty. It consists of works by George Stubbs painted in enamel on Wedgwood plaques and includes paintings entitled *Haymakers, Haycarting, The Farmer's Wife and the Raven,* and a *Portrait of the Artist on Horseback.* Stubbs was very interested in painting on enamel and induced Josiah Wedgwood to make him the thin panels of cream-coloured earthenware which he found best suited to his purpose. Of considerable interest in this room are the modelling tools used by John Flaxman, who produced many neo-classical designs for Wedgwood.

Lord Leverhulme's taste also included an appreciation of his contemporaries and thus many works from the Victorian period are to be found in the Gallery. Most remarkable of all perhaps is Holman Hunt's large version of *The Scapegoat* which encountered such adverse criticism when it was first exhibited in 1856 at the Royal Academy. Hunt's sources for the idea of *The Scapegoat* were the Talmud and Leviticus; an extract in the catalogue runs ' . . . the scene was painted at Oosdoom on the margin of the salt-encrusted shallows of the Dead Sea. The mountains beyond are those of Edom.' Ruskin, in his criticism, though praising Hunt's seriousness, ends, ' . . . in his earnest desire to paint the Scapegoat, [Hunt] has forgotten to ask himself first whether he could paint a goat at all.' But Ford Madox Brown called the picture 'one of the most tragic and impressive works in the annals of art'. *May Morning on Magdalen Tower,* painted by Hunt in 1890, portrays the celebration of the greeting of the sun on May morning which seems to be a relic of the rites of the Druids. *Sir Isumbras at the Ford* is a famous work by Sir John Millais, exhibited in 1857, which Ruskin, a former admirer, roundly condemned in his *Academy Notes.* (In the Gallery also is a satirical cartoon based on the picture from the *Westminster Gazette.*)

Later pictures by Millais include *The Black Brunswicker; Little Speed-well; Darling Blue*, deriving from Tennyson's *In Memoriam; The Violet's Message; An Idyll of 1745;* and a fine portrait of *Lord Tennyson* considered widely to be the finest portrait he did. Rossetti is represented by a version of *The Blessed Damozel* and one of his 'stunners', *Sibylla Palmifera*. Ford Madox Brown has here *Cromwell on his Farm, St Ives, 1630*, which in its scrupulous attention to detail recalls his famous *Work*, and two smaller pictures, *Windermere* and *Cordelia's Portion*.

Lord Leighton was also collected by Lord Leverhulme. Here are his *Fatidica, The Nymph of the Sands, The Daphnephoria*, painted 1876 and representing the triumphal procession held every ninth year by the Thebans in honour of Apollo, and *The Garden of Hesperides*, dated 1892. Of Lord Leighton his biographer Sir Wyke Bayliss wrote, 'He was a great painter, he was a sculptor, he was a scholar, he was a man of affairs, a linguist, a courtier, a fine speaker—but before all things he was President of the Royal Academy.' From Burne-Jones come two splendid works of a barely-distinguished eroticism, *The Beguiling of Merlin* and *The Tree of Forgiveness*—the latter deals with the story of Demophoon, son of Theseus and Phaedra and lover of Phyllis, daughter of the Thracian King. Demophoon was delayed in Attica and Phyllis, thinking she had been deserted, tried to kill herself but was turned into an almond tree; afterwards when he was consumed with sorrow she came to life again.

Other Victorians represented include William Etty with *Prometheus, The Judgement of Paris* and *Aurora and Zephyr;* Sir Luke Fildes with *An Alfresco Toilet;* Briton Rivière with *Fidelity;* and Sir Edwin Landseer with *Low Life*, which Ruskin called 'the intensest rendering of vulgarity, absolute and utter, with which I am acquainted'.

The sculpture in the Gallery forms a extremely varied collection ranging from examples from antiquity, a marble statue of *Antinous* found in the ruins of Hadrian's villa at Tivoli, to late-18th-century works such as Rysbrack's *Cromwell*, Flaxman's *Cephalus and Aurora*, and portrait busts such as the one of *Charles James Fox* by Nollekens. Nineteenth-century works include *Pandora* by John Gibson, *Sir Walter Scott* by Chantrey and pieces by Onslow Ford and Derwent Wood.

A group of Spanish primitive paintings should also be seen. They include a set from the early Catalan School of about 1420 illustrating *The Legend of St Ursula, St Michael and the Dragon* and *The Birth of St John*.

There is also an admirable collection of 18th- and 19th-century watercolours and drawings. Constable's watercolour of *East Bergholt Church* is among them, as well as a sketch of Lady Hamilton by Romney and works by Bonington, Girtin, Rowlandson, Varley, Burne-Jones and Turner, whose *Bolton Abbey* was owned and much valued by Ruskin.

PRESTON
Harris Museum and Art Gallery, Market Square
Tel.: 0772 53989
Open weekdays 10-5

This Gallery was built, together with a museum and library, through the bequest in 1877 of £300,000 for this purpose by a native of Preston, Edmund Robert Harris. The Art Gallery and Museum, under the care of the Corporation, were opened to the public in 1895; by this time a large bequest of 19th-century oil-paintings and watercolours, the gift of Richard Newsham, another Preston man, had been received. Since then many other benefactors have enriched the Gallery's collection.

Amongst the earliest works in the Gallery are a study for a portrait by Jonathan Richardson and studies by the sculptors Roubiliac and Rysbrack. Of considerable interest too is a crayon *Portrait of a Young Man* by Filippo Baldinucci, one of the first art historians. There is a portrait of *William Kent and his Wife* by Thomas Hudson. Kent was a celebrated architect and painter, one of his buildings being the Horse Guards in London. *Portrait of George Flaxman* is attributed to George Romney and there is a *Portrait of a Gentleman* ascribed to Joseph Highmore. There are several charming portraits and portrait groups by Arthur Devis, a popular 18th-century painter born in Preston whose sitters were mainly from the squirearchy or the merchant class. There are also some landscapes by his brother Anthony, and further portraits (notably *Portrait of an Actor)* by his son Arthur William Devis whose most famous work is however *The Death of Nelson* at Greenwich.

The great bulk of the collection is rooted in the 19th-century with an admixture of 20th-century works. There is a large dramatic work by Francis Danby, *Pharaoh and his Hosts Overwhelmed in the Red Sea;* and many works by David Cox, among them a splendid landscape, *Lancaster Sands.* Other painters represented are William Etty—*By the Waters of Babylon We Sat Down and Wept;* J. R. Herbert—*The Judgement of Daniel;* David Roberts—*Antwerp Cathedral;* Landseer—*Puppy Teasing a Frog* (famous for his animal paintings, Landseer also sculpted the lions at the base of Nelson's Column in Trafalgar Square). And here too are Augustus Egg, W. P. Frith, Paul Falconer Poole, Daniel Maclise, J. F. Lewis, G. F. Watts, Atkinson Grimshaw, Frederick Goodall. From the Pre-Raphaelites there is an Egyptian painting, *Back of the Sphinx, Gizeh* by Holman Hunt; and a domestic scene, *Bedtime,* exhibited at the Royal Academy in 1862, by Arthur Hughes.

Turning to the 20th-century here are *Two Women* by Sickert; *Roof Tops* by Charles Ginner; *Garden at Hertingfordbury* by Spencer Gore; *Eden Valley* by Lucien Pissarro; *Fishermen's Quarters, Venice* by Sir Frank Brangwyn; *Dorelia* by Augustus John; *A Game of Bowls* by Roger

Fry; *Channel and Breakwater* by Paul Nash; *Seine Valley Village* by John Piper; *Reflections* by Matthew Smith; *The Hill of Zion* by Stanley Spencer; *Swans, Cookham Bridge* by Spencer's wife Hilda Carline; *Crucifixion* by Carel Weight; *Rocky Landscape* by Graham Sutherland; and *Still Life with Sea Urchin* by Lucian Freud.

ROCHDALE
Rochdale Art Gallery, Esplanade
Tel.: 0706 49116
Open Monday to Friday 10-8; Saturday 10-5; Sunday 2.30-5

Rochdale's collection of paintings consist for the most part of a comprehensive group of works by Victorian artists of varying stature coupled with a selection of more recent paintings. The few European pictures in the Gallery are a *Charity* attributed to Bartolomeo Schedoni, a native of Modena who was Court Painter to the Duke of Parma in the early years of the 17th century; two landscapes by Jakob Philip Hackaert, Court Painter to Ferdinand IV of Naples and a friend of Goethe. English painting before the Victorian era consists of two works by J. S. Cotman, a landscape by John Crome and two attributed to Bonington. *Warkworth Castle* and *Furness Abbey* are by Thomas Girtin, and there are several works by Peter de Wint. Among the painters who emerged from the Victorian scene are William Collins, friend of David Wilkie and father of Wilkie Collins, who is represented by *The Sale of the Pet Lamb* and *Coast Scene with Boats,* and David Cox, who achieved early success as a watercolourist, only turning his attention to serious painting in oils about 1840; he is represented by several landscapes and a painting of Windsor Castle. There are several landscapes with cattle and sheep by T. Sidney Cooper, who was at one time employed by Queen Victoria to paint her Jersey cows. A comparable employment was given to J. F. Lewis, whose painting *The Heron* is here—he was required when barely 20 to paint game in Windsor Park for George IV. *The Convent Dole* and *Spanish Widow* are by John Phillip—'Spanish' Phillip as he was sometimes called; and *Ronda—Spanish Traveller,* dated 1864, by Richard Ansdell a Liverpool-born artist who accompanied Phillip to Spain. *Milan Cathedral* and *Winter on the Tiber* are some record of the extensive travels of David Roberts. In a different vein, attempting some sort of social comment, is a version of Frank Holl's *Newgate: Committed for Trial,* dated 1878. Other Victorian works include *The Marriage Procession: Rebekah* by Frederick Goodall; *Going to a Party* by J. C. Horsley; and there are works by many other Victorian painters.

From a later generation there is a large group by Sickert including *Dieppe Harbour, The Fair, Dieppe, Orchestra,* and *A Wicked Piece.* There are several by Wilson Steer—*Boats at Low Tide*, 1920, *The Needles*, 1919 and *Sandy Shore, Isle of Wight*, 1919. Therese Lessore, Sickert's third wife, is also well represented. There are two portraits by Ambrose McEvoy and of the Bloomsbury group there are works by Vanessa Bell, Roger Fry (*Studland Bay*) and Mark Gertler (*The Bokhara Coat*). A portrait of Eve Kirk by Augustus John dates from about 1928 and there are two paintings by Dame Laura Knight, *The Elder Sister* and *The Trick Act*. Also here are works by Matthew Smith, Stanley Spencer, C. R. W. Nevinson, L. S. Lowry, Lucien Pissarro, John Piper, Vivian Pitchforth, Ivon Hitchens, John Bratby. Appropriately enough there is a portrait by James Gunn of Rochdale's famous performer Gracie Fields.

SALFORD
Salford Museum and Art Gallery, The Crescent, Peel Park

Tel.: 061 736 2649

Open weekdays 10-6 (Oct.-March 10-5); Sunday 2-5

One of the most interesting features of this gallery situated adjacent to Salford University is its period reconstruction of a Salford street. Among the paintings in the Gallery are a portrait of William Beckford by the 18th-century painter John Hoppner; a Victorian depiction of medieval chivalry, *The Queen of the Tournaments*, by Philip H. Calderon; and two unusual subjects, *Defoe in the Pillory* by Eyre Crowe, and *Colombus and the Egg* by Benesch Knupfer. Most interesting however is the collection of works by L. S. Lowry, a native of the town. Here is an opportunity to study Lowry's development from his antique nude studies to his later, unmistakeable individual style. Among his works are *The Fight, Man Lying on a Wall, The Post Office, House on the Moor, The Cripples, Coming from the Mill*. Of considerable interest are a number of his drawings, particularly those of Salford and its surroundings.

SHEFFIELD
Graves Art Gallery, Surrey Street, Sheffield 1 and Mappin Art Gallery, Weston Park

Tel.: 0742 22624 and 0742 26281

Graves Art Gallery: open weekdays 10-8; Sunday 2-5. Mappin Art Gallery: open weekdays 10-5 (June, July, August 10-8.30); Sunday 2-5

The Graves Art Gallery owes its origin to Dr J. G. Graves, who contributed substantially towards the cost of the building and also presented the Gallery with a large collection of paintings and a distinguished group of watercolours. Additional bequests and gifts have been made since that time. The Gallery is also fortunate in possessing some of the pictures, drawings and documents formerly belonging to the now defunct Ruskin Museum. The pride of the collection used to be a *Virgin and Child* attributed to Andrea del Verrocchio and Leonardo da Vinci but this is now in the possession of Reading University where a considerable portion of the Ruskin material is kept. Still to be seen here however is another Ruskin possession, *Virgin and Child with Angels* by Cosimo Rosselli. There are other works from the Florentine school here including a circular *Nativity* by the 15th-century Master of the Borghese Tondo, *St Catherine of Alexandria* also from the 15th century and a number of other works by unknown artists. *Virgin and Child* from the studio of Giovanni Bellini should be noted and there are also a number of interesting works from 17th-century Italy, among them: *Death of St Francis* by Lodovico Carracci; *Madonna and Child* by the rather sentimental Sassoferrato; *The Mocking of Christ* by Procaccini. From the 18th century come *Cain and Abel* by Antonio Balestra; *Pool of Bethesda* by Leonardo Coccorante; *The Adultress before Christ* by the Venetian rococo painter Giovanni Pittoni; a portrait of Sir Thomas Reeve by Jacopo Amigoni who worked a great deal in England; and *The Arts* by Giandomenico Tiepolo.

The earliest work in the group of French paintings is a portrait of *Madame de Valentinois* by a member of the school of Francois Clouet. *Flight into Egypt* is by the 17th-century landscape painter Pierre Patel the Elder and there are a few unattributed works from the 18th century. Otherwise the collection is rooted in the 19th century. Here are *Landscape with Windmills* by Georges Michel; *The Holy Well* by Millet; *The Execution of Marshal Ney* by Gerôme; *Au Petit Chaville* by Corot; *Fishing Boats by a Stream* by Daubigny; *Farmhouses: St Aubin* by Harpignies; *The Echo in the Wood* and three other works by Monticelli; a *Portrait Study* by Manet's master Thomas Couture; *The Bend in the River* by Boudin; *The Young Craftsman* by Bastien-Lepage and a fine Cézanne, *Bassin du Jas de Bouffan*, painted about 1873-6. Other works are by artists such as Gustave Doré, Alphonse Legros, Théodore Rousseau, and James Tissot.

Spanish painting includes a Murillo, *The Infant Christ Asleep on the Cross; Head of an Apostle*, attributed to Ribera; and a striking *memento mori, Man with a Skull*, from the school of Ribera.

One of the earliest Dutch paintings in the Gallery is a portrait of Johanna de Witt by Michiel van Miereveld, the prolific painter to the House of Orange. Miereveld himself reckoned that he had done about 10,000 portraits. Also to be noted are *Cottages on the Dunes* by Jan van Goyen; *Portrait of a Lady* by Adriaen Hanneman; *Landscape* by Adam Pynacker; *The Ambuscade* by de Moucheron; *Landscape with Watermill* by Hobbema; and *River with Fishermen* by Salomon Ruisdael. There are also works by 19th-century artists such as Jozef Israels, Anton Mauve, Jongkind and members of the family of Koekkoek.

The selection of Flemish paintings includes a *Winter's Landscape* attributed to Joos de Momper and a *St Sebastian* given to Anthonis Mor. There is also a small group of works by German, Austrian, American and other artists.

Among the earliest English works at Sheffield are several Italian landscapes attributed to Richard Wilson; *Portrait of a Lady* by Lely; *Lady Mary Lyon* by Raeburn; *Portrait of a Gentleman* by John Downman; *A Ruined Abbey* by Joseph Wright. From the early 19th century come *A River Landscape* and *The Water Meadows at Salisbury* by John Constable; *Sunset* by Francis Danby and *Standing Female Nude* by William Etty. From later in the century come such paintings as: *Chevy Chase* by Landseer; *The Toilet* by W. P. Frith; *Persian Interior* by J. F. Lewis; *The Spirit of Chivalry* by Daniel Maclise; *Little Nell and her Grandfather* by Holman Hunt; *In the Grass* by Arthur Hughes; a long panel called *The Hours,* and two roundels, *The Guitar Player* and *The Mandolin Player,* by Burne-Jones; and numerous other works.

Later works include a *Portrait Study with Flowers, The Misses Vickers* by John Singer Sargent; *Portrait of a Man Seated on a Chair* by Sickert; *Chepstow Castle* by Wilson Steer; *Mushrooms* by Sir William Nicholson; *Mediterranean Scene* by Wyndham Lewis; *The Helter Skelter* by Stanley Spencer; *Tulips in a Blue Bowl* by Matthew Smith; *A Corner of the Artist's Room in Paris* by Gwen John; *Valley of La Hermida* by David Bomberg; *Tin Mine Prospect along a Level* by Graham Sutherland; and works by Harold Gilman, Spencer Gore, Victor Pasmore, J. D. Innes and others.

Sheffield is particularly rich and various in its collection of watercolours many of which are to be found in the Maplin Gallery. All the great names of the past are represented: Alexander Cozens, J. R. Cozens, Gainsborough, Cotman, Sandby, Girtin, Turner, Samuel Palmer, Constable.

SOUTHAMPTON
Southampton Art Gallery, Civic Centre
Tel.: 0703 23855

Open weekdays 10-7; Sunday 2-5

This gallery was first opened in 1939 but was forced to close again in the same year because of the outbreak of war. Many purchases for the Gallery have been made through the financial bequests of two former citizens of Southampton, Robert Chipperfield and Frederick William

Smith. To visit the Gallery is to be made aware of the extent of the municipality's achievement in acquiring an interesting and important collection even when, in comparison with many other towns, it has been late in the field.

The Gallery is well supplied with 20th-century British works but also among its possessions are the works of a number of 18th- and 19th-century artists. By Reynolds is a portrait of *Cornet Nehemiah Winter of the 11th Dragoons* with a depiction of the soldier's scene of action in one corner of the painting. From Gainsborough come a portrait of *Lord Vernon, Country Road,* and *The Edge of the Forest* and there is a portrait of *Lady Hamilton* by Romney. *Landscape with Figures and a Wagon* is by Joseph Wright of Derby; and a splendid panoramic view of Portsmouth and a *View on the Arno* are attributed to Richard Wilson. There is a lively illustration of a scene in *Clarissa Harlowe* by Francis Hayman, of whom Horace Walpole wrote that he was 'a strong mannerist, and easily distinguishable by the large noses and shambling legs of his figures'; nevertheless he was a very important artist in the middle of the 18th century. From the 19th century come a number of notable works: a watercolour, *Ruth Departing from Naomi,* by Blake; an important early Constable, *A View of Southampton* and a smaller work attributed to him, *On the Stour, Sunset; The Shipwreck* by de Loutherbourg and another sea piece, *The Wave* by Turner. A portrait of *Dr John Moore* is by Sir Thomas Lawrence and in a very different tradition is one of John Martin's bizarre fantasies, *Sadak in Search of the Waters of Oblivion.* Later 19th-century painting includes a variety of works: *Interior of St Stephen's, Venice* by David Roberts; *The World before the Flood* by William Etty; a series of paintings in body-colour by Burne-Jones on the theme of Perseus; *Lear and Cordelia,* and *The Traveller* by Ford Madox Brown; *On the Banks of the Dee* by Millais; *Afterglow in Egypt,* begun at Giza in 1854, by Holman Hunt; and two interesting parables of Victorian life by Abraham Solomon, *Third Class—Departure, First Class—Return.*

Painters of the New English Art Club and the Camden Town Group are well represented: there are a number of Sickerts, among them *The Mantelpiece,* and a self-portrait, *Juvenile Lead;* four excellent Impressionistic works by Wilson Steer, *Digging for Bait, Shoreham, Watching Cowes Regatta, Ludlow Walks,* and *Convalescent;* three paintings by Harold Gilman, *Interior, The Breakfast Table,* and a portrait of *Sylvia Gosse;* and three by Spencer Gore, *Panshanger Park, Brighton Pier,* and *View from a Window.* Charles Ginner is also represented and there are several paintings by Duncan Grant, Augustus John, Gwen John, and J. D. Innes. *Cyprus* by David Bomberg is very impressive and there are several other works by him on long loan to the Gallery. From Mark Gertler come four paintings, particularly notable *The Rabbi and his*

Grandchild, and *Family Group.* By Sir Matthew Smith there is a powerful *Still Life with Clay Figure* and several other paintings; by Robert Bevan *Cumberland Market,* and *Mydlow Village, Poland,* and there are several pastels by Gaudier-Brzeska, and watercolours by Wyndham Lewis. The *Resurrection with the Raising of Jairus's Daughter, Portrait of Patricia Preece* and *Pound Field, Cookham* are by Stanley Spencer, *The Rat Catcher* by his brother Gilbert. There is a large group of works by Graham Sutherland including *Green Lane, Red Landscape, Path through Woods* and *Santa Maria della Salute, Venice. Landscape near Malabata, Tangier, 1968* is an interesting example of the work of Francis Bacon, on loan to the Gallery. Other 20th-century artists represented include Michael Ayrton, John Bratby, Malcolm Drummond, Lucian Freud, John Golding, Josef Herman, Patrick Heron, Ivon Hitchens, L. S. Lowry, Paul Nash, John Nash, Ben Nicholson, Victor Pasmore, John Piper, Ceri Richards, William Roberts, Christopher Wood.

The collection of French painting contains but two early works; *Landscape with a Quiet River,* attributed to Gaspar Dughet and a landscape by Millet. From the early 19th century is a portrait of Napoleon by Baron Gérard. Then come two small works attributed to Corot; *Indian Warrior with Lance,* a watercolour by Delacroix; *Sea Piece at Honfleur* by Courbet; and *On the Loire* by Daubigny. The *Portrait of Herr Mühlfeld* by Renoir is very fine and there is an unusual night scene, *Moonlit Seascape,* by Boudin. From Alfred Sisley comes *In the Forest,* dated 1867, and from Camille Pissarro a painting of Louveciennes where he lived for a number of years, probably painted about 1890. Of considerable interest are *Children in a Landscape* by Henri 'Douanier' Rousseau; a snow picture, *Church at Longpoint,* by Maurice Utrillo; a landscape, *Outskirts of St Pierre, Yonne,* by Henri Harpignies, one of the original exhibitors at the Salon des Refusés of 1863; a *Nude* by Jules Pascin, a Bulgarian painter who committed suicide on the day on which an exhibition of his work was to open in Paris; *Two Poodles* by Pierre Bonnard; three delightful paintings by Vuillard, *Still Life on a Mantelpiece, Two People,* and *The Manicure;* and a remarkable work, *The Fisherman,* by J. L. Forain, of whom his friend Degas remarked, not altogether fairly, that 'he paints with his hand in my pocket.' Other French painters include Fantin-Latour, Othon Friesz, Lépine, Louis Vivin and James Tissot. There are also sculptures by Rodin, Degas and Artistide Maillol. Four examples of the work of the Belgian surrealist Paul Delvaux, among them an *Annunciation* and *A Siren in Full Moonlight* are very striking indeed.

Adding to the treasures of the Gallery are a *Virgin Adoring the Child* by Lorenzo di Credi and *Portrait of a Man* by Alvise Vivarini, on long loan from the National Gallery. Other Italian pictures include: *Mountain*

Landscape attributed to Salvator Rosa; *Madonna and Child* by Francesco Trevisani; *The Sacrifice of Jephtha's Daughter* by Pittoni; *Portrait of a Nun* by Sofonisba Anguisciola; two architectural fantasies by Alessandro Magnasco; and a seascape by Marco Ricci.

Dutch 17th-century painting is represented by *A Wooded Landscape with Peasants* by Salomon Ruisdael; *Dunes near Haarlem* by Jacob Ruisdael; *An Extensive Landscape* by Philips Koninck; *A River Scene* by Aert van der Neer; *A Woman with a Harpsichord* by Jacob Ochtervelt and several others. Some of these are also on long loan.

Of the Flemish school there is an interesting early work, *St Catherine Disputing with the Philosophers*, by Goossen van der Weyden, *A Hilly Landscape with a Shepherd* attributed to Paul Brill, a *Holy Family* by Jacob Jordaens, and two portraits of a man and of a woman attributed to Van Dyck.

SOUTHPORT
Atkinson Art Gallery, Lord Street
Tel.: 0704 5523 Ext. 149
Open weekdays 10-5; Sunday 3-5

The Atkinson Art Gallery is situated in Southport's famous tree-lined thoroughfare, Lord Street. It is a small gallery and like many provincial galleries possesses many more works of art than it can show, its collection amounting to about 1,300 items, some of them of great interest but only a small proportion able to be placed on view at any one time. There is no catalogue so authenticity of the works cannot be vouched for. The Gallery is also used for temporary exhibitions.

Of older works there is a portrait of the Duchess of Portsmouth attributed to Sir Peter Lely and a portrait of *A Courier* by Caspar Netscher. The Gallery also has a charming sketch of a child by Sir Thomas Lawrence, a landscape by David Cox, *On the Coast near Aberdovey*, a study of trees by John Crome, and a drawing by Bonington, *Palace of Prince Maffei, Verona*. Later painters represented include J. S. Sargent, Copley Fielding, Birket Foster, J. D. Harding; there is a small portrait by Ford Madox Brown and a drawing by Samuel Prout, formerly in the collection of Ruskin. Other works which should be mentioned include *Sinn Feiners* and *The Little Theatre* by Sickert; *The Slave Market* by Frank Brangwyn; *The Red Toque* and *Nude Girl Seated* by Augustus John; *Dressing-Room at Drury Lane* by Dame Laura Knight; *Street Scene* by L. S. Lowry; *The Teashop* by William Roberts; *The Palace of the Popes, Avignon* by Adrian Stokes. Roger Fry, Keith Vaughan, Philip Sutton, Michael Ayrton and Carel Weight are also represented and there is a bronze by Henry Moore, *Three-Way Points*.

STALYBRIDGE
Astley Cheetham Art Gallery, Trinity Street
Tel.: 061 338 2708

Open weekdays 10-4 (Wednesday 10-1)

Although there are a number of works attributed to unknown artists of
the Italian and Flemish schools it is to British painting for the most part
that this gallery owes its interest. By Richard Bonington is a work
entitled *Near Rouen;* by the Irishman Francis Danby, who at one time
challenged the fantastic paintings of John Martin, are three paintings:
Lake Scene; Ship on Fire; Isle of Arran. Sir Perceval is by G. F. Watts,
St Nicholas by Burne-Jones; and there are other paintings by John
Linnell, David Cox and William Collins. To be noted from the 20th
century are *Daffodils* by Mark Gertler and two works by Adrian Stokes.

STOCKPORT
Stockport Art Gallery, Wellington Road South
Tel.: 061 480 3668

Open Monday-Friday 12-6; Saturday 10-4

Among the paintings of interest here are two by the Salford artist L. S.
Lowry, *Crowther Street,* and *Old Steps, Stockport.* Here also are *Albert
Bridge* by Edward Bawden; *Ready for the Journey* by Frederick Goodall;
The Castanet Player by John Phillip, *Sheep-Gathering* by Richard
Ansdell; *Stoke Castle* by David Cox; and a collection of watercolours
together with a head of the musician Yehudi Menuhin by Epstein.

STOKE-ON-TRENT
Stoke-on-Trent Museum and Art Gallery, Broad Street, Hanley
Tel.: 0782 22714/5

Open weekdays 10-6; Sunday 2.30-5

Not surprisingly the Gallery at Stoke-on-Trent, in the heart of the
Potteries, is remarkable for its collection of pottery, slipware and porcelain. The development of the craft locally, illustrated by many fine
specimens, is traced in the Gallery, which also possesses examples of
such work from the Continent, South America and the Near and Far
East. Stoke Gallery also owns a considerable number of paintings,
watercolours, engravings etc. but as the space is limited only a small
proportion are on view at any one time. There are plans afoot for a much
larger and grander art centre which will enable more of the collection to
be shown.

Among the pre-20th-century works in the Gallery are *Woman in a White Hat* attributed to Frans Pourbus, *View of the River Thames looking towards Cookham* by Peter de Wint, and *A Greek Slave* by William Etty. Paintings by artists of the 20th century include *Rome* and *San Giorgio, Venice* by Frank Brangwyn; *The Lilac Dress* by Philip Connard; *Maurice Asselin* and *Idyll after Gilbert* by Sickert; *Freshwater Bay* by Wilson Steer; *The Young Sculptress* by Dame Ethel Walker; *Portrait of a Negress* by William Roberts; *Still Life* by S. J. Peploe, *Flatford-on-Avon* by Duncan Grant, *Lady in Red* by Bernard Meninsky; *Sandy Path* by C. R. W. Nevinson; *The Empty House* by L. S. Lowry, and a portrait of *Stephen Spender* by Wyndham Lewis. Other artists who should be mentioned include Robert Bevan, William Coldstream, William Nicholson, Roger Fry, Mark Gertler, Charles Ginner, Walter Greaves, James Holland, Dame Laura Knight, Henry Lamb, A. J. Munnings and Graham Sutherland.

Among the many watercolours in the Gallery are an unexpected group by the novelist Arnold Bennett, a native of this district. Other more accomplished artists represented include the architect Robert Adam, George Barret, Hercules Brabazon, William Callow, David Cox, Francis Danby, Edward Dayes, Constantin Guys, Samuel Palmer, Samuel Prout, David Roberts, John Varley, Peter de Wint and Turner.

Sculpture includes Epstein's *Head of Elsa Graves* and a Rodin bronze, *Eternal Spring*.

STRATFORD
Royal Shakespeare Theatre Memorial Gallery, Stratford
Open April-November: weekdays 10-1, 2-6 (November 2-4); Sunday 2-6.
November-March: Saturday 10-1, 2-4; Sunday 2-4

The first stone of the original Shakespeare Memorial Building to include Theatre, Library and Picture Gallery was laid on 23 April 1877, the anniversary of Shakespeare's birth, and the Theatre first commenced performances exactly two years later in 1879. In 1926 the Theatre was destroyed by fire but the Gallery survived and is still part of the original building. The smaller of the two rooms in the Gallery possesses a number of stained-glass windows, many of them commemorating the association of Sir Frank Benson and his company with the Theatre. The source of several of the paintings in the Gallery was the Shakespeare Gallery opened by John Boydell in Pall Mall in 1789, the year before he became Lord Mayor of London. Boydell wanted to enrich the tradition of historical painting in England and commissioned works illustrating Shakespeare from many of the leading painters of the day.

Of the greatest interest are the numerous portraits of Shakespeare here, none of them of course authentic, but rather for the most part approximations to ideas of his likeness. Here are a portrait derived from the Droeshout engraving which was a frontispiece to the first folio of 1623, a copy of the 'Chandos' portrait (the original is in the National Portrait Gallery) which has the longest reputation as a portrait of Shakespeare, and a number of other 17th- and 18th-century portraits and miniatures. There are also an *Ideal Portrait of Shakespeare* by the Swiss-born Angelica Kauffmann, who was a close friend of Goethe, and a cartoon for a portrait by Ford Madox Brown.

Most of the paintings in the Gallery represent either scenes from Shakespeare or actors who have performed his plays. There are two paintings by Fuseli, who was Swiss-born but who came to England and ended up as Professor of Art and later Keeper at the Royal Academy. He worked for Boydell for a time and the paintings here are *The Weird Sisters* (i.e. the witches from *Macbeth*) and *Henry V Discovering the Conspirators*. By Philip de Loutherbourg there is a very large painting, originally nearly twice its present size, representing the shipwreck in the first scene of *The Tempest*. There is a scene from *Richard III* by John Opie and *The Death of Cardinal Beaufort* from *2 Henry VI* by Sir Joshua Reynolds. Francis Wheatley painted two scenes, one from *The Comedy of Errors* and one from *A Winter's Tale*, and there is a picture of Titania from *A Midsummer Night's Dream* by Romney. By James Northcote there is a scene from *King John* and a portrait of *Master Betty as Hamlet*. Master Betty was an infant prodigy and the painting was executed when he was only fourteen. There is a mezzotint of *Lear and Cordelia* by the American-born Benjamin West, and a scene from Act I of *The Tempest* of *Miranda and Caliban* by James Ward, who chiefly made his name as an animal and landscape painter. Daniel Maclise has a watercolour of *The Play Scene in 'Hamlet'* and there is another watercolour of *Hamlet in the Churchyard* by Sir John Millais. There is also a portrait by Maclise of *Miss Priscilla Horton as Ariel*. By Henry Wallis, who was much influenced by Pre-Raphaelitism, there is a depiction of *A Sculptor's Workshop, Stratford* with the sculptor engaged upon the bust of Shakespeare to be found on his monument in Holy Trinity Church, Stratford.

Among the many portraits of actors are *Violet Vanbrugh as Lady Macbeth, The Kemble Family in the Trial Scene in 'King Henry VIII', Edwin Booth as Hamlet, Sir John Martin-Harvey as Richard III, Sir Laurence Olivier as Macbeth, Peggy Ashcroft as Imogen, Sir Michael Redgrave as Hamlet,* and *Paul Scofield as the Clown in 'The Winter's Tale'*. Many other actors are portrayed and there are numerous miniatures of, among others, David Garrick, Mrs Siddons, Roger Kemble and Ellen Terry.

SUDBURY
Gainsborough's House
Tel.: 078 73 2958
Open Tues.-Sat. 10.30-12.30, 2-5; Sunday 2-5. Closed Monday

This house, where Thomas Gainsborough was born in 1727, is main-
tained by the Gainsborough House Society and contains a number of his
paintings and drawings, all of them on loan. The House was originally
Tudor but Gainsborough's father, a cloth merchant, built the fine
Georgian front about 1723-4. Pictures in the gallery include a number of
landscapes, early portraits from his Ipswich period in the 1750s such as
*Sir Thomas Vere, John Vere, Mrs John Vere, Nathaniel and Mrs
Nathaniel Acton,* and later portraits from his time in Bath such as *Abel
Moysey,* dated 1771, and *Sir Thomas Rumbold and his Son,* dated about
1767. Other items of interest, letters etc. are to be found in the House.

SWANSEA
Glyn Vivian Gallery, Alexandra Road
Tel.: 0792 55006
Open weekdays 10.30-5.30

This gallery owes its origin to a gift of £10,000 donated to the Swansea
Corporation in 1905 by a local copper manufacturer, Richard Glyn
Vivian, who at the same time offered to present his own collection of
paintings, china and objets d'art as a nucleus for the Gallery. The
foundation stone was laid by him in 1909 but he did not live to see the
opening of the Gallery in 1911. The example of Richard Vivian was
followed by a number of other benefactors nd the collection has also
benefited from the efforts of the Contemporary Art Society, the Arts
Council and from purchases.

An early work here is *Susanna and the Elders,* which comes from the
Glyn Vivian collection; it was formerly thought to be by Guido Reni but
is more probably by his follower Simone Cantarini. Also here is a
Madonna della Scodella, after Correggio, attributed to the neo-classical
painter Anton Rafael Mengs. A *Holy Family,* originally ascribed to
Veronese, is now thought to be by one of his school. There is a portrait
of *Sir Robert Peel* by Sir Thomas Lawrence and an excellent David Cox,
Carreg Cennen Castle. Another work from the Glyn Vivian donation is
The Countess of Blessington as Juliet by C. R. Leslie, author of the
invaluable biography of Constable. From this collection also are a series
of eight paintings on Biblical and allegorical themes and a portrait of the
singer *Madame Patti* by Gustave Doré.

The Gallery has a good representation of Welsh artists. There is one

Richard Wilson, *Lake Avernus,* a version of the picture with the same title in the Tate; there are also a number of drawings by him. From Augustus John, who was born in Tenby, come several works: *The Tutor,* a portrait of John Hope-Johnstone, at one time tutor to the John children; *Arenig Mountain; Irish Coast* and *L'Hermitage Martigues.* Most surprising to the unprepared visitor is the room devoted to Evan Walters, a Swansea painter who died in 1951 and whose works reveal a decided gift. Among them are two fine portraits of *The Artist's Mother,* a *Self-Portrait with a Candle, Stout Man with a Jug, The Blind Pianist, Boy with a Feather.* Another room contains the work of Ceri Richards, whose work is much better known. Here are *Portrait of the Artist's Father, The Pianist, La Cathedrale Engloutie, Lion Hunt* and several others. *The Nun* and *Woman in a Coral Necklace* are typically subdued works by Gwen John. Other Welshmen are also represented: Kyffin Williams by *Snowdon in Winter, Deposition,* and *Highgate Schoolboy;* Alfred Janes by *Hyacinths, Still Life,* and a portrait of the poet Vernon Watkins.

Among works by other artists are *The Artist's Mother* by Mark Gertler, formerly in the collection of Sir Edward Marsh; *Marriage at Cana* by Stanley Spencer; *La Nera* by Sickert; *Winter Landscape, Cornwall* by Matthew Smith; *Selecting Calves* by the Vorticist painter William Roberts; *Portrait of Miss Close* by another Vorticist, Wyndham Lewis; *View in Venice* by Duncan Grant; *A View in Wales* and *Arenig* by J. D. Innes; *Essex River* and *Green Hill* by Ivon Hitchens; and *Mother and Child* by Josef Herman, painted while the artist was working in the Swansea Valley. There are paintings also be Frank Brangwyn, Carel Weight, Charles Ginner, Paul Nash, Derwent Lees, John Piper, Ruskin Spear, and a group of works by five Rouen Impressionists including *The Seine below Rouen* by Joseph Delattre.

The Gallery also possesses a large collection of prints, watercolours and drawings including works by Blake, Bonington, Cotman, Constable, Gainsborough and Turner.

SWINDON
Swindon Museum and Art Gallery, Bath Road
Tel.: 0793 27211
Open weekdays 10-6; Sunday 2-5

This collection concentrates mainly on 20th-century English art. There are two works by Duncan Grant, *Landscape* and *Seated Model; Nude with Paper Poppies* by Vanessa Bell; *The Black Sea Coast* by Roger Fry; and *The Artist's Sister Deborah* by Mark Gertler. Among other works which should be mentioned are *Welsh Hills* by C. R. W. Nevinson; *A London Church* by Robert Bevan; *Buildings in a Hilly Landscape, Palestine* by David Bomberg; *The Harbour* by John Nash; *Composition in Black and White* by Ben Nicholson; *Spring in Eden* by Ivon Hitchens, and *Roman Window* by Michael Ayrton. Represented also are Jankel Adler, Bernard Cohen, William Coldstream, Lawrence Gowing, L. S. Lowry, Christopher Wood and Kyffin Williams. In addition there are watercolours by such artists as Wilson Steer, Henry Moore, Graham Sutherland, Paul Nash and John Nash.

TUNBRIDGE WELLS
Royal Tunbridge Wells Museum and Art Gallery, Civic Centre
Tel.: 0892 26121
Open weekdays 10-5.30

The Museum here houses the Ashton bequest of Victorian pictures which unfortunately, owing to the demands made upon available space by travelling and local art exhibitions, are only on view for about six weeks of every year. The collection was formed by Mr Ashton, a resident of Tunbridge Wells, between the years 1852 and 1863, being bought for the most part straight from the exhibitions of the Royal Academy or the British Institution, or occasionally from the painter's studio. It seems clear that he did not favour the Pre-Raphaelites as there are no paintings of that school here.

Among the paintings are three by the very popular Abraham Solomon: *Waiting for the Verdict*—this had an immense success when engraved during the last century and it is at present being reprinted as a paperback cover for Dickens's *Bleak House; The Acquittal;* and *Brighton Front,* which seems not altogether successfully to aim at an almost Impressionistic style. There are two oils by John Linnell, *The Cornfield Shelter* and the pleasing *A Surrey Lane*. There is fine observation in F. D. Hardy's *The Young Photographers* and historical echoes in Frederick Goodall's *A Letter from Papa* inspired by the outbreak of the Crimean War. There is a landscape by Thomas Creswick, *Autumn Leaves,* and a *Riverscape* by Clarkson Stanfield. *The Toilette* and *The Lazy Girl* are by Henry O'Neil and *The Bridesmaid,* dated 1860, by John Phillip. J. B. Burgess, who like Phillip painted many scenes in Spain, has here *Spanish Girl* and *Portrait of Girl*. There are works by, among others, T. Sidney Cooper and Richard Ansdell, and on the stairs leading to the Gallery is a portrait of Charles II by Jacob Huysmans.

WAKEFIELD
Wakefield City Art Gallery, Wentworth Terrace
Tel.: 0924 75402

Open weekdays 12-5; Sunday 2-5

Paintings in the Wakefield Art Gallery, which like many other provincial galleries is frequently used for loan exhibitions, include portraits by Romney, Philip Mercier and Sir Godfrey Kneller. There are also works by Sickert and James Tissot and more recent paintings and drawings by such artists as Henry Moore, Barbara Hepworth, Epstein, Keith Vaughan, Graham Sutherland, John Piper, Ivon Hitchens, Roger Fry, Edward Bawden, Michael Rothenstein, Jacob Kramer, Wyndham Lewis.

Among the sculpture in the Gallery are works by Henry Moore, Barbara Hepworth, Bernard Meadows, Reg Butler and Jacob Epstein.

WALSALL
Walsall Art Gallery, Central Library, Lichfield Street
Tel.: 0922 21244 Ext. 135

Open Weekdays 10-7; Saturday 10-5.30

The collection of paintings in the Walsall Art Gallery was considerably enhanced in 1973 by the gift of the Garman-Ryan collection. This was donated by Lady Kathleen Epstein, widow of Sir Jacob Epstein, formerly Kathleen Garman, and comprises the collection of sculpture, paintings, drawings etc. formed by her together with Miss Sally Ryan, the American sculptor and collector. This group of works contains many of the greatest interest. Before the advent of this collection the Gallery already owned a group of 19th-century paintings. Among these are works by the 19th-century Dutch painters Jozef Israels and Barend Cornelis Koekkoek. George Morland is represented by *Rural Scene* and *The Sleepers,* and other paintings are by John Crome, David Cox, Thomas Barker, W. P. Frith and Daniel Maclise.

The Garman-Ryan collection abounds in works by Epstein. Among the sculptures are *Kathleen,* 1921; *Head of Kitty with Curls,* 1949; *T. S. Eliot; Heads of Children—The Sisters, Ann and Annabel Freud,* c. 1952; *Frisky, the Sculptor's Dog,* 1953, and several other portrait busts. Also by Epstein are two bronze masks, *Mask of St Francis* and *Mask of Tagore,* and numerous pencil drawings and watercolours. Other sculpture in the collection includes a small Degas bronze, *Femme Se Levant sa Jambe Gauche;* a small Rodin, *Woman's Mask;* a plaster bas-relief by Gaudier-Brzeska, *Women Bearing Sacks;* and a number of works by Sally Ryan herself.

Among fine examples of French painting are a portrait of *Chateaubriand* by Girodet; *La Seine à Vernon* by Bonnard; *Portrait of*

Marguerite, Sister of the Artist by Degas; *Study of a Nude Man* by Géricault; *Le Chemin Creux dans la Falaise à Varangeville* by Monet; *Les Oliviers à Cagnes-sur-mer* by Renoir; *The Wood Gatherer* by Diaz; *Woman Reading* by Corot; and a portrait of *Igor Stravinsky* by Robert Delaunay. In addition there are many watercolours, drawings and etchings etc. by painters such as Jacques Callot, Domenichino, Rembrandt, Goya, Delacroix, Millet, Manet, Renoir, Monet, Redon, Pissarro, Vuillard, Puvis de Chavannes, Van Gogh, Gauguin, Modigliani, Constantin Guys and Charles Meryon. A self-portrait in watercolour is attributed to Bernini.

Among the English paintings are a *Landscape with Clouds* by Constable; a watercolour, *Christ in the Carpenter's Shop* by Blake; a female nude by William Etty; and *Portrait of Kitty,* and *Kingcups, Souvenir of Glen Artny* by Lucian Freud. Numerous other works in various media are by Gainsborough, Turner, Romney, Ruskin, Burne-Jones, Rossetti, Whistler, Augustus John, Ambrose McEvoy, Matthew Smith and others.

WHITBY
Pannett Art Gallery, Pannett Park
Open May - September weekdays 9-1, 2-5.30; Sunday 2-5. October - April weekdays 10.30-1; Wed., Sat. and Sunday 2-4

This gallery was built through the bequest of Alderman Pannett, who died in 1920; in 1928 the building housing his art collection was opened to the public. The collection of oil-paintings consists mainly of undistinguished 19th-century works though a recent acquisition has been a portrait of the writer Leo Walmsley by Dame Ethel Walker. The main gallery contains, however, a selection of watercolours by some of the most distinguished exponents of that art. Among them are *Criccieth Castle, North Wales* by Turner; *Fécamp, Normandy* by Richard Bonington; *Loch Kiltearn, Scotland* by Thomas Girtin; *An Old Mill, Stratford St Mary's, Suffolk* by Constable. In addition there are works by David Cox, Peter de Wint, John Varley and others.

WINDSOR
Windsor Castle
Tel.: 95 68286

Open weekdays May-Sept. 11-5; March-April and Oct. 11-4; Nov-Feb. 11-3; Sundays April-Oct. from 1.30-4 (or 5 May-Sept), State Apartments usually closed approx. 6 weeks for Easter, 3 weeks for Ascot, 3 weeks around Christmas.

Windsor Castle, erected by William the Conqueror about 1070 as one of a series of strategic fortresses designed to subjugate the local population, has been used at least since the reign of Henry III in the 13th century as one of the royal residences, being in fact the only one that has remained in continuous use from the Middle Ages to the present day. During this time radical alterations and enlargements to the Castle have been carried out. A large programme of rebuilding was undertaken under Charles II, directed by the architect Hugh May, and again a hundred years later under George III. Further reconstruction took place in the reign of George IV. Three rooms now remain as they were originally decorated for Charles II with ceilings painted by the Italian decorator Antonio Verrio and ornamental woodwork by Grinling Gibbons. But the present impressive general outline and appearance of the Castle and its comfort as a residence are owed to George IV's architect Sir Jeffrey Wyatville.

The paintings available for public view at Windsor are to be found in the State Apartments. Occasionally they may be moved for the special exhibitions of works of art owned by the Queen which are held in the Queen's Gallery, Buckingham Palace, but as a general rule they are to be found as described below.

The King's Dining-Room, remarkable for the wood-carving of Gibbons, contains several portraits: a painting of Catherine of Braganza, Charles II's Queen, by Jacob Huysmans; *The Duke of Richmond and Lennox* by Daniel Mytens, for a time Court Painter to Charles I; *Louis XIII of France* from the studio of Philippe de Champaigne; *The Chinese Convert* by Sir Godfrey Kneller, considered by him, according to Horace Walpole, to be his masterpiece; and an unexpectedly plebian portrait for these grand surroundings, a full-length portrait of *Bridget Holmes Chambermaid to James II* by John Riley done in 1686 when she was in her 96th year. Riley for a short time shared the office of Principal Painter with Sir Godfrey Kneller.

The next room, the King's Drawing Room, contains a masterpiece by Van Dyck, *St Martin Dividing his Cloak with a Beggar*. This large impressive picture, painted when Van Dyck was 21 or 22 years of age, was given by him to Rubens, whose *Holy Family*, a very fine example of his religious work, hangs above the fireplace. On each side of the fireplace is a landscape ascribed to Rubens—one of *Summer*, the other of *Winter*—but neither is as fine as those in the National Gallery or Wallace Collection and they probably owe a great deal to studio assistants. Another Rubens studio work, *The Family of Sir Balthasar Gerbier*, is also here (perhaps Rubens was responsible for the central group); and there is an equestrian portrait after Rubens of Philip II of Spain.

In the King's State Bedchamber are to be found a portrait by Gainsborough of his son-in-law *Johann Christian Fischer*, difficult to see in its present position; two double portraits by Zoffany of royal princes and princesses; a Canaletto—*The Old Library and the Church of Santa Maria della Salute;* and *The Finding of Moses* by the 18th-century Italian artist Francesco Zuccarelli, who came to England in 1761 and was a founder-member of the Royal Academy. The bed in this room was especially made for Napoleon III on his state visit in 1855.

The small King's Dressing-Room contains an overwhelming collection of masterpieces, all of them portraits. Here is a rare oil-painting by the Frenchman Jean Clouet, painter to Francis I, *Portrait of a Man Holding a Volume of Petrarch.* Equally remarkable is a Dürer *Portrait of a Man,* painted in 1506 on his second journey to Venice. Also here are a *Portrait of a Man* by Hans Memling and two portraits by Holbein of members of Henry VIII's entourage: the first is of Sir Henry Guildford, Comptroller of the King's Household; the second of William Reskimer who for a time was a Page of the Chamber. From Rubens comes a magnificent, flamboyant self-portrait, painted in 1623 for Charles I, who was then Prince of Wales; also by him are a *Portrait of a Young Lady,* possibly the sister of his second wife, and an intriguing portrait of *Van Dyck.* By Van Dyck himself there is the famous triple portrait of *Charles I* which he did for Bernini to work from in sculpting a portrait bust of the King. The resulting bust was probably destroyed by the fire at Whitehall Palace in 1698. A portrait by Andrea del Sarto probably of his wife brings to mind Vasari's dislike of that lady. In addition there are three portraits by Rembrandt: a self-portrait done in middle age; a *Portrait of a Young Man in a Turban,* dated 1631; and an astonishing portrait of his mother, dated about 1629, which was given to Charles I by Sir Robert Kerr, later Earl of Ancram, and was among the first works of Rembrandt to come to this country.

Outstanding among the splendid paintings to be seen in the next room, the King's Closet, is Claude's landscape *The Rape of Europa.* Sir Joshua Reynolds's portrait of *David Garrick in the Part of Kitely* is a study in browns and greys; there is also a lively portrait by Hogarth of Garrick and his wife. But the greater number of works in this room are by Canaletto, among them being *The Colleoni Monument and the Church of SS Giovanni e Paolo, The Piazza and Campanile,* and *The Ducal Palace and Prison at Venice.* The large number of Canalettos and some of the other Venetian paintings in the royal collection were bought by George III from Joseph Smith, a wealthy merchant who lived in Venice, became British Consul there in 1740 and devoted himself to building up a collection of works of art.

Van Dyck is the dominating master to be found in the Queen's Drawing-Room. Here are two portraits of Henrietta Maria, Charles I's Queen, one full face, the other in profile; together with another they were intended for Bernini to enable him to make a companion bust to that of Charles I, but they were never sent to Rome. A portrait of Charles I by

Van Dyck captures a look of anxiety in the King as well as a distin-guishing grandeur. There is a group portrait of the five children of Charles I by the same artist, painted for Charles and placed by him in his breakfast room at Whitehall. Also very fine is a portrait of two courtiers of the time, *Thomas Killigrew and William, Lord Crofts.* These two were painted while in mourning for a lady who was the sister of the one and wife of the other and the picture is replete with symbols of grief and loss. Another double portrait, also by Van Dyck, is that of *George, 2nd Duke of Buckingham and his brother Francis.* There are also two single portraits by him; one is of *Beatrice, Duchess of Lorraine;* the other, of *Mary Villiers, Duchess of Richmond,* seems like a refined forerunner of many of Lely's later works; indeed, at one time it may have belonged to Lely. By Lely himself is a portrait of *Catherine of Braganza,* and by William Dobson, called by John Aubrey 'the most excellent painter that England hath yet bred' there are two portraits, one of *Charles II when Prince of Wales* and the other of James II when he was the young Duke of York. Two earlier portraits—of *Anne of Denmark* by Marcus Gheeraerts and *James I* by Paul van Somer—present the contrast of an earlier style.

In the Queen's Ballroom can be found more of the Canalettos in the Royal collection, among them *The Church of S. Giorgio Maggiore,* and a Capriccio view of the *Monastery of the Lateran Canons,* and also two landscapes by Marco Ricci. There is a charming portrait by John Singleton Copley of the youngest daughters of George III with their King Charles spaniels together with a portrait of George III himself and one of *Queen Charlotte* by Benjamin West, painted about 1776-9. By Gainsborough there is a striking full-length portrait of *Colonel John Hayes St Leger* who in 1784 was appointed Groom of the Bedchamber to the Prince of Wales, who called him 'one of ye best fellows yt. ever lived'. By Honthorst, the Utrecht painter who modified his earlier Caravaggesque style and became a popular court painter, are two por-traits, one of *William II, Prince of Orange* as a boy and the other of his father *Frederick Henry, Prince of Orange.* A portrait of Mary, Queen of Scots by an unknown artist, contains an inset representation of her execution.

Most remarkable in the Queen's Present Chamber are busts of Handel and Field-Marshal Lord Ligonier by Roubiliac and busts of Marshal Vauban and Marshal Villars by Coysevox. There is also a group portrait of members of the French Royal House by Pierre Mignard, the 17th-century artist who became First Painter to Louis XIV in 1690. The Queen's Guard Chamber contains busts of the Emperor Charles V, Philip II of Spain and the Duke of Alva by Leone Leoni. There are also busts of the Duke of Marlborough, Wellington and Winston Churchill, the latter in a siren suit.

St George's Hall is lined with portraits and busts of Stuart and Hanoverian monarchs in Garter Robes. (They were all members of the Order of the Garter, the most ancient order of knighthood in Great Britain, whose motto is *Honi soit qui mal y pense*—'Shame be to him who thinks evil of it'.) Notable amongst this series are a Van Dyck of James I copied from an original by Van Somer, a portrait of Charles II by Lely, and a portrait of William III by Kneller. Among the busts are those of George II by Rysbrack, George IV, William IV and Queen Victoria by Sir Francis Chantrey, Frederick, Duke of York by Nollekens, and George II by Roubiliac.

The Waterloo Chamber contains a remarkable collection of portraits by Sir Thomas Lawrence which the Prince Regent commissioned him to execute in order to commemorate all those who had contributed to the defeat of Napoleon. Of it Roger Fry wrote not unjustly, 'It is the English counterpart of Marie de' Medici's great decorations with Lawrence playing the part of Rubens.' The portraits were painted in two sizes, full-length for the monarchs, the Pope and the most important generals, and half-length for the lesser lights. Among them are splendid full-length paintings of Wellington and of the Archduke Charles of Austria, but particularly remarkable is that of Pope Pius VII, which possesses great power and subtlety. Among the half-lengths a number are very fine—in particular those of the Duc de Richelieu, the Count of Capo d'Istria and Prince Metternich.

Always on view at Windsor is a selection from the enormous collection of drawings in the Royal Library. Among these is an unrivalled group of drawings by Leonardo and Holbein as well as numerous examples of the work of artists such as Michelangelo, Raphael, Poussin, Claude and many others. There is also an interesting group of watercolours and drawings of Windsor and the Castle by Paul Sandby.

WOLVERHAMPTON
Wolverhampton Art Gallery, Lichfield Street
Tel.: 0902 24549

Open weekdays 10-6

Wolverhampton Art Gallery, housed in an imposing classical building, was opened in 1884, the money for this purpose having been donated by a former Burgess of Wolverhampton, Philip Horsman. Works of art or money for their purchase were given by other citizens of the town, and a collection was formed consisting mainly of products of the 19th century. In recent years the Gallery has been attempting to build up its collection of 18th-century works and also to purchase paintings by contemporary artists.

From the 18th century are two works by Gainsborough, a portrait of *Sir Edward Turner* and *The Travellers; The Watershot Wheel* and a *Landscape* by J. C. Ibbetson; *Love and Charity* by Francis Wheatley; *Miss Eliza O'Neill* by Arthur Devis; *The Coming Storm* and *Landscape* by George Morland; *Jason and Medea* by John Downman, at one time a pupil of Benjamin West; *Boy Blowing a Bladder* attributed to Wright of Derby; a group of watercolours by Paul Sandby; and several landscapes by Thomas Barker of Bath.

From the early 19th century are several works by Richard Bonington including *The Doge's Palace, Venice, Fort Rouge* and *Coast Scene.* Three landscapes are attributed to John Crome and two are by another Norwich painter, James Stark. A large work, *Destruction of the Cities of the Plain,* is by John Martin and *Athens by Moonlight* is by his rival Francis Danby. Many of the well-known painters of the Victorian age are here. Paintings include *A Scotch Market Place* by David Wilkie; *Castle of Ischia* and other works by J. B. Pyne; *Lady Playing the Mandoline* by Daniel Maclise; *A Market Girl* by William Mulready; *At the Opera* and others by John Phillip; *The Rejected Poet* by W. P. Frith, a scene representing Alexander Pope and Lady Mary Wortley Montague; and works by, among others, David Roberts, Frederick Goodall, J. R. Herbert, William Collins, Paul Falconer Poole and Landseer.

Contemporary paintings recently purchased include *Jackie* by Andy Warhol and *Tandoori Restaurant* by Patrick Caulfield.

WORCESTER
Worcester Museum and Art Gallery, Foregate Street
Tel.: 0905 22154

Open weekdays 9.30-6 (Thursday and Saturday 9.30-5)

The collection in this town consists in the main of works by Peter de Wint, William Marlow, Thomas Woodward, Thomas Baxter, and William Callow, who studied for some years in Paris and whose partiality was for painting watercolours of picturesque old churches and houses.

YORK
York Art Gallery, Exhibition Square
Tel.: 0904 23839

Open weekdays 10-5; Sunday 2.30-5

York Art Gallery was opened in 1879, owing its origin to an Industrial and Fine Arts Exhibition in 1866. It was known as the York Fine Art

Institution and was managed by an association of citizens until 1891, when it was sold to the Corporation of York. In 1882 came its first substantial acquisition when John Burton, a local merchant and mine owner, bequeathed his collection consisting mainly of late-19th-century English paintings and some older Dutch works. Various bequests of no great quality continued to be received by the Gallery and a Museum and Art Gallery Committee was formed in 1912 whose accent was on the purchase of works by local artists or those connected with local history. During the Second World War the Gallery suffered considerable bomb damage which necessitated the reconstruction of the building. The new Gallery was re-opened in 1948 and in 1955 it received a bequest which transformed its character from that of a minor institution to the status of a major provincial gallery. The bequest consisted of the collection of F. D. Lycett Green which included many fine European paintings as well as a number of English ones. Over the years the Gallery has also acquired a considerable group of works by William Etty, who was a native of York. Much work has been done in recent years, as is of course the case in many other galleries, on the revision of attributions of paintings so that many of those given in Volume I (*Foreign Schools 1350-1800*) of the catalogue have been altered. The foreign pictures mentioned here are the ones likely to be seen permanently in the Gallery.

Among the earliest Italian paintings in the Gallery are the wings of a triptych, the *Virgin and Child Enthroned* and *The Crucifixion* by the Master of the Fabriano Altarpiece, who was active in Florence between 1335 and 1365; this was formerly attributed to a follower of Bernardo Daddi. *The Baptism of Christ* is considered to be from the workshop of Bicci di Lorenzo, who was active in Florence from 1373 to 1452; and by Bartolommeo di Giovanni, in Florence 1485-1510, are panels of two saints who were invoked against the plague, *St Sebastian* and *St Roch;* these panels were formerly thought to be by Biagio di Antonio. Two other panels of saints, *St Anthony Abbot* and *St Bridget of Sweden,* are attributed to Tommaso Manzuoli, called Maso da San Friano, active in Florence 1536-71; and there is a tondo of *The Agony in the Garden* by Pier Francesco Foschi, who was in Florence about 1545. Sienese works include two predella panels of *St Peter* and *St Paul* by Martino di Bartolommeo, active in Siena 1389-1434; and *St Clement Striking the Rock* by Bernardino Fungai, which depicts St Clement, exiled to the stone quarries, obtaining water from a rock. A predella panel of *St Peter Released from Prison* is attributed to the Lucchese Master of the Immaculate Conception, named for his altarpiece in the church of San Francesco, Lucca.

Among Venetian works are a *Portrait of a Man with a Missal,* dated 1524, by Bernardo Licinio; *Christ and Veronica,* attributed to Dirck Barendsz, who was active in Amsterdam and Venice; *The Sacrifice of*

Polyxena and *St Prosdocimus Baptizing Daniel* by G. B. Pittoni; a small
landscape, *Il Rio dei Mendicanti,* by Guardi; and *The Piazza, San
Martini and Duomo, Lucca* by Bernardo Bellotto. Other Italian works
include: *The Risen Christ* by Nicola di Maestro Antonio, active in
Ancona 1470-1500; *The Circumcision of Christ* by the Milanese artist
Bernardino Luini; *Portrait of a Man* attributed to Parmigianino; *The
Annunciation,* dated 1605, by Giulio Procaccini; *Landscape with Diana
and Endymion* by Agostino Tassi; *Rest on the Flight into Egypt,* attributed to Agostino Carracci, which one catalogue describes as having
been so highly esteemed by Reynolds that he offered £2,000 for it; a
small *Pietà* attributed to Guido Reni; a self-portrait by Andrea Soldi; *St
Agatha* by Bernardo Cavallino; *The Parable of the Mote and the Beam* by
Domenico Feti; *The Last Supper* by Luca Giordano; and most outstanding of all a *Portrait of Monsignor Agucchi* by Domenichino. Agucchi
was a Papal Secretary and Papal Nuncio who wrote an important treatise
on aesthetic theory.

The earliest Dutch painting at York would appear to be a *Portrait of
a Gentleman* ascribed to Jan van Scorel, an early-16th-century artist who
travelled widely and was instrumental in bringing back the ideas of the
Italian Renaissance to Holland. There is also an early-16th-century
triptych, the wings painted with scenes from the Old Testament. By Van
Baburen, who belonged to the Caravaggisti circle of painters in Utrecht,
is *Roman Charity: Cimon and Pero*—the subject derives from a chapter
on filial piety by Valerius Maximus and was treated by Caravaggio
himself in his *Seven Works of Charity.* Another work from Utrecht is
Joachim Uytewael's *Venus and Cupid* and by Jan de Bray, chiefly known
as a portrait painter in Haarlem, is an Old Testament scene, *Jael and
Sisera.* There is a *Portrait of a Lady* by Frans van Mieris; a *Vanitas* by
Juriaan van Streek, who was active in Amsterdam; and *An Old Woman
Asleep,* dated 1655, by Esias Boursse. There are various landscape scenes
including *Landscape with Cottage and Bridge* by Cornelis Decker; *Coast
Scene with Lobster Catchers* by Nicolaes Berchem; *Landscape with Cattle*
by Karel Dujardin; *Peasants and Horsemen at an Inn* by Jan van Goyen;
and *Battle Scene* by Philips Wouwerman. Other paintings are *The
Butcher's Shop* by Jan Victors; *Tavern Scene* by Cornelis Bega; *Banquet
Piece* and *Seascape with Galliots* by van Beyeren; and from the 19th
century comes *A Dutch Watering-Place* by Jacob Maris.

Paintings by Flemish artists include *St Bruno* by Caspar de Crayer;
Still Life with Fish and Cat by Alexander Adriaensson the Elder, dated
1631; *Portrait of a Young Girl,* attributed to Cornelis de Vos; *Landscape
with St George* and *Landscape with Venus and Adonis* by Gillis Nyts;
Portrait of a Lady by David Teniers the Younger; *Military Encampment*
and *Soldiers Resting in a Village* by Pieter van Bloemen, both dated 1697.

From the German school come *The Flagellation of St Barbara* from the workshop of the Younger Master of the Schotten Altarpiece, active in Vienna 1475-1500, and *A Sleeping Soldier* by Bernhard Strigel.

The Spanish group contains a portrait of *A Knight of the Order of Santiago* attributed to Juan del Mazo, son-in-law of Velazquez; *A Jesuit Conversion* by Juan de Valdes Leal—it has been suggested that the convert represented here was Don Miguel de Manara, the original Don Juan—and a *Still Life with Lemons and Nuts* by Luis Menendez, an 18th-century painter active in Madrid and Italy.

Representative of French painting before the 19th century are *The Nobleman of Capernaum* by Jean Francois Millet, and by the engraver and caricaturist Gravelot a small work, *Le Lecteur* of about 1750. Gravelot was in England from 1733 to 1753, taught drawing at St Martin's Lane Academy and helped considerably to introduce the French rococo style into England. Early-19th-century works include *Boat in a Storm* by Eugène Isabey; *On the Beach* by Anton Mauve; *Plain of St Denis* by Georges Michel; and *Landscape with Red Sunset* by Théodore Rousseau. A *Swiss Landscape* by Courbet was probably painted on his return to Ornans by way of Switzerland from Munich, where he had been awarded the Cross of the Order of Merit of St Michael. *Forest of Fontainebleau* and *Woman Washing by a Stream* are by Diaz and *The Waterfall* by Daubigny is possibly dated around 1870-5. A *Head of a Woman* by Eugène Carrière is dated 1870. From both Monticelli and Fantin-Latour come paintings entitled *Roses;* there is a *Still Life*, 1879, by Bonvin, and *Still Life with Jug* and *Still Life with Oysters* are by Auguste Ribot. A 20th-century work here is *La Vallée* by Jean-Paul Riopelle.

The rich choice of English pictures begins with some strange panels from the early 16th century which derive from St Lawrence's Chantry, Leake in Lincolnshire. There are a number of portraits by unknown 16th- and 17th-century artists but identifiable are a portrait of Mary Denton, née Martyn, aged 15 in 1573, by George Gower, and by Edward Bower, who was a servant of Van Dyck, two portraits of Ferdinando, 2nd Lord Fairfax, and Lady Elizabeth Drake, painted in 1646—she was an ancestress of Winston Churchill and her own husband actually bore that name. On loan is a portrait of Endymion Porter attributed to Van Dyck. A portrait by Sir Peter Lely here is of the little girl Charlotte Fitzroy, fourth child of Barbara Villiers, Duchess of Cleveland, by Charles II, attended by an Indian servant. From Lely also comes a *Portrait of an Unknown Gentleman.* By John Riley is a portrait of John Cholmley, and from Kneller's pupil Michael Dahl comes a painting of *The Magdalen.* By Kneller himself is a portrait of Dr Thomas Gale, who was made Dean of York in 1697 and is buried in York Minster. Marcellus Laroon, another pupil of Kneller, is the painter of a naive little scene, *Le Rencontre.* By Philip Mercier, who was the son of a refugee

French tapestry worker and who lived in Yorkshire for 11 years, there are a portrait of Miss Adams, *Portrait of an Unknown Gentleman,* and a *Scene from 'The Careless Husband'.* Lent to the Gallery by York Minster are Francis Wheatley's *The Baptism* and *The Communion,* both painted in 1791. The Gallery is the fortunate owner of three works by Sir Joshua Reynolds: there is a portrait of *Captain John Foote in Indian Costume*—the costume is also now in the possession of the Gallery; a half-length of *Sir Conyers D'Arcy,* executed in 1858; and a *Landscape with Goatherd* of about 1788. From Fuseli comes a fragment, *Prospero,* which is part of a larger work, *Prospero, Miranda and Caliban,* he painted for Boydell's Shakespeare Gallery. *The Wreckers,* dated 1767, and *Mountain Landscape,* 1784, are by de Loutherbourg; from George Morland there is a characteristic *Gypsy Encampment,* and from his brother-in-law James Ward a painting entitled *The Disobedient Prophet,* inspired by some verses in the Book of Kings. An *Evening Landscape* is by Julius Caesar Ibbetson, who after an adventurous life finally settled in Yorkshire; *Old Ouse Bridge* is by William Marlow; and by Thomas Barker of Bath is *Crazy Kate,* derived from a poem by Cowper. There is a derogatory reference by Ruskin to *Christ Stilleth the Tempest* by John Martin. Martin's excessively dramatic works were only rivalled by those of the Irishman Francis Danby whose *The Deluge,* painted about 1828, also hangs here.

Most widely represented of all at York is William Etty, who was born there and after a varied life died there in 1849. Examples of all aspects of his work are here: Biblical, historical, mythological, nudes, portraits, landscapes, still lives. To mention but a few here are *Venus and Cupid, The Bridge of Sighs, The Wrestlers, Mlle Rachel* (a portrait of the famous actress, probably painted on her first visit to England in 1841) and *The Strid, Bolton Abbey.*

Other 19th-century works include *The Harvest Cradle* by John Linnell; *Collecting the Offering in a Scottish Kirk,* dated 1855, by John Phillip; a landscape by Richard Dadd, dated 1837, before he entered the R. A. Schools; *The Bay of Naples, Progress,* and *Ararat* by G. F. Watts; *Venus, Kingcups,* and *End of a Sofa* by Albert Moore; and marine landscapes by his brother Henry—both these painters were born in York. From Sickert comes *The Butcher's Shop,* dated 1885, but also in the collection by him are *Visitor* and *Old Heffer,* dated 1908 and 1916 respectively. *Boats on the Beach at Southwold* by Wilson Steer is dated 1894 and *Kimono* and *Dover Coast,* 1920, are also by him. From Harold Gilman come several works, among them *The Artist's Daughters* and *Beechwood, Gloucestershire,* dated 1917. *View from a Canal Bridge, Chalk Farm Road* is an example of the work of Spencer Gore; *Girl in a Red Shawl,* dated 1912, comes from Gwen John; and by David Bomberg there are two works, *The Bath,* 1922, and *Man's Head. Winter Sea* by

Paul Nash is a culmination of studies of the sea on the edge of Romney Marsh; from Stanley Spencer comes a painting divided horizontally depicting *The Deposition* and *The Rolling Away of the Stone,* and dated 1956. By L. S. Lowry there is a picture of a local scene, *Clifford's Tower, York,* as well as *The Bandstand: Peel Park,* and other artists represented include Mark Gertler, Charles Ginner, Matthew Smith, Ethel Walker, Josef Herman, Bryan Kneale and Fred Uhlman.

Among the sculpture in the Gallery is a bust of Alfred Wolmark by Gaudier-Brzeska, a bust of Paul Robeson by Epstein and a *Working Model for Locking Piece* by Henry Moore.

Index